Labour and unions
in Asia and Africa

$45.00

LABOUR AND UNIONS IN ASIA AND AFRICA

Labour and Unions in Asia and Africa

Contemporary Issues

Edited by
Roger Southall

St. Martin's Press   New York

First published in the United States of America in 1988

Printed in Hong Kong

ISBN 0–312–01362–0

Library of Congress Cataloging-in-Publication Data
Labour and unions in Asia and Africa/edited by Roger Southall.
p. cm.
Includes index.
ISBN 0–312–01362–0 : $45.00
1. Trade-unions — Asia.   2. Trade-unions — Africa.   I. Southall,
Roger.
HD6796.L3 1988
331.88′095—dc19   87-21475   CIP

Contents

Contents

Preface

This collection is a third and final volume of papers emerging out of the conference on 'Third World Trade Unions: Equity and Democratisation in the Changing International Division of Labour' held at the University of Ottawa in October 1984. The previous volumes, both edited by myself, were a special issue on South African labour of *Labour, Capital and Society*, vol. 18, 2, 1985 and *Trade Unions and the New Industrialisation of the Third World* (Zed Press and Ottawa University Press, 1987). Whilst the present collection stands on its own as a set of studies addressing issues similar to those raised previously, it is obviously more fruitfully located within the context provided by its predecessors while simultaneously complementing them by allowing for a much sharper contrast to be drawn between the situation of labour in two major regions not usually juxtaposed. What it demonstrates, I believe, is the pressing need for yet further comparative surveys of labour and unions if we intend to build upon present progress currently being made towards a more dynamic study of labour in the third world.

The conference was a large one and attracted considerable interest amongst trade unionists and scholars associated with what is becoming known as 'the new international labour studies'. In the course of organising it I inevitably contracted many debts. Not least of all, the Institute for International Development and Cooperation at the University of Ottawa provided me with the opportunity to present the conference as its fourteenth annual colloquium, and provided me thereafter with considerable logistical support. Ali Ayari, the Administrator, was particularly helpful in this regard, and I could not have done without the help of all the other administrative and secretarial staff. Equally, I would have been out of my depth without the support of Bill Paton, my assistant, whose humour before the event was as widely known as his prodigious bureaucratic skills were not. And, of course, the Institute and myself are greatly indebted to the Canadian International Development Agency, the International Development Research Centre, the (Canadian) Social Sciences and Humanities Research Council and Labour Canada for providing the very considerable financial backing without which the conference could not have been held. I must express appreciation, too, to John Harker, Director of the International Department of the Canadian Labour Congress for endorsing the conference by recommending it to the international trade union

vii

Preface

network. The conference was delighted, *inter alia*, that Cyril Rama-
phosa, General Secretary of the South African National Union of
Mineworkers, was able to use the opportunity of his presence to address
the annual convention of a major Canadian union.

Department of Politics
University of Leicester ROGER SOUTHALL

Notes on the Contributors

Debashish Bhattacherjee is currently completing his doctoral dissertation on 'The Economic and Political Effects of the "New" Unionism in India: An Interindustry Study of Bombay' at the Institute of Labor and Industrial Relations at the University of Illinois. He has previously published in the journal *Industrial Relations*.

Michel Chossudovsky is Professor of Economics at the University of Ottawa. He has contributed to many scholarly journals, and is author of *La Disoccupazione su Scala Mondiale* and *La Miseria en Venezuela*. His most recent work is *Towards Capitalist Restoration? Chinese Socialism after Mao*.

Tayo Fashoyin is Associate Professor and Head of the Department of Industrial Relations and Personnel Management, University of Lagos. He has published several scholarly works, among them *Industrial Relations in Nigeria* and *Incomes and Inflation in Nigeria*. He is Secretary of the Nigerian Industrial Relations Association.

Julius O. Ihonvbere is Senior Lecturer in International Relations at the University of Port Harcourt in Nigeria. He is co-author of *The Rise and Fall of Nigeria's Second Republic 1979–84*, co-editor of *Nigeria Power: The Political Economy and Foreign Policy of Oil* and author of essays in *Africa Spectrum*, *Odu*, *West Africa* and other journals.

Jon Kraus is Professor of Political Science at the State University of New York, Fredonia. His most recent of numerous publications include articles in *Current History*, *Labour, Capital and Society*, and *African Studies Review* and chapters in a number of recent collections on Africa's crisis. He is editor of *Radical and Reformist Military Regimes*.

Leslie O'Brien is a Research Fellow at the Research School of Pacific Studies, Australian National University, Canberra. Her publications include *Australian Manufacturing Capital in Peninsular Malaysia* and an article in *Kajian Malaysia*.

Jane L. Parpart is Associate Professor of History at Dalhousie University, Halifax, Nova Scotia. She is author of *Labor and Capital on the*

African Copperbelt and several chapters on women in collections on Africa. She is co-editor of *Women, Employment and the Family in the New International Division of Labour*.

Jaganath Pathy is Reader in Sociology at South Gujerat University, Surat, India. He is author of *Tribal Peasantry: Dynamics of Development* and numerous articles on agrarian structure in India and Marxist theory and practice.

Timothy M. Shaw is Professor of Political Science and Director of the Centre for African Studies and Executive Director, Lester Pearson Institute for International Development at Dalhousie University, Halifax, Nova Scotia. He is author of numerous articles on Africa and *Towards a Political Economy of Africa: the dialectics of dependence*. He is also co-editor of various works including *Africa Projected, Political Economy of African Foreign Policy* and *Regional Development in Africa and Canada*.

Roger Southall is Lecturer in Politics at the University of Leicester. He is author of *South Africa's Transkei: The Political Economy of an 'Independent' Bantustan* and *Federalism and Higher Education in East Africa*. He is author of various articles on Africa and is editor of a special issue of *Labour, Capital and Society* (vol. 18, 2, 1985) on South African labour and *Trade Unions and the New Industrialisation of the Third World*.

1 Introduction

Roger Southall

The chapters in this book were originally offered to a conference called to examine the impact of changes in the structure of international capitalism upon trade unions in the contemporary third world. Central to the problem as posed were two key issues (Southall, 1984). The first was to consider the structural effect upon labour in third world countries of a widely postulated transition from a 'colonial' to what is now commonly referred to as the 'new' international division of labour; and the second was to discuss the likely role and potential of third world trade unions in a changing situation widely construed as deleterious to the conditions and defensive capacities of labour globally.

In their influential proposition of a new international division of labour (NIDL), Frobel, Heinrichs and Kreye (1980) argue that three major developments have fundamentally transformed the conditions for the expansion and accumulation of capital on a world scale. These are: (i) the growth of a virtually inexhaustible world wide reservoir of labour consequent upon the relentless penetration of the third world by capitalism and the resulting dissolution of pre-capitalist socio-economic structures; (ii) the fragmentation of complex production processes into elementary tasks easily learned and performed by an unskilled work-force; and (iii) advances in communications and transport technology which allow production processes to be spatially separated and the simpler tasks to be relocated to sites where labour is cheap. As a result, the relative deindustrialisation of traditional industrial centres has been matched by the expansion of export-oriented manufacturing in the third world, alongside a marked trend towards the transnationalisation of production processes and increased domination of the global economy by transnational corporations (tncs). As a result:

> the previous division of the world into industrialized centers and non-industrialized periphery will be superseded by a new dispensation. The contrast will be between highly sophisticated production (development of advanced technologies, soft-ware, and so forth) and industrial production using standard technologies. Sites of this second type will be established and then disappear at an unheard of rate. Capital may be attracted to one region today, leave again tomorrow, and possibly return the day after. (Frobel *et al.*, 1978, p. 857)

1

If, at one level, this may generate the conditions for a classical confrontation between capital and labour (and thereby point the way to international solidarity between workers), at another level the more immediate result for labour is seen as unambiguously disastrous. Unemployment and pressure on real wages and working conditions will increase virtually everywhere, and workers will become increasingly subject to harsh factory discipline and political repression as (especially third world) states compete to attract internationally mobile capital.

NIDL theory has been roundly criticised on a number of grounds. *Inter alia*, it overstates the extent and prospects of a general relocation of jobs from developed to developing countries, and by focusing almost exclusively upon the export-led growth of a rather small number of 'Newly Industrialising Countries' (NICs) such as Taiwan, Singapore, Malaysia, South Korea and Mexico has understated the level of industrialisation achieved at the (semi-) periphery of the capitalist system (e.g. Argentina, Chile, India and South Africa) prior to the 1960s (the decade in which the NIDL is said to have become a reality). Likewise, it overestimated the role of tncs whilst underestimating the extent to which the state and even indigenous bourgeoisies have played in mobilising capital in the third world. Similarly, whilst at one level it may be argued that a surplus of labour in developing countries is nothing new, at another it can hardly be assumed that either governments or workers themselves can be expected to remain passive in the face of employment losses. Even so, notwithstanding these and other telling criticisms, NIDL theory has pointed the way to a widespread recognition that transformations in the global economy have significantly affected labour in many parts of the world for the worse.

If it is the case that progress towards a globalisation of production implies a deterioration in the condition of (some) workers in the third world, then it becomes important to reassert the importance of their trade unions. I say 'reassert' for two reasons. Firstly, because in the period following the independence of most of Asia and Africa trade unions in the third world received an overall 'bad press', from the right on the consumptionist grounds that wage leverage by a 'selfish' minority of organised workers diverts scarce resources away from investment in the public good ('development'), and from the left on the grounds that they had too often proved bureaucratic, representative principally of 'labour aristocrats', and subject too readily to Western (or Soviet) 'labour imperialism'. And second, corresponding disappointment amongst radicals with the performance of third world trade unions, along with discontent at the appropriateness of concentrating analysis upon organisations serving only a small proportion of still predominantly rural work forces, produced a shift from the traditional concerns of 'labour studies' (industrial relations, union structures, wage rates, employment levels, labour mobility and so on) towards emphasis upon broader processes such as proletarianisation, the political character of worker struggles, the role of the urban poor, labour migration and, critically, the subordination of women as producers and 'reproducers' in peripheral societies.

This 'new international labour studies' (as Robin Cohen (1980a) dubbed it) notwithstanding, the role of trade unions in the third world has recently been coming under renewed scrutiny as writers such as Peter Waterman have emphasised that, for all their limitations, unions are fundamental organisations of the working class, ones which workers 'cannot do without' if they are to resist exploitation by capital and 'thereby impose themselves upon society' (Waterman, 1977; p. 58). In tandem, writers such as James Petras (1978) and Mark Selden (1983) have argued the need to write the working class back into the history of third world transformation from whence it has been too dismissively banished 'in favor of preoccupations with landlord, peasant, bourgeoisie, and the state' (Selden, 1983, p. 59). Hence whilst the conference at which the papers which compile this volume were angled specifically at considering the position and potential of third world unions in relation to changes in the international division of labour, it none the less was similarly premised upon the growing appreciation (e.g. Kraus, 1976) that focus upon worker organisation is critical to any understanding of the defensive and offensive capacities of the third world poor, even (perhaps especially) in conditions that are not revolutionary.

In retrospect, the objective of the conference was similar to that of recent attempts to marry the global perspective pioneered by Immanual Wallerstein (1974, 1979) with international labour studies (Wallerstein, 1983; Portes and Walton, 1981; Bergquist, 1984), even though the conception of the NIDL is much more time-bound (in the late twentieth century) and much less grand in its historical sweep than the full-blown 'world-systems' approach.

In a recent critique of these attempts, Cohen and Waterman (1986) argue that hitherto world systems analysis has failed to deal adequately with labour struggles, first because its roots lie in radical trade theory and the circulation of commodities unconnected with labour power, and second because it has difficulty in accounting for human agency in a deterministic, causative schema (entailing rhythms, cycles, wages and capital movements) which operates at a very high level of abstraction.

However, rather than abandoning world systems theory, they commend it for having transcended nationalist historiography, for having activated internationalist and global thinking and for having transformed a concern for world areas (centre, semi-periphery and periphery) into a concern for world classes so that *social* relationships have become more important than *spatial* relationships. What world systems theory can contribute therefore is a mapping out of the constraints faced by differentially located labour movements. But what we need to do in addition is to 'situate and describe the connecting, dynamic and moving parts of the international system, to find where ideas are traded, politics are fought and social forces assert themselves'. They conclude: 'the economic determinism of the world system theorists . . . must be replaced by a concern for the role of politics, ideology, consciousness and class organisation' (Cohen and Waterman, 1986, pp. 7, 15). In other words, if we are to marry global approaches to international labour studies, we need to ensure that the marriage is well founded, that either partner does not talk past the other and that there is sufficient compatibility to make the liaison intimate and fertile.

In the companion volume to this collection a concerted attempt was made to overcome this tension between global level analysis and international labour studies. Hence in my overview and introduction (Southall, 1986), having argued that continuities in the global economy caution strongly against any exaggeration of the extent of the shift towards a new away from the 'old' international division of labour, I none the less proposed that the increasing extent to which production is becoming restructured at the global level indicates a major threat to world labour. In particular, I argued that four overlapping areas of concern could be identified with regard to third world trade unions:

1. The shift to global surplus population wrought by changes in the international division of labour implies un(der)employment and pressure on real wages and working conditions everywhere, and thereby undermines trade unions' defensive potential.
2. The forms of segmentation of the global workforce implied by the changing international division of labour may widen divisions between workers in hi-tech industry in the North and labour-intensive industry in the South, as well as between higher paid and higher skilled workers and low paid, lower skilled, marginally employed or unemployed labour *within* countries (North *and* South), thereby rendering united working class resistance to exploitation newly problematic.

3. Industrialisation in the third world generally takes place under highly repressive state and despotic production forms which unions are hardpressed to counter.
4. Although the internationalisation of production posits an extending depth of global proletarianisation and may thereby facilitate more extensive international labour links, it simultaneously throws up new obstacles to international labour solidarity.

If this was only a rough mapping out of the terrain on which third world trade unions are constrained to operate, the collection then sought to make progress towards engaging global approaches and international labour studies in a fruitful union, not only by considering the requirements for a 'new labour internationalism' going beyond mere international trade union co-operative (i.e. economistic) forms, but also by considering the prospects for trade union and worker alliances with other social movements and classes within the related contexts of both national and global economy. Hence, in trite summary, what was suggested by widely differing case studies of unions in Argentina, Nigeria, Sri Lanka, Malaysia and Iran was, *inter alia*: (i) summoned up historically by the process of import-substituting industrialisation, Latin American working classes provide a counter to capitals which now urgently argue the imperative of disorganising labour if continental competitiveness is to be restored, yet without indicating a concerted capacity to carry through an offensive socialist project; (ii) locked into the colonial rather than the new international division of labour, Nigerian unions' strength (and, by implication, that of the bulk of unions in Black Africa) is closely tied to their strategic location in national economy, and the prospect is that their muscle will be eroded over the long term to the extent that the continent is restructured disadvantageously by transformations in the global economy; (iii) export-oriented industrialisation in Asia asserts the underlying imperative which causes labour to struggle and combine, yet tends – not least through state machination and intervention – to a division and disorganisation of the working class which is particularly attractive to international investors; and (iv) the pattern of development pursued by the oil-exporting countries of the Middle East (entailing a 'rentier' form of state together with inward-looking import-substitution industrialisation) requires a reorganisation of social production relations centring around the accelerated growth of an industrial proletariat strategically located within the economy, yet in conditions (as in Iran) in which the political consciousness of the working class blends with Islam to allow a

Introduction

blunting of its revolutionary impetus by the social agencies of repressive theocracy. In sum, what is argued is the value of locating working class struggles within the context of the international redeployment of capital, with emphasis being given to how patterns and strategies of industrialisation are both acted upon and simultaneously restructure the nature of the labour market (whether by expanding the reserve army or by segmenting it along ethnic or skill-based lines) and how they encourage a shift to authoritarian state and production forms.

The problem with any such generalisations, of course, is that they soon break down when confronted by contrary instances and the sheer diversity of reality. Further, as an excellent (as yet unpublished) overview by conference participant Ronnie Munck (1987) makes clear, we simply cannot reduce such varied aspects as employment patterns, changes in the labour process, class formation, trade union forms and practices, systems of labour control, union–state relations and so on to a function of changes in the international division of labour (about which there remains much controversy anyway).

Munck takes issue with the approach of Hobart Spalding (another conference contributor) whose work had done much to structure the theme of the gathering (Southall, 1984, p. 150) by proposing that Latin American labour movements have tended to pass through similar periods (pre-formative, formative, expansive and explosive, and co-optive), these stages being strongly conditioned by two variables: (i) the mode of integration of national economies into the world economy; and (ii) the specific nature of national elites, these being largely dependent upon foreign markets, capital and technology. But the problem with this line of arguments, says Munck, is that if general trends are located across a whole continent they will tend to be superficial and devoid of explanatory power, whilst an emphasis upon elites undervalues the ability of workers to participate in making their own destinies. Then, in a related observation later in his text, Munck questions James Petras's generalisation that the emergence of what he terms neo-fascism in a number of NICs with diverse historical backgrounds and internal structures (Chile, Brazil, Uruguay, Argentina, Indonesia, South Korea and the Shah's Iran) is a function of 'the growth of capital accumulation on a world scale' (Petras, 1980, p. 124; also featuring in Southall, 1984, p. 153). Rather Munck cites regional diversity and national peculiarities, stressing also labour movements' capacity to resist authoritarianism (Munck, 1987, ch. 9).

Munck's critique is well taken: the questions which the conference posed were valid, legitimate and important, but the answers do not fit neatly into pre-determined 'world system' or 'dependency theory' packages, and certainly not those of area-studies. This is further demonstrated by the papers offered here which although constituting a small number of country and thematic case studies, illustrate variety in labour's settings, struggles and strategies. That said, the collection does not dissolve into disparate stories and issues, nor does the international labour studies. Rather, as Munck himself argues, concentration upon

> a given geographical area of the world does not imply that labour is 'different' there. Rather the emphasis is on international labour studies, with the third world being simply the area we focus on. This perspective is essential because workers and peasants in the third world are part of a global economic, political and social process. (Munck, 1987, Preface)

In other words, the international dimension remains crucial, and in seeking to overcome the unhelpful compartmentalism of 'area studies within labour studies', the comparative thrust of the present volume may be suggestive in providing further indication of the advantages to be wrought by seeking out the global conditioning of diverse yet historically specific labour situations and strategies.

I THIRD WORLD AREA LABOUR STUDIES

Munck begins his overview of third world workers by observing that the NILS perspective has developed on the back of a wave of labour studies carried out in Africa and Latin America over the last fifteen years. In contrast, Asian labour studies have lagged behind, only more recently having put on a late spurt as Asia has provided the major area-focus for debate concerning the new international division of labour. It is not without relevance that in the related sphere of political economy there has been a much more explicit and concerted joint focus upon Africa and Latin America (Stallings, 1972; Ehrensaft, 1967; Shaw, 1982), with rather few attempts having been made to systematically compare Asian incorporation into the global economy with that of other world areas.

At one level (and this is a statement which in the presence of African and Latin American specialists I would not wish to push too far!) this lack of comparative focus would appear to be a reflection of the greater diversity of historical experiences, socio-economic structures, political struggles and state forms found in Asia (if we take into account the fact that we have to include such varying states as India, China, Malaysia,

Vietnam and the Philippines under the same continental rubric). As Munck (1987; ch. 7) observes in relation to the industrial relations sphere, the experience of Asian workers is characterised by enormous unevenness ranging from spectacular struggles on the one hand (China, Vietnam) to apparently quiescent labour movements (Singapore) on the other.

This unevenness finds little echo in one of the few attempts to compare the characteristics of the working class in Africa and Asia wherein Soviet writer Dimitry Kucherenko (1983) reduces enormous diversity to order by identifying three key aspects of what (significantly) he terms 'Afro-Asian' society. These are: (i) the broad tendency, out of the complexity of widely varying precapitalist social relationships, for societies to move towards common class patterns (notably the historical evolution of the working class); (ii) the fact that the working class as yet forms a relatively small proportion of the total labour force and articulates with what he terms 'transitional' social strata; and (iii) the resultant historical weakness of the proletariat (despite the disproportionate influence it brings to bear upon society) and its consequent need to forge alliances with other oppressed and democratic classes if it is to become a developed revolutionary force. As a result, concludes Kucherenko, proletarian parties have been practically non-existent, and workers have consequently joined petty-bourgeois or even bourgeois dominated parties. Thus even though trade unions have assumed a political role (reflecting the inherently political nature of the proletariat), their progressive possibilities are inhibited by their organisation of only a small proportion of the working class, their tendency towards bureaucracy, their dispersal through small industrial units and their division between competing trade union centres. Hence although increased proletarianisation will promote the incorporation of the wider masses into the labour movements, this may lead to a dilution of 'the fine process of the qualitative ripening of the proletariat as a whole', even though the working class will remain 'the most consistent revolutionary force of anti-imperialist struggle' (Kucherenko, 1983, p. 247).

The point does not need much elaboration that if reality can be glimpsed through such formalistic analysis, then it is simultaneously diffracted in such a way as to avoid any assessment of revolutionary experiences in such countries as China, Vietnam and Angola which might prove awkward to Soviet cosmology. We clearly need some sense of world historical process, but the role of the working class cannot be imposed upon reality precisely because the *commonality* of third world subjection to imperialism is simultaneously *differentiated* in terms of the diversity of national forms, historical experiences and modes and levels of integration into the global economy. Development may well be combined, but it is also remarkably uneven. We may well be able to say with Samir Amin that 'the national question, which in the nineteenth century was principally that of oppressed European nations was transferred in the twentieth century to Asia and Africa' (Amin, 1980, p. 173), yet the variegated responses of the veritable cacophony of nations and quasi-nations to even this issue allows no reduction to any such homogenised entity as 'Afro-Asian' society. This can be clearly illustrated by very brief reference to the rather different (yet not unconnected) trends and developments in third world area labour studies.[1]

Latin America

As far as Latin America is concerned, the emphasis in labour studies shifted in the 1960s from historical to the structural analysis of labour, ideological accounts of labour movements by diversely politically-oriented activists giving way to sociological analyses of initially the modernisation and later the dependency school. These approaches centred around two dualisms, the one addressing the dichotomy of urban/industrial and rural life (in terms of workers' origins, consciousness, cleavages and so forth) and the other the issue of whether the working class was reformist or revolutionary (Munck, 1987; ch. 1).

A principal concern – where it was not to detail the extent of labour repression – was to specify the characteristics of trade unions which had made so many of them susceptible to incorporation by the state. In particular, this required analysis of working class mobilisation by populist regimes, and how working class militancy had been variously manipulated and contained by populist leaderships and/or more reactionary forms of corporate state. At one level, this led to a focus upon trade union organisation (labour bureaucracy, 'parallel' union structures and pervasively, a lack of rank and file democracy) and structural ties of unions with the state; at another, more advanced level, it led to attempts to establish relationships between trade union developments and forms of state required by the changing nature of local economies' insertion into the global system, there being a shift away from 'welfare populism' – which facilitated the development of national capitals on the basis of expanding markets – to more regressive (often military) regimes associated with the post-war inflow of foreign capital oriented to export-led growth (Almeida and Lowy, 1976;

Epstein, 1979; Harding and Spalding, 1976; Moises, 1979). A growing sophistication of debate was subsequently encouraged not only by studies of the changes in the labour process brought about by the transnationalisation of production (Humphrey, 1982; Vellingra, 1979) but also by a wave of labour insurgencies in countries like Argentina, Brazil and Chile which illustrated that mobilisation of the working class may proceed beyond the structural limits established by reformist union leaderships to more radical forms of political action (Erickson, Peppe and Spalding, 1974; Jelin, 1979; Petras, 1970; Spalding, 1979).

Africa

In contrast to the Latin American experience, bibliographic overviews of African labour studies (Cohen, Copans and Gutkind, 1978; Freund, 1985; Munck, 1987) indicate, apart from a very limited communist engagement (Nzula, Potekhin and Zusmanovitch, 1979; Simons and Simons, 1969), an almost total absence of known participant written history. What is demonstrated in its place is a movement away from an early preoccupation of colonial writers with the 'problem' of labour supply to a post-independence concern by radicals with the elaboration of the coercive essence of colonial labour policies, this matched by a transition via labour migration studies from an earlier colonial- -sociological emphasis upon tradition/modern dualities to stress upon working-class formation and proletarianisation of the peasantry.

Independence brought with it a wave of studies of trade unions, assessing their political role in the national struggle and their likely contribution to development. Inevitably, the initial focus was upon union relations with the state, debate focusing upon the level of autonomy retained by trade unions as a function of their strategic location in the economy, their relation to ruling and opposition political parties, and the extent to which their internal structures continued to serve the class interests of their members (Ananaba, 1979; Berg and Butler, 1964; Cohen, 1974; Sandbrook, 1975). In retrospect, what such case studies demonstrate is that although the muscle of African trade unions (as befits countries integrated into the global economy as suppliers of raw materials) lies in the mines, railways, docks and public services, post-independence import substitution industrialisation (limited though it has been) has considerably strengthened the working class as a political constituency which governments can ill afford to ignore (Bates, 1971; Grillo, 1973; Jeffries, 1978; Parpart, 1983; Peace, 1979; Waterman, 1983).

Kraus noted some time ago that many of the early studies of trade unions' performance were couched in terms of a dominant radical paradigm whose bias presupposed, *inter alia*, co-option of union leaderships by the state, bureaucratisation of union organisations and the unresponsiveness of union organisations to rank and file pressures from below. This followed not just from widespread concern about unions having been transformed from representative/consumptionist into productionist/welfare organs in the 'new states', but also from the centrality which the labour aristocracy notion came to assume in the late 1960s and 1970s, the principal thesis being that the most highly organised strata of the working class materially and culturally identified with emergent neo-colonialism (Arrighi and Saul, 1973; Saul, 1975; Waterman, 1975). However, successive later studies demonstrated that the most highly paid and skilled urban workers were not necessarily less militant than other workers, whilst the endemic economic crisis throughout Africa in recent years has exposed the fragility and relativity of 'aristocratic' privilege and re-emphasised the legitimacy of employment and wage protection as the basic trade union function (Howard, 1987; International Confederation of Free Trade Unions, 1984).

The radical paradigm offered inadequate consideration of the question of how union leaders and workers should cope with often overbearing state power to which they could usually counterpose only meagre resources. Thus it was that later work dealt more sympathetically with the ambiguous contexts in which African unions were located, with there being a reaffirmation of the role of trade unions as the only remaining mass organisations of the labouring poor in the majority of African countries which have succumbed to the military or other demise of democratic rule (Waterman, 1975). New emphasis upon the question of how workers are to develop their muscle to alter power relations in their favour, along with a developing interest in union democracy and the labour process, now combine to produce a more sophisticated theoretical approach which suggests that African workers can secure progressive change even in politically and economically restrictive contexts (Crisp, 1984, p. 12).

This more nuanced appreciation of the possibilities as well as the limits of union power has meshed with growing interest in relations between organised and non-unionised workers (who still form the overwhelming majority of the working population). Seminal to this development has been the increasingly sophisticated delineation of labour protest and understanding of the emergence of class consciousness, with earlier concentration upon overt reaction to the impositions of capital (ranging from constitutional petitioning to strikes) being supplemented by emphasis and discovery of the variety of forms, tactics and strategies utilised by workers in covert protest (Cohen, 1980b; Gutkind *et al.,* 1978; Sandbrook and Cohen, 1975). And whilst at one level this advance has been associated with an increasing number of studies of the labour process (Buroway, 1982; Crisp, 1985), at another it reflects the interest which burgeoned in the 1970s in the 'informal' sector of the economy, this entailing elaboration of the complexity of the social composition of the African working population and its engagement in small-scale commodity production (Gerry, 1976; Sandbrook and Arn, 1977; Waterman, 1984).

It goes almost without saying that no survey such as this could conclude without reference to the enormous impact made by the flowering of the historiography of southern Africa and the maturation of the critically engaged contemporary analysis which has taken place around the growth of the independent trade union movement in South Africa since the early 1970s. Pioneered above all by Van Onselen (1976; 1982), the new approach to labour history which stresses the infinite variety and subtlety of forms of worker resistance to the coercive work environments has found loud echo in studies well beyond the region, whilst a recent shift away from concentration upon the disentangling of class and race has allowed a greater understanding of the 'immensely complex and often painful making of (the) working class in all its cultural specificity' (Marks and Rathbone, 1982, p. 7). Meanwhile, centred around the *South African Labour Bulletin* (which has emerged as the major forum for progressive debate concerning the direction in which the independent unions are moving and the issues which black workers must confront) has emerged a labour-orientated and committed tradition of analysis and monitoring devoted as much to practical issues (e.g. health and safety) as the strategic dilemmas the movement has continuously to resolve. Emerging from this at the Ottawa conference was a set of studies relating the development of working class organisation and transformations in the labour process and working class culture to the transition from competitive towards monopoly capitalism (Southall, 1985).

Asia

Noting the paucity of analysis of Asian labour and labour movements, Mark Selden (1983, p. 58) observes: 'the proletariat has not fared well in the hands of social scientists and historians of Asia'. Given also, as noted above, that the experience of Asian labour has been so variegated, we clearly need to approach the very notion of an 'Asian labour studies' with some caution lest we impose a contrived coherence upon a very disparate reality. Yet whatever the situation in the past, it can now be argued with some confidence that a number of common themes are beginning to distinguish a new approach to labour throughout Asia. Despite the difficulties, therefore, it is useful to identify a move from a traditional to a 'new labour studies' parallel to advances made in the analysis of third world labour elsewhere.

Given that it was the peasantry and not the proletariat which was deemed central to the great transformations which took place in China and Vietnam, the traditional approach was forged more or less by default around the study of labour in those countries in which the impetus towards revolutionary change was avoided, suppressed or diverted along nationalist lines. Thus it was that in India, where research into labour issues was most detailed and extensive (and where, correspondingly, the 'new labour studies' is today most deeply rooted), the principal concerns were at first with employment statistics, wages, social security, industrial relations, formal trade union history, labour productivity and the labour policies of the colonial and post-colonial state (Das, 1980, pp. 1–2; Gupta and Kharbas, 1984, pp. 139–41). Cursory survey of the literature on countries such as Malaysia and Thailand (O'Brien's bibliography below; Mabry, 1977) indicates that this experience was replicated elsewhere, if rather unevenly, with considerable emphasis being laid upon the emergence of workers and their organisations as reflecting the modernisation of 'traditional' society (Wehmhorner, 1983). However, what was notable about these early forays was that the emergent working class was not treated so much as an historical agency but as a factor of production from which all political content was wrung dry (despite the irony, in the Malaysian case, that trade unionism in its origins had been closely associated with the development of 'communist insurgency').

Despite this depoliticisation of the working class (notably by government and academic analysts) what is particularly distinctive about the Indian case is the extent to which even the early study of labour was dominated by nationals. There were many reasons why this was so, but the overwhelming one was simply that labour studies developed very much in tandem with the nationalist struggle, the primary motivation being to expose the devastating impact of colonialism upon Indian workers. If initially this meant that the approach was largely taxonomic (detailing the extent and causes of poverty), after independence it was reflected in a number of autobiographical and partisan accounts of early trade union politics by activists, although Das observes that ferment among the peasantry during the 1930s had shifted nationalist attention to peasant questions during that era.

Following independence, in India and elsewhere, growth of state involvement in national economies meant that primary emphasis was laid upon study of the labour market, productivity, union–state relations and so on. But the subsequent crisis in post-colonial political economy was to stimulate different perspectives. Hence Das (1980, p. 3) writes that in India 'the bulk of the new labour studies started almost at the same time as a severe economic recession, breakdown of the Congress monolith, passing of political power into the hands of 'opposition' parties, splits in the communist and social democratic parties, the outbreak of the massive "Naxalite" (Maoist) peasant and youth movements, and the forging by industrial and other workers of the innovative weapon of *gherao*' (an agitational form in which workers surround and humiliate factory owners, managers and supervisors to advance their struggles) (Aggarwal, 1968). Much more attention was now paid to 'labour protest', not least because both state and capital founded research institutes to study ways and means to secure worker discipline and industrial harmony, although labour struggles simultaneously stimulated wider interest in workers as a major force of social change.

Within the latter context the analysis of the Naxalites ushered the labouring population in agriculture to centre stage and focused attention upon the plight and potential of workers in the rural areas. This much was welcome, but in so far as the 'peasant messianism' (Waterman, 1982, p. 478) of the Naxalites was to sideline industrial workers in the wings it provoked a counter-reaction and impelled an urgent analysis of the relationships between the different class elements of the oppressed (what Das correctly identifies as the crux of the new labour studies). As Pathy details in his chapter, this was to become caught up in the intricacies of the 'modes of production' debate and result in a somewhat arid discussion of whether or not the peasantry was becoming proletarianised. Even so, despite its drawbacks, this was to pave the way for a more radical approach which found expression in worker–intellectual engagement in popular struggles, a labour-based journalism and a resurgence of socialist labour studies.

This is, of course, too tidy a picture of a very uneven Indian reality. None the less, it offers a broad outline of trends which found its echo in the study of labour elsewhere in Asia, for instance, in application of the concept of marginality (e.g. Ronasinghe, 1982, on Sri Lanka) and in more nuanced exploration of the notion of worker–peasant alliance (e.g. Post, 1979, on China). Furthermore, although organised labour in Thailand–by 1976 'the most credible spokesman for the urban masses' (Mabry, 1977, p. 948)–still awaits its historian, strike waves in such countries as Pakistan and Sri Lanka began to generate interest in the long-term effects of an accumulation of experience of struggle upon worker organistation and consciousness (Fernando, 1983; Kearney, 1979; Shaheed, 1979). In contrast, the post-colonial withering away of strike activity in Singapore encouraged analysis of the systematic repression of overt labour protest (Luther, 1978; 1979).

It is, of course, the connection between authoritarian regimes, forms of labour control and 'new' industrialisation which has become the major focus of the new labour studies in South and South East Asia. In brief, the shift towards a NIDL under which tncs have relocated aspects of their production to low wage countries such as Singapore, Malaysia, South Korea, the Philippines and Taiwan (whether via subsidiaries or joint ventures with local capitalist firms) has generated an explosion of research upon the nature of the capitalist labour process as it has been transferred to the third world, the sexual division of labour and the capacity of workers to fight back against the despotic conditions which capital imposes.

The greatest single stimulus to the new labour studies in this context has been the widespread establishment throughout Asia of export processing zones in which concessions by host countries to tncs regularly imply minimal wages, appalling work conditions, a denial of social benefits and, of course, a suspension of trade union rights. Whilst much preliminary work was done on outlining the extent of state support for what was (and is) a strategy of primitive accumulation, later work has centred rather more upon analysis of the fragmentation of the produc- tion process by tncs and their mode of employment and control of third world workers to undertake semi- and unskilled labour-intensive work at a cost lower than in countries of the industrialised West. Indeed, it is precisely because tncs have sought out malleable, vulnerable and adaptable workforces that they have so often turned to women, and it is to the elaboration of why women are deemed to have the required dexterity and passivity that much recent study has turned (Elson and Pearson; 1981), particular attention being paid to how women's work in the domestic and agricultural economy underpins their participation in wage labour (Nash and Fernandez-Kelly, 1983; Pineda-Ofreneo, 1982).

Necessarily, studies of the labour process in Asian NICs have taken their lead from Buroway's (1982; 1985) elaboration of how different mixes of coercion and consent in the labour process have forged different forms of labour control in colonial and post-colonial (market and state socialist) societies, and in turn they have contributed much to the elaboration of the variant ways in which Taylorist work principles are applied by capital to the third world (Lipietz, 1982; 1984; Norlund, Wad and Brun, 1984). But equally important has been the stress laid upon the way in which the production process shapes working class struggles and resistance to managerial control. In turn, this has resulted in emphasis being laid upon the important role by women in collective struggle, within the factory and beyond, the particular forms of resistance they espouse, and what is too often the incapacity or unwillingness of male-dominated trade unions and other organisations to respond to their needs (Halim, 1983; Omvedt, 1980).

As yet we await study of the labour process (and much besides) in the socialist countries of Asia. However, growing dissatisfaction with the manner in which the working class has been overlooked because of overwhelming preoccupation with the peasantry in the study of Asian revolutions is leading to a reassessment of both the historical and contemporary role of the proletariat. To be sure, few query the judgement of historians that, ultimately, the small Chinese proletariat played a peripheral part in the main drama of the Chinese civil war between Chinese Communist Party (CCP) forces and the Guomindang and the liberation of 1949 (Bianco, 1967, p. 83). Nevertheless, increasing attention is now being paid to elaborating just how crucial the activities of workers were in the development of anti-imperialist nationalist activity and in providing a base for the nationalist revolution of 1911, whilst new emphasis is being laid upon the conjuncture of nationalist issues with the post-1918 'golden age' of the Chinese working class (notably the strike waves of 1919–22 and 1925–7) which accelerated the growth of the CCP and its challenge to imperialism, the warlords, the landlords and the bourgeoisie (Chesneaux, 1968). 'Perhaps no working class movement has ever matured so rapidly or carried to such intensity the natural thrust of its struggle as did the Chinese labour movement between 1919 and 1927' (Selden, 1983, p. 95). The subsequent smashing of organised labour in the reactionary counterthrust by the Guomindang in 1927 was of course to drive the revolution into the countryside, workers playing only a minor role in events thereafter. However, the suggestion by Petras (1978) that the mass of recruits to the revolutionary forces were in fact *former* peasants (uprooted from the land) and were hence a proto-proletariat, even if exaggerated, should encourage a honing of the debate about the nature of class forces and the class alliances required for successful socialist transformation.

Finally, as Selden (1983, p. 112) observes, the irony of the CCP coming to power by a route which bypassed the industrial working class in favour of a close relationship with the peasantry in arms should not be allowed to obscure the fact that the revolution of 1949 opened a new cycle of industrialisation featuring the growth of the proletariat and its improved material position. However, as yet, the consensus is that it is the socialist state which has made this expanded working class, not vice versa (Walder, 1984). The contribution of Chossudovsky in the paper below in which he argues that a recent reorientation of Chinese industry to the world market is premised upon the exploitation of cheap labour hence not only gives rise to classic questions about the necessity of working class engagement as a vanguard in the struggle for socialism, but points the way to a greater integration of Asian labour studies by inviting extension of the analysis of the labour process, worker resistance and the sexual division of labour under the NIDL to China after Mao.

II CONTRIBUTIONS TO A DEVELOPING APPROACH

However cursory the survey, enough has been said to indicate that the labour studies of Latin America, Africa and Asia each have their distinctive traditions reflecting the different forms of exploitation of labour historically, and the uneven and varied experiences, modes and levels of working class formation, resistance, organisation and so on. At the same time it becomes clear that certain common themes and problems have defined foci of interest in each case. Critical to all, of course, has been delineation of the relation of unions to political forces and governments. Whilst this has found prominence in the Latin American case in the theorisation of corporatism, it has been matched by the 'radical paradigm' in African labour studies and has more recently found echo in discussion of the dictatorial politics which seems the most widespread accompaniment of new industrialisation in the countries of Asia. A closely related issue has been that of discerning labour's political tendency (the debate having been most rigorous in connection with the notion of labour aristocracy in Africa), whilst necessarily the themes of migrancy and workers' continuing associations with the land (inhibited proletarianisation) feature prominently especially in African and Asian labour studies (although note Laite, 1981, and Nash, 1979, for Latin America). In turn, the modes of production debate has meshed with intense interest in changes in the labour process wrought by the transnationalisation of production to stimulate a new awareness of the fundamental importance of analysing the nature of the multi-layered exploitation and domination of women and their relation to unions and other social movements. And common to third world labour studies generally has been an insistence upon progressing beyond the simplicities of whether workers are good for 'reform or revolution', emphasis now being laid upon the contested nature of the terrain between capital and labour.

What is unsatisfactory, of course, is any suggestion that we should go on 'thinking labour studies' in continental terms. The artificiality of even such an apparently established term as 'Asia' has already been noted, whilst the utility of the notion of a 'third world' as merely a convenient conceptual hold-all has often been commented upon. But what is important to stress is the increasing weight of third world workers in the world system and the need for international labour studies to take account of the specifics as well as the general conditions of third world labour if we are to make progress towards forging what Waterman (1984) has called a 'new labour internationalism'.

The papers that follow were all selected to that end. They seek to flesh out our understanding of unions and labour in Africa and Asia and enable us to make useful comparisons, but the intention is not that they should be construed narrowly as contributions to 'Oriental and African Studies'. Rather, they reflect the much more vital concern of the Ottawa Conference to analyse the restructuring of labour markets occasioned by changes in the international division of labour and the limits this imposes upon and the opportunities it opens up for workers in the third world. Yet not surprisingly, even though we must accept that the small number of countries dealt with necessarily inhibits any emergent cross continental comparisons, what does come through very clearly in the contrast between the overwhelming continuity of Africa's location in the old division of labour and the differentiated nature of Asian countries' location in the new.

This is demonstrated initially by the papers on China and Nigeria. Michel Chossudovsky opens his analysis on the former with an uninhibited outline of the global tendency towards a NIDL, proposing that the post-Second World War transnationalisation of production has resulted in a migration of productive capital away from the advanced capitalist centres to the periphery of the world economy where labour is cheap. However, his particular theme is that world systemic integration is brought about by capital's juxtaposition of competing labour reserve countries. In historical terms, therefore, as the dynamic rate of export-led development in the first wave of NICs in South East Asia has led to an increase in the average level of industrial wages, so have traditional labour-intensive industries moved on to competing cheap labour countries. The world relative surplus population characterised by the juxtaposition of national industrial reserve armies becomes the lever of accumulation on a world scale, thus necessitating state intervention against organised labour to secure the international competitiveness of national labour markets.

Within this context Chossudovsky provides a fascinating account of how the opening of the Chinese economy to foreign investment capital in the post-Mao period is re-establishing the pattern of trade relations with the imperialism which obtained before 1949, this centring around the re-emergence of comprador relations within the network of the state bureaucracy and party apparatus as well as a mediating role between China and Western capital by the expatriate Chinese bourgeoisie in Hong Kong and elsewhere. Conditions in China for foreign investors are now more favourable than in other (capitalist) cheap labour countries in South East Asia and, in addition, the Chinese state is now becoming active in the sale of Chinese migrant labour to foreign contractors abroad. In brief, with some 25 per cent of the global population, 'socialist' China's reinsertion into the capitalist world economy signifies a new and important historical phase in the development of the international division of labour.

It has recently been argued by Jenkins (1985) that the existence of a virtually inexhaustible supply of labour on a world scale can hardly contribute to a NIDL in that the reserve army at the periphery had made its appearance well before the 1960s. What he would appear to overlook, however, is Chossudovsky's point that the significant shift to world market production that has taken place since then has pitted previously disarticulated national labour reserves against each other via world market competition. Fashoyin's contribution goes on to amply demonstrate the extremely uneven nature of that process.

In examining the labour market consequences of labour mobility within the Economic Community of West African States (ECOWAS), Fashoyin addresses the apparent contradiction that a seeming labour surplus economy like Nigeria simultaneously draws upon supplies of unskilled migrant workers from neighbouring countries. His basic answer is that migrant labour is largely complementary to and non-

competitive with indigenous labour. Hence, although he does not use the
term, he is arguing that the labour market in Nigeria is segmented; that
is, it is divided between a formal sector characterised by monopoly
employers who use high technology, require high as well as lower skilled
workers, and offer career opportunities and higher wages; and an
informal sector, characterised by highly competitive conditions, ease of
entry, a preponderance of family labour and ownership, small scale
operation, use of limited capital and labour-intensive technology, and
offering minimal wages. In other words, whilst accepting that prevailing
conditions in the informal sector do serve ultimately to restrain wage
levels in the formal sector, he none the less maintains that formal sector
labour (which is reserved largely to citizens) is not significantly
threatened by non-citizen migrant labour precisely because the latter is
effectively barred from advance employment spheres by its non-posses-
sion of skills and national exclusivity. He therefore concludes that
Nigerian trade unions, which have hitherto organised only formal sector
workers, should abandon any hint of labour market protectionist
policies and now seek to incorporate migrant workers in order to achieve
improved working conditions within the informal sector whilst simultaneously assisting the integration of ECOWAS. In particular, the
labour movement can afford to take a more vigorous internationalist
stand against periodic expulsion of non-citizen workers by the government without fear for the jobs and employment prospects of citizens.

There are clearly aspects of this which are troublesome, not least the
conditional vision of labour internationalism which Fashoyin projects.
But what is particularly germane to the present interest is his insistence
that Nigerian informal sector employers offer work to non-citizens
precisely because their labour is cheaper. For what Fashoyin also argues
is that labour shortages in key employment spheres following the 1983
wave of non-citizen labour expulsions (officially motivated in part to
free jobs for citizens) indicates that at the wages offered Nigerian
replacements were not prepared to come forward, the implication being
that many of the citizen 'underemployed' are in fact 'fully employed' in
the informal sector or agriculture. Obviously, what is needed is a more
sensitive exploration of labour market segmentation than Fashoyin's
neo-classical dichotomy of formal and informal sectors allows; but at
another level it becomes clear that in Nigeria it is foreign migrants, not
citizens, who at present compose the preponderant body of the *active*
reserve army of the unemployed.

Ihonvbere and Shaw go some way towards this more detailed
specification of the Nigerian labour market in their study of Nigerian oil

workers. Because of their strategic location in the oil dependent economy, these are apparently well placed for militant action. What the authors seek to explain is why these workers have been less volatile than the energy source they extract and distribute.

They find the answer at a number of levels, but critical is the restructured colonial shape of the economy. In other words, whilst they identify Nigeria as a NIC at the semi-periphery of the global economy, they stress its continued reliance upon the export of raw materials. Nigeria is clearly *not* located in the NIDL in the sense described by Chossudovsky, but rather is a provider of fossil fuels subject to cyclical demands. The 'petroleum proletariat' is therefore only in a position to realise its strategic potential when the oil price is high and the effects of the strong demand for oil have reverberated throughout the rest of the economy soaking up alternative surplus labour.

To be sure, Ihonvbere and Shaw acknowledge other important factors that impinge upon the character of the 'petro-proletariat'. For a start, they accord rather more importance to the informal sector and migrant labour as a reserve army of labour than Fashoyin allows, and in addition they stress the coercive labour controls exercised by the oil companies under the auspices of a 'triple alliance' between international capital, Nigerian compradors and the state, this entailing *inter alia* the incorporation of an aristocratic stratum of oilworkers whose conservative dispostion centres upon the benefits accorded to them by virtue of their higher skills and levels of seniority. But what may most usefully be stressed here is that the political space allowed Nigerian oil workers is hedged in by the marginality of their labour market situation.

What the Nigerian and Chinese case studies point to is the differing global function of surplus population in Asia and Africa. In brief, despite an already critical situation in Africa where in 1977 some 12 million people or 8 per cent of the total workforce were unemployed and another 60 million of 40 per cent of the labour force were under-employed (International Confederation of Free Trade Unions 1974), multinational capital is not greatly attracted to the continent, which presently contributes only about 1 per cent of world industrial output. Hence, with only a handful of countries having developed export-oriented manufacturing sectors, the mass of potential labour can be said to constitute only a *latent* surplus population – a global reserve army of labour largely held in reserve, and one which *actively* functions as such only around nodes of advanced industrial production (notably South Africa, but to a lesser extent countries like Nigeria and Kenya). In contrast, there is in Asia – where unemployment rates remain endemically high yet are lower overall than in Africa[2] – a greater *tendency* for the surplus population to assume a *floating* form. That is, to the extent that Asian economies are differentially incorporated into the NIDL, labour is alternately repelled and attracted by industry according to its cyclical requirements, whilst a growing resort to outwork (the use of mainly female and child labour in the home) by export industries such as clothing and electronics indicates a *stagnant* element forming part of the active labour force, dispersed well beyond the factory gates, yet irregularly employed and subject to extensive exploitation for minimal wage return.

It goes without saying that such contrasts between Africa and Asia can only be pushed so far. This point is driven home by a reading of Jaganath Pathy who in fact argues against the utility of describing the masses of semi-pauperised peasants and urban underemployed in India as a reserve army of labour. Rather, he suggests, the maintenance of a vast informal sector (characterised by the existence of precapitalist social relations of production) is crucial to the very functioning of capitalism in Inida (although he notes the simultaneous contrary tendency for pre-capitalist agrarian relationships to act as a fetter upon capitalist development). Clearly, stress upon the juxtaposition of national reserve armies, whilst a useful indicator, must necessarily take very careful account of pre-existing levels of industrialisation, state strategies, working class formation and organisation, and so on.

Given the dangers inherent in generalising about a sprawling sub-continent of infinite complexity, Pathy's is a bold attempt to elucidate the organisational situation and potential of 'the world's major unstudied working class' (Waterman, 1982, p. 464). Placing himself firmly in the camp of those who argue that capitalism in India has developed not by destroying pre-capitalist structures but by adjusting to them, Pathy argues that the increasing association of the Indian bourgeoisie with transnational capital is creating a surplus population which cannot be absorbed either by agriculture or the formal industrial sector. In turn, the inability of the Indian bourgeoisie to transform production relations (because of its ties to landed elements) is matched by entrapment of major segments of the Indian working class in pre-capitalist relationships. Contrary to interpretations which stress the inevitable proletarianisation of the rural workforce, he argues that no inherent trend towards an homogenisation of the labour market can be identified. Rather, the conservation-dissolution of precapitalist relations, the resultant inhibited proletarianisation of large numbers of labourers, and the coexistence/articulation of diverse segments of the workforce make the conventional distinction between formal and informal sectors redundant precisely because of the overlap of the working conditions between them.

It follows from this that Pathy should focus upon the severe limits of 'conventional' trade unionism in India as it has developed historically. That is, based upon the organisation of only formal sector workers, divided between competing party policital tendencies, otherwise fragmented along caste, religious, regional, linguistic and other primordial grounds, and heavily compromised by internal bureaucratisation and control/co-option by the state, the traditional unions have been rendered incapable of presenting a labour-based challenge to capital. The way forward therefore lies in strategies associated with what have been termed 'social movement' unions whose recent emergence and militance is premised not just upon working class grievances but also upon the linkage of these to the oppressions borne by the non-proletarianised workforce.

It is to the limitations of trade unionism as presently constituted to which Leslie O'Brien directs herself in her study of relations between capital and labour in Malaysia where the state has played a highly interventionist role in attempting to restructure the economy and its relation to international capitalism by encouraging export-oriented manufacturing alongside import-substitution industrialisation and the processing of natural resources for export. Under the auspices of a New Economic Policy inaugurated in the early 1970s, official strategy has sought to promote ethnic Malay ownership and control of a corporate economy previously dominated by colonial and minority Chinese ethnic capital as part of a broader project to eliminate the identification of Malay subordination with economic function.

Within the framework of the NEP, a further objective has been to promote a movement of ethnic Malay farmers off the land into urban and industrial occupations (previously the reserve of Chinese and Indian workers). Yet such a project of officially sponsored proletarianisation has necessarily held dangers for the ruling Malayan political coalition which has founded its post-colonial dominance upon the Malay masses thinking and acting along ethnic lines rather than in terms of any class position which they might share with Chinese and Indian workers. Not surprisingly, therefore, under the NEP the trade union movement is subject to a battery of state controls designed not merely to secure the normal advantages to capital and enhance Malaysia's attraction as a site for investment in world terms, but also to maintain the fragmentation of organised labour as far as possible along ethnic lines.

O'Brien locates all this within the context of the development of Malaysian trade unionism (which historically has seen the suppression of principally Chinese ethnic unions associated with the Chinese and Malaysian Communist parties and the subsequent state sponsorship of 'responsible' unionism representing mainly Indian workers). But what is particularly important about her analysis (despite her pessimistic conclusion that circumstances will hardly allow workers to find themselves as a class through labour as currently organised) is her insistence that we do not write off the existing unions as agencies of struggle. As with Wad (1987), who has explored the potentialities of worker activity within the constraints of Malaysian company unionism, she identifies unions as being of some real (albeit marginal) benifit to those who are organised within them. Malaysian labour studies will clearly need to move beyond depiction of union–state relations towards analysis of the shop floor if we are to comprehend the nuances and mode of worker struggles.

It appears that the same should be said for the study of capital–labour relations in Africa. In any case, this is the conclusion of Jon Kraus who offers a wide-ranging comparative survey of union-state relations in four countries of Africa (Algeria, Ethiopia, Ghana, and Tanzania) with the particular objective of examining whether radical and/or populist regimes, dedicated to strategies which *have* sought to advance certain popular class interests, have in practice safeguarded the interests of workers within the related contexts of both national political economy and the changing international division of labour.

Insisting that trade unions in Africa are the only mass organisations potentially capable of imposing the interests of the popular classes on state power, Kraus draws three major conclusions: (i) implementation by radical/populist regimes of labour repressive policies is directly related to their need to attract foreign capital, maximise foreign exchange and accept International Monetary Fund policy prescriptions in exchange for debt relief; (ii) developed strength and autonomy of a union movement prior to the establishment of radical and populist regimes increases the capacity of trade unions to retain a degree of independence from party and state; but (iii) despite any such residual autonomy, unions under populist/radical regimes have not been able to safeguard or significantly advance the material interests of workers, to extend their participation in national level politics or to influence the organisation or management of the means of production. In sum, the 'radical paradigm' of union–state relations in Africa which Kraus has criticised previously fails to take into account the high levels of coercive and co-optive capability of the state, and in consequence we should examine workplace authority relations if we seek to develop our comprehension of working class struggle.

Such an approach draws support from Debashish Bhattacherjee's analysis of the 1982 Bombay textile strike, the largest such confrontation in Indian urban labour history. In the Indian case, of course, we are dealing not with a radical or populist state but one whose social-democratic pretensions have encouraged the incorporation/co-option by the regime of the dominant trade union federation (which is closely aligned to the long-ruling Congress Party). Not surprising then that the legitimacy of the state sponsored union textiles affiliate should be rejected by workers when it failed to project their interests at a time when the textile industry was being restructured to cope with a decline in profitability and increase its world competitiveness, nor that militant shop floor struggle should unite different segments of the textile workforce (skilled and unskilled, permanent and temporary) in un-precedented rank and file efforts to wrest control of the capital–labour bargaining relationship.

The strike itself met with defeat, yet Bhattacherjee none the less marks it out as a major working class event, closely connected as it was with the 'new unionism' featured by Pathy. In particular, it points to the analytical utility of the concept of 'production politics' (Buroway, 1982) which, centring around the mesh of labour control institutions and practices employed by both management and state, pushes beyond the common but sterile distinction between economic and political aspects of the production process. It is therefore to capital–labour relations at the point of production (rather than to union–state relations) to which we should turn our attention if we wish to comprehend the determinants of worker activity.

That said, there is a danger: exclusive concentration upon production politics should not deflect us from consideration of how specifically worker grievances and protests articulates with other forms of oppression and struggle. If, at one level, such articulation finds expression in social movement unionism, it must also concentrate our attention upon the role of women in collective labour action.

This latter point is the subject of the closing essay by Jane Parpart who stresses time and again the need for more research to redress the gender-biased manner in which women have not so much been written out as not written in to African (and, we could equally well add, Asian) labour history. If this call is now becoming increasingly widespread, the jig-saw which Parpart has so painstakingly put together offers a sharp reminder of the fragmentary nature of our knowledge about women and work in the third world. Women have been ignored, she says, because historically they have been disproportionately excluded from wage labour, and when they have entered the wage labour force it has typically been in the least skilled, the most insecure and overwhelmingly ill-paid positions. Hence, except to a rather lesser extent in South Africa (where the role of women in wage labour has been most advanced), women have taken a back seat in trade unions, whose partiarchal inclinations have remained insensitive to women's needs and demands as women as well as workers. Even so despite the enormous obstacles they have faced in both the labour market and labour organisations, women have historically played a crucial, not merely supportive but often a highly active role in both colonial and post-colonial collective protest. It is therefore critical to overcome all forms of patriarchal bias within trade unions if gender divisions are not to impede worker solidarity and effective collective action, whilst students of labour clearly must embed gender into their analysis of class and worker struggles.

III   A CONCLUDING COMMENT

What does this all add up to? What can we draw out which is common to a small collection of diverse papers on different countries and topics? There are, I think, three very simple points I would like to make to conclude an already too lengthy introduction.

First, however we choose to interpret the notion of a changing international division of labour, we live in a world where production is becoming increasingly internationalised and in which, correspondingly, third world workers are becoming increasingly engaged in industrial production. Correspondingly, the study of their trade unions must remain central to any labour studies. In other words, despite all the limitations of third world trade unions as they actually exist, we must not throw the baby out with the bathwater in our enthusiasm to analyse labour in its broader societal context of oppression, survival and resistance.

Second, we need to centre our study of labour in the third world around the capital–labour relation and not, as has happened too much in the past, around a narrowly constructed relationship between the working class and the local state. Not only is the latter usually derivative from the former, but it encourages too concentrated an emphasis upon only the most visible of those who labour and toil. Our objective must be to link the study of direct exploitation by capital to associated relations of oppression and domination in a broader sense. Our focus upon unions must be production centred yet located in the context of workers' relations to and involvement in other social and political movements. Third, even if we do not go so far as Munck (1987, ch. 11) who argues that the tendency towards differentiation of the conditions of production is stronger than that towards its universalisation, we need to recognise that pre-capitalist relations of production are restructured as much as dissolved by the shift towards a globalisation of production. Correspondingly, even whilst we specify the impact of such uneven development in the third world (as this collection's focus on Asia and Africa sets out to do), we must simultaneously identify the developing linkages between and interdependence of spatially separated national working classes and theorise the problems of and possibilities for a new labour internationalism.

Notes

1. In what follows I attempt only a very brief sketch of trends and developments in area labour studies, not a full bibliographical essay. Accordingly I have tried to economise on references, drawing freely from Das (1980), Munck (1987) and Southall (1984).
2. Obviously, generalisation is dangerous as the employment situation in Asia is so varied. However, for a measure of employment and unemployment in the states of the Association of South East Asian States, see Table 1.4 ASEAN Employment and Unemployment 1983 in ICFTU, *The Trade Union Role in ASEAN/EC Relations* (Brussels: ICTFU, 1984), which indicates unemployment rates of zero [*sic*!] in Brunei and Singapore, and 4.3 in Indonesia, 5.9 in Malaysia, 4.6 in the Philippines and 2.0 in Thailand.

Bibliography

Aggarwal, A. (1968) *Gheraos and Industrial Relations* (Bombay: N.M. Tripathi).
Almeida, A.M. and Lowy, M. (1976). 'Union Structure and Labor Organisation in the Recent History of Brazil'. *Latin American Perspectives*, III, 1.
Amin, Samir. (1980) *Class and Nation, Historically in the Current Crisis* (New York and London: Monthly Review Press).
Ananaba, W. (1979) *The Trade Union Movement in Africa* (London: Hurst).
Arrighi, G. and Saul, J. (1973) 'International Corporations, Labour Aristocracies, and Economic Development in Tropical Africa' in *Essays on the Political Economy of Africa* (New York: Monthly Review Press).

Bates, R. (1971) *Unions, Parties and Political Development: A Study of the Mine-Workers in Zambia* (New Haven: Yale University Press).

Bergquist, C. (1984) *Labour in the Capitalist World Economy* (Beverly Hills: Sage).

Berg, E. and Butler, J. (1964) 'Trade Unions' in J. Coleman and C. Rosberg (eds) *Political Parties and National Integration in Tropical Africa* (Berkeley: California University Press).

Bianco, L. (1967) *Origins of the Chinese Revolution, 1915–1949* London, Stanford: Oxford University Press and Stanford University Press.

Buroway, M. (1982) 'The Hidden Abode of Underdevelopment: Labour Process and the State in Zambia', *Politics and Society*, 11, 2.

—— (1985) *The Politics of Production* (London: Verso).

Chesneaux, J. (1968) *The Chinese Labour Movement, 1919–27* (Stanford: Hoover Institution Press).

Cohen, R. (1974). *Labour and Politics in Nigeria* (London: Heinemann).

—— (1980a) '*The "New" International Labour Studies: A Definition*', Centre for Developing Area Studies, McGill University, Working Paper Series No. 27.

—— (1980b) 'Resistance and Hidden Forms of Consciousness among African workers', *Review of African Political Economy*, 19, 8.

Cohen, R. and Waterman, P. (1986) 'World Systems Theory and International Labour Studies, A Review Article', mimeo.

Crisp, J. (1985) *The Story of an African Working Class: Ghanaian Miners' Struggles, 1870–1980* (London: Zed).

Das, A. (1980) The 'New' Labour Studies in India, *Newsletter of International Labour Studies*, 8, 1–4.

Ehrensaft, P. (1976) 'Polarized Accumulation and the Theory of Economic Dependence: The Implications of South African Semi-Industrial Capitalism' in P.C.W. Gutkind and I. Wallerstein (eds), *The Political Economy of Contemporary Africa* (Beverly Hills, London: Sage).

Elson, D. and Pearson, R. (1981) 'The Subordination of Women and the Internationalization of Factory Production' in K. Young, C. Wolkowitz and R. McCullagh (eds) *Of Marriage and the Market* (London: CSE Books).

Epstein, E.C. (1976) 'Control and Co-optation of the Argentine Labour Movement' *Economic Development and Cultural Change*, 27, 3.

Fernando, L. (1983) 'The State and Class Struggle in Sri Lanka: The General Strike of July 1980', *Labour, Capital and Society*, 16, 2.

Frobel, F, Heinrichs, J. and Kreye, O. (1978) 'The World Market for Labor and the World Market for Industrial Sites', *Journal of Economic Issues*, XII, 4.

——, ——, —— (1980) *The New International Division of Labour* (London: Cambridge University Press and Paris: Edition de la Maison des Sciences de l'Homme).

Gerry, C. (1976) 'The Wrong Side of the Factory Gate: Casual Workers and Capitalist Industry in Dakar, Senegal' *Manpower and Unemployment Research*, 9, 2, 17–27.

Gupta, B. and Kharbas, D. (1984) *India* (Oxford, Santa Barbara: Clio Press, World Bibliographical Series, Volume 26).

Gutkind, P. Cohen, R. and Copans, J. (1978) *African Labor History* (Beverly Hills, London: Sage).

Halim, F. (1983) 'Workers' Resistance and Management Control: A Comparative Case Study of Male and Female Workers in West Malaysia', *Journal of Contemporary Asia*, 13, 4, 121–50.

Harding, T. and Spalding, H. (1976) 'The Struggle Sharpens: Workers, Imperialism and the State in Latin America: Common Themes and New Directions', *Latin American Perspectives*, III, 8.

Howard, R. (1986) 'Third World Trade Unions as Agencies of Human Rights: The Case of Commonwealth Africa' in Southall (ed.) 1987.

Humphrey, J. (1982) *Capitalist Control and Workers' Struggle in the Brazilian Auto Industry* (Princeton: Princeton University Press).

International Confederation of Free Trade Unions (1984) *The African Worker and the World Economic Crisis* (Brussels: ICFTU).

Jeffries, R. (1978) *Class, Power and Ideology in Ghana: The Railwaymen of Sekondi* (Cambridge: Cambridge University Press).

Jelin E. (1979) 'Labour Conflicts under the Second Peronist Regime, Argentina 1973–76', *Development and Change*, 10.

Jenkins, R. (1985). 'Latin America and the New International Division of Labour; a critique of some recent views' in *Latin America, Economic Imperialism and the State*, edited by C. Abel and C. Lewis (London and Dover, New Hampshire) 415–29.

Kearney, R. (1979) 'The Political Impact of Strikes and Disorder in Ceylon', in *Peasants and Proletarians: The Struggles of Third World Workers* edited by R. Cohen, P. Gutkind and P. Brazier (London: Hutchinson) 248–64.

Kraus, J. (1976) 'African Trade Unions: Progress or Poverty?' *The African Studies Review*, XIX, 3, 95–108.

Kucherenko, D. (1983) 'The Working Class of Asia and Africa in the 1970s' in Wallerstein, I. (ed.) 1983, 237–48.

Laite, J. (1981) *Industrial Development and Migrant Labour in Latin America* (Manchester: Manchester University Press).

Lipietz, A. (1982) 'Towards Global Fordism', *New Left Review*, 132, 41–53.

—— (1984) 'Imperialism or the Beast of the Apocalypse', *Capital and Class*, 22, 10.

Luther, H. (1978) 'Strikes and the Institutionalization of Labour Protest: The Case of Singapore', *Journal of Contemporary Asia*, 8, 2: 219–30.

—— (1979) 'The Repression of Labour Protest in Singapore: Unique Case or Future Model?' *Development and Change*, 10, 287–99.

Mabry, B. (1977) 'The Thai Labor Movement', *Asian Survey*, XVII, 10, 931–51.

Marks, S. and Rathbone, R. (eds) (1982) *Industrialisation and Social Change in South Africa: African class formation, culture and consciousness 1870–1930* (London, Longman).

Moises, J. (1979) 'Current Issues in the Labour Movement in Brazil', *Latin American Perspectives*, VI, 4.

Munck, R. (1987) *Third World Workers and the New International Labour Studies* (London: Zed).

Nash, J. (1979) *We Eat the Mines and the Mines Eat Us: Dependency and Exploitation in the Bolivian Tin Mines* (New York: Columbia University Press).

—— and Fernandez-Kelly, M. (eds) (1983) *Women, Men and the International Division of Labour* (Albany: State University of New York Press).

Norlund, I. Wad, P. and Brun, V. (eds) (1984) *Industrialization and the Labour*

Process in Southeast Asia (Copenhagen, Institute of Cultural Sociology).

Nzula, A.T., Potekhin, I. Zusmanovitch, A. (1979) *Forced Labour in Colonial Africa* (London: Zed).

Omvedt, G. (1980) *We will Smash this Prison: Indian Women in Struggle* (London: Zed).

Parpart, J. (1983) *Capital and Labor on the African Copperbelt* (Philadelphia: Temple University Press).

Peace, A. (1979) *Choice, Class and Conflict: A Study of Southern Nigerian Factory Workers* (Brighton: Harvester).

Petras, J. (1970) *Politics and Social Structure in Latin America* (New York: Monthly Review Press).

—— (1978) 'Towards a Theory of Twentieth Century Socialist Revolutions', *Journal of Contemporary Asia*, VIII, 2, 167–95.

—— (1980) 'Neo-Fascism: Capital Accumulation and Class Struggle in the Third World', *Journal of Contemporary Asia*, 10, 1/2.

Pineda-Ofreneo, R. (1982) 'Philippine Domestic Outwork: Subcontracting for Export-Oriented Industries', *Journal of Contemporary Asia*, 12, 3, 281–93.

Portes, A. and Walton, J. (1981) *Labor, Class and the International System* (Florida: Academic Press).

Post, K. (1979) 'The Alliance of Peasants and Workers: Some Problems Concerning the Articulation of Classes (Algeria and China)' in *Peasants and Proletarians* edited by Cohen, Gutkind and Brazier (London: Hutchinson) 265–86.

Ronasinghe, S.W. (1982) 'Plantation Economy and the Marginalization of Labour with Special Reference to Sri Lanka', *Labour, Capital and Society*, 15, 1, 64–79.

Sandbrook, R. (1975) *Proletarians and African Capitalism: The Kenyan Case 1962–70* (Cambridge: Cambridge University Press.)

—— and Arn, J. (1977) *The Labouring Poor and Urban Class Formation: The Case of Greater Accra* (Montreal: Centre for Developing Area Studies, McGill University).

—— and Cohen, R. (1975) *The Development of an African Working Class* (Harlow: Longman).

Selden, M. (1983) 'The Proletariat, Revolutionary Change, and the State in China and Japan, 1850–1950' in Wallerstein (ed.) 1983, 58–120.

Shaheed, Z.A. (1979) 'Union Leaders, Worker Organization and Strikes: Karachi 1969–72' *Development and Change*, 10, 181–204.

Shaw, T. (1982) 'Beyond Neo-colonialism: Varieties of Corporatism in Africa', *Journal of Modern African Studies*, 20, 2.

Southall, R. (1984) 'Third World Trade Unions: Equity and Democratization in the Changing International Division of Labour', *Canadian Journal of Development Studies*, V, 1, 147–56.

—— (1985) (ed.) 'South African Labour', *Labour, Capital and Society* (Special Issue), 18, 2.

—— (1987) (ed.) *Trade Unions and the New Industrialisation of the Third World* (London: Zed and Ottawa University Press).

Spalding, H. (1977) *Organized Labor in Latin America 1850–1960* (New York: New York University Press).

Stallings, B. (1972) *Economic Dependency in Africa and Latin America* (Beverley Hills, London: Sage).

Van Onselen, C. (1976). *Chibaro, African Mine Labour in Southern Rhodesia* (London: Pluto).
—— (1982) *Studies in the Social and Economic History of the Witwatersrand* Vol. I, New Babylon; Vol. II, New Nineveh (London: Longman).
Vellingra, M. (1979) *Economic Development and the Dynamics of Class: Industrialization, Power and Control in Monterrey, Mexico* (Netherlands, Van Gorcum).
Wad, P. (1987) 'The Japanization of the Malaysian Labour Market', in Southall (ed.) 1987.
Walder, A. (1984) 'The Remaking of the Chinese Working Class 1949–1981', *Modern China*, 10, 1.
Wallerstein, I. (1974) *The Modern World. Capitalist Agriculture and the Origins of the European World-Economy in the Sixteenth Century* (New York: Academic Press).
—— (1980) *The World Capitalist System* (Cambridge: Cambridge University Press).
—— (ed.) (1983) *Labor in the World Social Structure* (Beverly Hills, London, New Delhi: Sage).
Waterman, P. (1975) 'The "Labour Aristocracy" in Africa: Introduction to a Debate', *Development and Change*, 6, 3.
—— (1977) 'Workers in the Third World', *Monthly Review*, 29, 4.
—— (1982) 'Seeing the Straws: Reading the Whirlwind: Reflections on Unions and Popular Movements in India', *Journal of Contemporary Asia*, 12, 4, 464–83.
—— (1983) *Aristocrats and Plebians in African Trade Unions? Lagos Port and Dock Workers' Organisation and Struggle* (The Hague: Institute of Social Studies).
—— (1984) 'A New Focus in African Worker Studies: Promises, Problems, Dangers, *Cahiers d'Etudes africaines*, 95, XXIV-3, 343–62.
Wehmhorner, A. (1983) 'Trade Unionism in Thailand – A New Dimension in a Modernising Society', *Journal of Contemporary Asia*, 13, 4, 481–97.

2 World Unemployment and China's Labour Reserves[1]

Michel Chossudovsky

This chapter examines the role of world unemployment in the development of the low wage economy in China and the Far East.

Part I examines briefly the internationalisation of productive capital and the process of international integration and juxtaposition of the 'reserves' of cheap labour in different third world countries brought about, in the post-Second World War period, though the 'migration' of productive industrial capital to the periphery of the world economy.

Part II examines the foregoing problematic in the context of China's reintegration into the structure and logic of the world capitalist economy in the post-Mao period. In this regard, the development in China of trade and foreign investment relations 'along capitalist lines' signifies a new phase in the development of the post-war capitalist international division of labour characterised by the subordination of 'socialist' China's manpower reserves to the needs and requirements of world capital. Concurrently, the 'integration' of cheap third world labour has important implications regarding the economic articulation and development of the third world low wage industrial export economy in the global structure of capital accumulation.

I THE MIGRATION OF CAPITAL AND LABOUR

Historically, the formation of a relative surplus population in the 'old' centres of industrial development played an important role in the national and international migration of labour. In the early nineteenth century, the floating surplus population was the lever of capital accumulation which enabled the rapidly expanding branches of industry to appropriate fresh labour power (Marx, 1907, p. 704). Both nationally and internationally, the migration of labour followed that of capital:

> Only a very small number continue to find employment in the same branches of industry while the majority are regularly discharged. This

majority forms an element of the floating surplus population growing with the extension of these branches of industry. Part of them emigrate following in fact capital which has emigrated (Marx, 1907, p. 704).

The export of capital in the late nineteenth century and early twentieth century coincides with the waves of emigration: where capital migrates so does labour, the floating surplus population in the 'old' centres flows to the 'new' labour scarce centres of capital accumulation. The international movement of labour was, therefore, closely related both to the movement of capital and the structure of the international division of labour.

The process of transnationalisation after the Second World War substantially modifies the patterns of migration of both capital and labour. The migration of labour (after the Second World War) has become increasingly 'selective', largely characterised by the movement of professional and skilled manpower from the third world to the advanced capitalist countries. On the other hand, productive capital will increasingly 'migrate' towards the labour reserves – i.e. from the advanced centres of capital accumulation to the 'cheap labour reserve countries' of the third world.

Prior to the Second World War, the industrial and manufacturing base was largely located in the advanced capitalist countries. The movement and structure of wages in these industries was, therefore, 'regulated' by the upward and downward movement of the level of national unemployment. The role of the colonies and overseas territories was essentially to provide raw materials and agricultural staples for the advanced centres of capital accumulation.

The transnationalisation of industrial production after the Second World War, characterised by the transfer of the 'old' labour intensive assembly and transformation industries to the periphery of the world economy substantially modifies the structure of accumulation in the advanced capitalist countries as well as the role and functions of the national relative surplus population in the national process of capital accumulation.

The process of transnationalisation (after the Second World War) is characterised by a *tendency* towards the integration of the various phases of commodity production on a world level. In turn, the internationalisation of productive capital coincides with the parallel *juxtaposition* of the national reserve armies in different countries, i.e. the 'national labour reserves' in different social formations are internationalised through the 'integration' of the national markets for labour in different geographical locations. This 'integration' is brought about through the mobility of productive capital (i.e. through industrial relocation) rather than through the international mobility of labour.

Off-shore productive capital in the assembly and transformation industries is extremely mobile, moving from one geographical location to another in accordance with the relative scarcity or abundance of cheap third world industrial labour power. In this process, the national relative surplus population (in distinct third world countries) not only regulates the internal national wage structure (and hence the cost of labour for international capital) but also the process of *'migration'* of international productive capital from one cheap labour location to another, and, therefore, *indirectly* the levels of industrial wages in alternative 'competing' cheap labour locations.

The Transnationalisation of Productive Capital

The transnationalisation of productive capital (and its international relocation), the international 'buying and selling' of labour power in different national labour markets and the international division of labour are parallel and interdependent processes.

The 'migration' of distinct branches of industry from one region of the world to another has proceeded (after the Second World War) through *sequential displacements* in the international division of labour. In the 1960s, many of the 'old' labour intensive industries, (requiring essentially unskilled labour) of the advanced capitalist countries are relocated to the cheap labour free trade zones of South East Asia (Taiwan, Hong Kong, South Korea and Singapore). Rapid capital accumulation in these countries and regions was conducive throughout the seventies to an increase in the level of wages (in these cheap labour locations) which substantially counteracted the initial impetus of an economic growth process based almost exclusively on the development of cheap labour industrial exports.

The succession of economic growth and stagnation in the so-called 'semi-industrial countries' of South East Asia is functionally related to the 'migration' and mobility of productive capital. 'Export-led development' is characterised by a contradictory movement: dynamic growth of the export industries in the semi-industrialised countries of South East Asia becomes an obstacle to further growth because the increase in industrial wages which accompanies the dynamic development of the export sector modifies the patterns of 'migration' of productive capital. In other words, this process is conducive to the international *relocation* of these 'traditional' cheap labour export industries to yet *cheaper* supplies of unskilled labour in Sri Lanka, Malaysia, Indonesia, the Philippines, the People's Republic of China, etc.

While this process will gradually displace the traditional labour intensive industries in South Korea, Singapore, Korea and Taiwan, new (and more sophisticated) areas of economic activity hitherto exclusively located in the advanced capitalist countries will 'migrate' towards the so-called 'semi industrialised countries of the Third World'.

These *sequential* displacements in the structure of the international division of labour not only modify the underlying industrial fabric of the 'semi-industrialised countries' but also that of the advanced capitalist countries. Increasingly, 'skill intensive' industries as well as certain areas of heavy industry are transferred to the third world's 'industrial periphery'. In Taiwan, for instance, 'skill intensive' industries are being developed in Hsinchu Science Base Industrial Park. Hsinchu belongs to a 'new generation' of export processing zones in which investment is promoted in areas such as information systems, microprocessors, communications' equipment and computer software. The underlying rationale of the new 'skill oriented' free trade zones, however, is remarkably similar to the 'vintage cheap labour model', i.e. wages for skilled labour are at least four times lower in Taiwan or Singapore than in the advanced capitalist countries.

Structural Recession in the Advanced Capitalist Countries

The sequential shifts in the international division of labour after the Second World War which result from several phases on international relocation of industry, is conducive to a process of *structural recession* in the advanced capitalist countries. *Structural recession* characterised by high unemployment, stagnation and decline of the 'old' labour intensive manufacturing sectors is an important (although not essential) feature of the economic crisis.

The international division of labour is characterised by a bi-polar structure. In the advanced industrialised countries, the new high technology industries are replacing the 'old' manufacturing base of centre capitalism. The low technology 'hardware' manufacturing industries are transferred to the third world (Chossudovsky, 1981).

The World Relative Surplus Population

In each of the national economies, 'the relative surplus population is the pivot upon which the law of demand and supply of labour works' (Marx,

1907, p. 701). The national relative surplus population thereby conditions the structure of wages *between* the various branches of a national economy as well as the movement of labour from one branch of activity to another. In third world social formations, the low wage economy is often sustained through the reproduction of those so-called 'traditional' or 'non-capitalist' sectors which provide and set free their surplus population. The miserable conditions of material existence in so-called 'traditional subsistence agriculture' (and urban petty commodity production) act as an instrumental lever in maintaining low levels of industrial (and agricultural) wages in the 'modern' capitalist sectors.

The *world relative surplus population* characterised by the juxtaposition of the national industrial reserve armies becomes the lever of capital accumulation on a world level. On a world level, *the world relative surplus population conditions the international movement (migration) of productive capital in the same branch of industry between different countries.* International capital (the direct or indirect purchaser of labour power) 'moves' from one national labour market to another. From the point of view of capital, the national reserves of labour (in different countries) are integrated into a single 'international reserve pool' where workers in different countries are brought into overt competition with one another.

The maintenance of third world poverty and underdevelopment constitutes the basis upon which the national and world relative surplus populations are reproduced and sustained.

The Low Wage Economy

Transnationals producing or subcontracting (with independent national capitalists) in the third world, will relocate their productive activities in accordance with the international structure of wage disparities. According to ILO statistics, the cost of industrial labour power in the third world is on average one tenth that of the advanced capitalist countries (Frobel, Heinrichs and Kreye, 1977, pp. 633–34; Sharpstow, 1975, p. 105). Important disparities in the cost of labour power also exist *between* countries of the third world: In South and East Asia the effective cost of industrial labour is on average four times higher in Hong Kong, Singapore, Taiwan and South Korea than in Sri Lanka, Indonesia, the Philippines and the People's Republic of China. In China, the average cost of industrial labour (at the official exchange rate) in the State sector is of the order of US$21 a month, in Sri Lanka's Katyunake free trade zone, the average monthly wage is US$36.

Whereas (according to ILO statistics) the overall average disparity in the industrial wage between centre and peripheral social formations is of the order of one to ten, *the absolute disparity is of the order of one to thirty*. For instance, in the People's Republic of China, the wage rate for unskilled labour in the State sector is 40–60 yuan a month (14–21 dollars)–i.e. less than 13 cents an hour as opposed to 5–10 dollars an hour in North America (for the same category of labour and skill).

Namely, the *daily* cost of labour in the advanced capitalist countries (in the same branch of industry) is often of the same order of magnitude as (or in excess of) the *monthly* cost of labour in the 'labour reserve countries' of South and East Asia.

International disparities in labour costs are also accompanied by important differences in the length of the working week, the intensity of the labour process and the working conditions in industry. In South Korea, Taiwan, Singapore and Hong Kong, the length of the working week (without overtime) varies from 48 to 60 hours. In South Korea, factories in the export garment, footware, electronics assembly, etc. industries operate on the basis of an eleven-hour day (including a one-hour break for lunch) and six-day working week. In the People's Republic of China, the statutory working week is 48 hours over 6 days. Apart from public holidays and Chinese New Year, there are no paid holidays in China.

Third world manufacturing industry reproduces many of the conditions which were prevalent historically during the Industrial Revolution in the advanced capitalist countries. The Korean garment and footware industries, for instance, rely heavily on female labour from rural areas in the 15–25 year age group; after several years of intensive factory work, long working hours and despotic factory supervision, workers will either abandon employment or be dismissed by the factory. This process enables the frequent replacement of 'used' labour by a fresh supply of 'new' labour which flows into the urban industrial labour market from rural areas.

In the 'labour reserve countries' of South East Asia and the Far East, the supply of unqualified labour released from rural hinterland is abundant and the costs of maintenance and upkeep are extremely low. Real wages are often below the level of subsistence, i.e. the reproductive process in both peripheral industry and commercial agriculture is characterised by the *non-renewal* of human labour power.

State Controls on the Level of Wages

The maintenance of a low wage structure is implemented through the operation of the labour market (as discussed above) as well as through the enforcement of State controls on the level of industrial wages and/or other political instruments which enforce the 'free and competitive' operation of the labour market. The elimination of trade unions as well as the consolidation of traditional techniques of state repression (e.g. in the Philippines, South Korea or Indonesia) become the means for enforcing an industrial wage rate substantially below subsistence.

II   CHINESE LABOUR AND EXPORT ORIENTED INDUSTRIALISATION

The foregoing section described the role of world unemployment in the process of international relocation of productive capital. The latter enables transnational capital to minimise labour costs through the international redeployment of its productive interests. In many low technology and assembly industries, this process does not require direct foreign investment or the setting-up of a subsidiary. In a wide range of manufacturing industries, international corporate capital (performing essentially commercial and merchant functions) *sub-contracts* with a national enterprise.

In the following sections we examine the role of China's 'reserves of labour' in the development of the low wage industrial export economy. In this regard, China's 'opening up of trade along capitalist lines' in the post-Mao period signifies not only the 'integration' of its large 'reserves' of labour into the 'international reserve pool' of cheap third world labour, but also a new phase in the process of international redeployment (relocation) of productive capital. The following sections will (a) outline China's 'open door' policy; and (b) examine the implications of China's economic reinsertion into the structure of world capital accumulation.

China's Open Door Policy

China's 'open door' policy should be understood in the overall context of the economic and social reforms implemented in China since 1977. In turn, the latter are the expression and consequence of the changes in the political power structure during the Cultural Revolution and since the death of Mao Zedong and the downfall of the 'Gange of Four'.

In other words, the liberalisation of foreign trade proceeds alongside major reforms in the management and organisation of China's state enterprises. The adoption of 'capitalist type' managerial technology in industry interacts with the development of foreign trade and investment relations. The reforms in the structure of wages, the tendency towards individualised work according to the leadership's new interpretation of the principle 'to each according to his work', the adoption of material incentive schemes and labour discipline, the reforms in the system of state assigned jobs, etc., proceed alongside the development of technology transfer and licensing agreements, joint ventures with foreign capital, compensation trade and the formation of 'special economic zones' and trading areas. In turn, the internal reforms reinforce and consolidate the development of trade and foreign investment relations along capitalist lines by creating the appropriate social and organisational conditions at the level of the individual factory.

Whereas the liberalisation of trade and foreign investment relations with the capitalist world economy constitutes a major departure in relation to the structure and policies of foreign trade prevalent since Liberation, the open door policy adopted under Dengxiaoping is at the same time the expression of historical continuity in China's foreign trade relations with the imperialist powers.

The term 'open door' policy was first used by the United States in the settlement rising from the Yi He Tuan uprising of 1900. Washington had advocated the liberalisation of trade and foreign investment according to the principle of 'equal opportunity'. The Anglo-Japanese agreement of 1905 stipulated in somewhat similar terms:

> . . . the preservation of the common interests of all the powers in China by ensuring the independence and integrity of the Chinese empire and the principle of equal opportunities for the commerce and industry of all nations in China. (Hu Sheng, 1980)

In other words, the opening of trade in the post-Mao period does not take place in an historical vacuum. The 'open door' policy, while emerging from decisions of the Chinese Communist Party, is in some respects conducive to the rehabilitation of many features of China's foreign trade relations which existed prior to 1949. Whereas the structure of the world economy–characterised by new patterns of multinational corporate expansion –has evolved considerably since the Second World War, China's 'open door' policy in the late 1970s takes place against a long historical background of commercial and bureaucratic practices with foreign capital. Moreover, the regional configuration of China's foreign trade (in the coastal provinces and former treaty ports), the transport network and industrial base established since the later part of the nineteenth century, constitute an articulate infrastructure which conditions the scope and direction of foreign trade in the post-Mao period. Comprador relations which developed in China historically re-emerge in a new form within the network of China's state bureaucratic and party apparatus.

The liberalisation of foreign trade, the establishment of joint ventures, the development of cheap labour export processing industries and the setting up of free trade zones (i.e. 'special economic zones' and 'trading areas') along China's coast-line according to a new system of extra-territorial rights, constitute the essential features of the CCP Central Committee's 'open door policy'.

The liberalisation of foreign trade was initiated in 1978. The following year, the National People's Congress (NPC) gave special rights in foreign trade to the two Southern provinces of Guangdong and Fujian thereby approving the formation of China's 'special economic zones', a modern blend of extra-territoriality combining China's colonial tradition with South East Asia's export platforms (free trade export processing zones).

In 1979, the National People's Congress adopted China's Law on Joint Ventures which enables foreign companies 'to join with Chinese companies, enterprises or other economic organisations in establishing joint ventures in the People's Republic of China in accordance with the principle of equality and mutual benefit'.[2] The Joint Venture Law also enables the setting-up in China of fully owned subsidiaries. The first subsidiaries of multinational companies started operating in 1984.

Provisions for 'Labour Management in Chinese–Foreign Ventures' were adopted in 1980 to regulate 'the employment, dismissal and resignation of the staff and workers of joint ventures and their production and work, wages and awards and punishments' (People's Republic of China, 1982, p. 20).

In 1984, the Central Committee outlined a project for the establishment of 'special trading areas' in China's coastal cities (i.e. former treaty ports) in which foreign capital may either invest in joint ventures or set up fully owned subsidiaries. 'Special trading areas' will be set up in fourteen coastal cities many of which were treaty ports under extra-territorial colonial jurisdiction prior to Liberation (e.g. Dalian, Tianjin, Qingdao, Ningbo, Guangzhou, Shanghai, Fuzhou).

The Institutional Framework

The authority to conduct foreign trade in a wide range of activities is transferred from the central government level to the provincial and local levels. The foreign trade procedures increasingly enable individual Chinese state enterprises to enter directly, without government approval, into trade, joint ventures and other co-operative arrangements with foreign capital. Concurrently, major changes are implemented in China's international financial, banking and commercial structures.

New comprador relations are developing in China as a result of the 'open door' policy. The social class base of this policy is complex. It involves an understanding of the political struggle within the Communist Party during the Cultural Revolution, which was ultimately conducive–after Mao and the downfall of the Gang of Four–to the consolidation of the 'Rightist' line. In this context, the development of a comprador bureaucratic and managerial elite in the party and state apparatus as well as in industry, financial institutions and trading corporations interacts with the implementation of the open door policy to foreign capital and the development of trade and foreign investment along capitalist lines.

The Expatriate Bourgeoisie

The expatriate Chinese bourgeoisie consititutes a vital link in the establishment of trade, joint ventures and international financial operations. These relations are not solely commercial or economic links *stricto sensu*, they are characterised by family and class ties within the Chinese bourgeoisie, i.e. between members of the so-called 'national patriotic bourgeoisie' who remained in China after Liberation and expatriate bourgeois families in Hong Kong, Singapore, Taiwan and elsewhere. Moreover, a Chinese bourgeoisie of merchant extraction, constitutes the dominant national economic elite in Thailand, Indonesia, Malaysia and Burma (and to a lesser extent the Philippines). These national groups of Chinese extraction are not isolated from one another: the Chinese (expatriate) bourgeoisie in the various countries in South East Asia are integrated in commercial, banking and financial undertakings as well as through family and class ties.

The Hong Kong Chinese bourgeoisie plays, in this regard, an important role as a contractual intermediary in financial and commercial undertakings and joint ventures between the People's Republic of China and Western capital. Moreover, Hong Kong capitalists are directly involved in developing on the Chinese mainland (through compensation trade, sub-contracting or direct investment) cheap labour export processing industries similar to those which already exist in Hong

Kong, Taiwan, South Korea and elsewhere in the capitalist third world.
The expatriate bourgeoisie is invited by the Central Committee Politburo to invest in the Motherland and develop privately owned business interests in manufacturing, services, construction and the tourist industry.

The Modalities of Foreign Trade

The various contractual foreign trade and investment procedures express the concrete conditions of the law of unequal exchange and China's reinsertion into the capitalist international division of labour in a wide range of cheap labour export industries.

Whereas the 1979 Law on Joint Ventures *de facto* enables multinational enterprises to establish corporate subsidiaries in the People's Republic of China under a formal structure of joint ownership, compensation trade and sub-contracting arrangements are the most prevalent contractual forms in light industry and export processing.

In compensation trade, the 'foreign partner' will provide a Chinese state factory with equipment and technology. In turn, the Chinese factory will supply (through a government import–export corporation) a finished commodity at a so-called 'friendship price' over the period of repayment of the equipment. The official export price is regulated by the provincial government import–export corporation. The 'friendship price' is, however, substantially below the regulated price, i.e. the differential between the two prices constitutes repayment (over x years) of the machinery supplied by the foreign contractor. In many compensation trade transactions, however, the agreement is not clearly specified in value terms. In the garment industry, for instance, highly-priced second hand equipment is often exchanged for low-priced finished output.[3]

Wages and the Cost of Labour to Foreign Capital

Conditions for the foreign entrepreneur in 'socialist' China are more favourable than in other 'capitalist' cheap labour locations in South East Asia. At the official exchange rate, the effective cost of labour (for international capital) is less than one fifth that paid in Hong Kong, Singapore and South Korea.

Wages in China in the state sector are on average (without bonuses and overtime) of the order of 60 yuan a month (US$21). Industrial wages for unskilled categories range from approximately 40 yuan (US$14) to 90 yuan a month (US$32). Wages in joint venture factories are *in principle* established at a rate which is 50 per cent above average rates in comparable industries. In the co-operative sector (i.e. municipal and neighbourhood factories) and in rural factories the level of wages is substantially below that of the state sector.

However, foreign capital contracts with a state (or municipal or rural) enterprise; the costs of maintenance and reproduction of labour power are met by the 'socialist' State, i.e. the social distribution of housing and essential social services – a major achievement of the Chinese revolution – constitute in a sense an implicit 'subsidy' to a foreign capitalist enterprise investing (in a joint venture) or subcontracting (e.g. with a state enterprise) in China.

Foreign capitalist enterprises do not generally purchase labour power directly in the market; they purchase the services of labour along with the other factors of production (factory space, land, etc.) in a contractual arrangement with the Chinese State authorities. In this case, no direct money (or social relationship) exists between foreign capitalists and Chinese workers.

The management and supervision of the labour force, the length of the working day and the reproduction of labour power are ensured by the State and the various State social programmes. In joint ventures (between a foreign company and a Chinese State enterprise), the hiring and firing of workers, the determination of wages and the management of the labour force is entirely under the jurisdiction of the Chinese partner. Moreover, wages in joint ventures and/or enterprises producing for the export sector are regulated by a national statutory wage scale.

China's Manpower Exports

As discussed in Part I, the post-war international division of labour is characterised by the international 'migration' of productive captial towards abundant sources of cheap third world labour. This process – which is characterised by the internationalisation of the sale and purchase of labour – has been conductive to the relocation of labour intensive transformation industries in South East Asia and the Chinese mainland. In other words, in industrial processing industries, capital 'moves' towards cheap sources of labour in China and elsewhere in South East Asia. On the other hand, in productive activities which by their very nature are not mobile internationally (e.g. public works, construction, mining, etc.) an important market for the export of *contractual* third world labour has developed in the Second World War period.

Manpower exports have taken on different forms. For instance, Mexico exports a contractual seasonal agricultural workforce to Southern California; France, West Germany and Switzerland have imported cheap industrial manpower from Southern Europe, North Africa and Turkey. The sale of manpower by the Portuguese colonial authorities (prior to Liberation in Angola and Mozambique) has provided South African mining with cheap supplies of contractual labour, etc.

The contractual sale of manpower after the Second World War should be distinguished from the pre-war international migration of labour. Manpower exports are not generally characterised by the permanent (international) migration of labour. Moreover, whereas (contractual) manpower exports are conceptually distinct from the development of cheap labour export processing industries within the geographical boundaries of third world countries, the development of an overseas contractual manpower market is characteristic of the overall post-war process of internationalisation of production. The same processes which govern the relocation of industry towards cheap labour locations in the third world are concurrently conducive to the rapid development of an 'internationally mobile reserve army' of cheap contractual manpower which is used in economic activities which by their very nature are not mobile internationally (e.g. construction, public works, etc.).

In recent years, an important overseas (contractual) manpower market has developed primarily in the Middle East in construction and public works projects. China has entered the contractual sale of manpower in competition with Korean, Pakistani, Philippino and other third world 'suppliers' of cheap labour.

The export of Chinese manpower for overseas construction work takes place through:

1. the direct sale of labour power to a foreign construction company;
2. contractual agreements with a Chinese construction company. In this case, the Chinese company will supply the labour and will undertake part of the construction work.

In 1982, China had more than 30 000 overseas workers employed either with a Chinese overseas construction company or directly with international construction multinationals:

They [the workers] are on production and construction projects mainly in the Middle East in co-operation with Middle-East petroleum exporting countries and also from contractor companies from France, West Germany, Italy, Japan and Spain. Competition is strong in the field of supply work forces. (*China Daily*, 4 November 1981).

The sale of Chinese labour power to a foreign buyer is often negotiated through the intermediary of a Hong Kong manpower firm. The sale of labour power is conducted both by the central and provincial governments. Guangdong province exports manpower through the Guandong Manpower Service Corporation. Negotiations with foreign contractors are undertaken by Chronicle Consultants of Hong Kong on behalf of the Guangdong State manpower firm. In Fujian province, Fujian Provincial Investment Enterprise established in 1979 (to promote foreign investment in Fujian) has expanded its activities to include overseas construction contracts and manpower export sales. In Beijing, the central government ministries have also entered the manpower export business: the Ministry of Metallurgical Industry, for instance, supplies manpower to Japanese and US companies as well as to Italy's giant construction multinational IRA.

Labour power for overseas construction projects is generally sold at a contractual price agreed between the Chinese and Hong Kong manpower firm and a foreign contractor. The length of the working day and the various conditions of employment are set out in the contract. The contractual price for unskilled, semi-skilled and specialised categories varies from US$300 to US$450 a month for a six-day week. The actual wages paid to the workers are regulated by the Chinese State manpower company and are somewhat higher than industrial wages paid in China. Japanese engineering companies which approached the Hong Kong manpower firm Chronicle Consultants (acting on behalf of the Guangdong government) will in some cases provide Japanese–Mandarin speaking supervisory personnel. 'The proposal assures potential employers that the Chinese will be diligent and obedient to their employers' reasonable instructions' (Breeze, 1979, p. 69).

Rather than purchasing the services of labour directly from a Chinese manpower firm, foreign companies in the multinational construction business often favour direct contractual arrangements with a Chinese construction firm. In this case, the foreign company sub-contracts part of the construction work to the Chinese enterprise which, in turn, is responsible for the supervision and management of its overseas workforce. For instance, China Construction and Engineering Company (CCEC) and its Hong Kong subsidiary Overseas Building

Company has a work force of 80 000 workers. CCEC is involved in industrial and construction projects in the Middle East.

III   CONCLUDING REMARKS

With close to 25 per cent of the world's population, a sizeable heavy industrial sector and manufacturing base, vast reserves of conventional and strategic raw materials, China's reinsertion into the world capitalist economy signifies a new and important historical phase in the development of the post-war international division of labour. Concurrently, the reintegration of China's 'reserves' of labour into the 'international reserve pool' of third world labour substantially modifies the structure and functions of world unemployment as a lever of capital accumulation of a world level.

The 'migration' of productive capital in the same branch of industry from one country to another is conductive to important dislocations in the industrial fabric of the advanced capitalist countries. 'Structural recession' in the advanced capitalist countries characterised by the international transfer of productive capital was initially conductive to the phasing out (and in some cases disappearance) of several important branches of manufacturing industry. In a second historical phase, the internationalisation of production has proceeded in heavier and more sophisticated sectors of economic activity leading to the development in many third world countries and China in particular, of 'off-shore' heavy industry (e.g. the automobile industry, shipbuilding, etc.) as well as so-called 'skill intensive' industries.

In other words, the process of internationalisation of productive capital is not limited solely to conventional assembly and transformation industries: monopoly capital tends to disengage itself from many areas of *material hardware production* while maintaining its control over the technology and production designs used in the various phases of *material* production (as well as over the channels of commodity trade, distribution and marketing). Whereas the ownership and control over high technology (and its production) are centralised in the advanced capitalist countries, the actual process of material production does not necessarily require direct corporate control and, therefore, can be transferred or relocated internationally.

'Third World semi-industrialisation' does not, in this regard, constitute an autonomous and independent process of industrialisation in any way comparable to the historical experience of the advanced capitalist countries, i.e. the setting up of industry is dependent and subordinate to the requirements of international monopoly capital.

The process of juxtaposition and international integration of the 'national reserve armies of unemployed' in different social formations modifies the role and 'regulating' functions of the national reserve army in the process of national capital accumulation. The internationalisation of production capital interacts with the internal structure of national accumulation and conditions the movementof employment, wages and economic activity in the advanced capitalist economies. The international relocation of industry also counteracts pressures on the average national rate of profit evident in the advanced capitalist countries since the 1960s.

While the process of migration of productive capital responds to the decline in the national average rate of profit, the internationalisation of productive capital is as the same time conducive to organic, institutional and organisational changes in the structure of capital which modify the significance of the national average rate of profit and the national level of unemployment as economic categories i.e. in the understanding and analysis of capital accumulation.

Notes

1. A Professional Development Award from the International Development Research Centre (IDRC) is gratefully acknowledged. The views are those of the author.
2. The Law of the People's Republic of China on Chinese–Foreign Joint Ventures, adopted by the Second Session of the Fifth National People's Congress, 1 July 1979 (People's Republic of China, 1982, p. 1).
3. In many cases, the 'foreign partner' will establish a long term agreement with the Chinese manufacturer through the provincial import–export corporation. Whereas the cost of the machinery (often over-valued in relation to its world market price) is repaid over a period of say three years, the Chinese factory agrees to supply its foreign partner at a friendship price over a period of say seven to eight years. This means that the imported machinery is paid several times over.

Bibliography

Breeze, R. (1979) 'Peking's People Exports', *Far Eastern Economic Review*, 30 November.
China Daily (Beijing).

Chossudovsky, M. (1981). 'The Politics of World Capital Accumulation', *Canadian Journal of Development Studies,* 2, 1, 9–40.
Frobel, F., Heinrichs, J., Kreye, O. (1977). *Die neue internationale Arbeitsteilung* (Rowohlt: Reinbeck bei Hamburg).
Hu Sheng (1980). *Imperialism and Chinese Politics* (Beijing: Foreign Language Press).
Marx, K. (1907). *Capital,* Volume 1 (New York: Random House).
People's Republic of China (1982). *China's Foreign Economic Legislation,* Volume 1 (Beijing: Foreign Language Press).

3 Trade Unions, the State and Labour Mobility in ECOWAS[1]

Tayo Fashoyin

In January 1983 an estimated 2 000 000 aliens mostly of West African origin, were expelled by the Nigerian state for over-staying their legal residency permit. The expulsion order naturally raised many issues of international interest, not least of which is international labour mobility and solidarity, on which this chapter focuses. Labour internationalism, a highly-valued tradition, acquired great importance in the post-war period in response to the power and influence of multinationals which have pitted workers in one country against those in another. To face this challenge international solidarity becomes crucially important in the struggle of workers across national boundaries (Martens, 1978; Wright, 1981; Bienefeld *et al.*, 1977).

International labour solidarity is equally important particularly where economic co-operation and integration is actively encouraged by public policy. In the case of the Economic Community of West African States (ECOWAS),[2] closer economic relations between nations in the community is seen as an effective means of achieving regional economic development. In fact, this kind of regional co-operation pre-dated political independence and has received considerable boost in Africa in recent years (Usoro, 1982; Onwuka, 1982; Ojo, 1975; Hazelwood, 1967). Unfortunately studies on economic co-operation and integration in Africa have focused on the narrow areas of international trade and customs union, and although broad issues such as resource utilisation are often examined, the discussion generally relate less to human resource mobilisation than to capital and natural resource mobilisation.

Yet, in any policy on economic co-operation within a community the labour process plays an important role because of the inescapable role of human efforts within the particular framework. This view however poses certain labour market questions. For example, how does the employment of migrant workers[3] in a particular country enhance or undermine union objectives on job security, improved wages and conditions of service, and the equally important task of maintaining organisational cohesion? In the case of trade unions in the ECOWAS issues concerning employers' preference for foreign labour, and the likely tendency to pay migrant workers low or substandard wages, which inevitably reduces the bargaining power of trade unions, and the possibility of organising migrant workers, are crucially important. It is in this respect useful to understand unions' response to labour mobility in the community and also the labour market implications of economic co-operation and integration in the sub-region.

This chapter examines the labour market consequences of labour mobility within West Africa drawing mainly on the recent experience of migrant labour in Nigeria. It is hypothesised that trade unions will be tempted to respond to migrant labour by developing a protectionist strategy although they are handicapped by prevailing institutional constraints. In reality a protectionist policy seems unnecessary because migrant worker are, by and large, a complementary or non-competing group. On the other hand, the failure of the Nigerian labour movement to pursue a policy of international labour solidarity by standing up for the expelled aliens was due to the internal and external challenges to the movement's legitimacy and existence. In any event, it is argued that a design to incorporate migrant workers into the orbit of trade union influence will enhance both the organisational objectives of the unions and labour's contribution to economic integration in the ECOWAS. The chapter is in 5 sections. Section 1 introduces the formal – informal sector phenomenon as a framework of analysis while Section 2 examines the issue of public policy and labour mobility. Section 3 discusses the employment patterns among immigrants while Section 4 looks at the responses of trade unions to the employment of migrant workers. The final Section gives a summary and conclusion of the discussion.

THE LABOUR MARKET AND THE FORMAL – INFORMAL SECTOR THESIS

The formal and informal sector thesis in the labour market distinguishes between jobs that are accessible to different elements of the working population. The formal sector which is variously referred to as modern, employment or ILO sector, describes organisations which have monopolistic control of basic means of production in both the private and public sectors. It has the peculiar nature of high technology which is not always accessible to the informal sector in which a dependent society predominates. In this formal sector employment is stable, wages are high and there is opportunity for career development (Bremen, 1980). Also, workers are engaged in jobs where the mode of operation is, as noted, high technology. The high wage levels in the sector are due to the unequal power relationship between capitalist employers and workers, but high wages do not necessarily reflect the level of labour productivity. Besides, a dependent mass of unemployed or underemployed people in the informal sector ensures that the supposedly high wages are kept low.

The informal sector, on the other hand, though a rather ambiguous concept, is used variously to describe the unorganised and unregistered enterprises, with characteristics such as low capital and technology, low earnings, ease of entry and preponderance of family labour and ownership, small-scale operation, labour intensive and adopted technology. Additionally, the sector has people with low skill which is generally obtained outside the formal educational system. The sector is usually unregulated though it is surprisingly competitive (Sethniaman, 1981; Fapohunda, 1978; ILO, 1972). Those in the sector have no access to the means of production, and their attachment to the labour market is unstable and irregular while working conditions are extremely poor.

One other important distinguishing characteristic of the informal sector is that it encompasses two employment possibilities; those in wage employment in the relatively small business enterprises owned and operated by indigenous capitalists, and non-wage employment in any of the imaginable occupations: street trading, road-side repairs (in different trades), tailoring, shoe shining, etc. People in these occupations are, by and large, self-employed.

In the context of international labour migration, jobs in the formal sector are reserved for a small proportion of the natives while migrant workers are found mainly in the informal sector. Applying the conceptualisation offered by Obregon (1974, p. 406), the two principal factors influencing the allocation of labour power between the two levels of production as outlined above are:

1. the type of productive resources they employ, and
2. the social interests which control those resources and the mechanisms which they make use of for this purpose.

According to this framework technology which has an overriding influence among the means of production is under the monopoly of the modern sector establishments where capitalists from the industrialised countries are dominant. Given the tacit support and collusion of the ruling elites in the LDCs who seek to promote foreign investments at all costs, and the indigenous entrepreneurs who form a subordinate association with Western capitalists, a social interest group which restricts entry into the formal sector emerges. Thus, there is often no interface bewteen the two levels of production except that, as noted earlier, employment conditions in the formal sector are sensitive to prevailing conditions in the formal sector.

PUBLIC POLICY AND LABOUR MOBILITY IN THE ECOWAS

Economic Conditions and Mobility

International labour mobility in West Africa was quite common before and during the colonial periods. Though opinion might differ on the forces compelling labour migration from one country to another, it was evident that during this period labour mobility was mainly a result of colonialists' policy of forced labour and slavery. For example, Orde-Browne (1967) has outlined several efforts made by the colonialists not only to conscript labour but also to recruit labour from India, Sierra Leone and Ghana. Quite apart from this, labour mobility in the sub-region was instigated by the repressive attitude of landowners and feudalists who denied peasants the right to own land. Though with few exceptions (such as emigration of Nigerian peasants to Equatorial Guinea in the late 1950s) migration was generally internal, that is, within a particular country.

While labour migration within West Africa during the pre- and colonial periods might have been due to the draconian policies of the feudal lords, landowners and colonialists, there is irrestistible evidence that in the post-colonial period, migrants, by and large, make their move in response to economic incentives (OECS, 1979 p. 21; Vletter, 1978). As Piore (1979, p. 54) has argued, labour migration and the work performed by the migrant 'are a means to gather income, income that can be taken back to his or her home community and used to fulfil or enhance his or her role within that social structure'. In the West African sub-region, there is little to gain in arguing that recent migration is not a conscious response to economic decline in the migrants' home country and a relatively brighter economic opportunity elsewhere.

The data in Table 3.1 will undoubtedly provide a partial confirmation of this development. To begin with the table shows the region has a high population growth rate. With the exception of Cape Verde, population

growth rate ranged from 2 per cent in Upper Volta to 5.1 per cent in
Ivory Coast. Yet, economic performance during the last decade has not
been impressive. Cape Verde is the only country that attained a relatively
encouraging growth in per capita GNP during the period. Gambia and
Nigeria obtained a growth rate of 3.1 per cent and 3 per cent respectively.
Nigeria's performance during the period was largely due to the windfall
in oil revenue, but taking account of the failure of non-oil sectors in the
country, one can explain the sudden near-collapse of the economy since
the beginning of the 1980s. Other countries in the community such as
Mali, Benin and Upper Volta attained modest growth rates while
Ghana, Liberia, Mauritania, Niger, Senegal and Sierra Leone experienced a decline during the decade 1970–80.

The case of Ghana is of particular interest to our analysis. During the
1965–74 period, the Ghanaian economy performed satisfactorily. Real
manufacturing output increased by 69.6 per cent, representing an
annual growth rate of 9.1 per cent (Ewusi, 1980, pp. 59–60). However,
between 1971 and 1977, manufacturing contribution to the GDP

Table 3.1 Population growth and GNP per capita in ECOWAS, 1970–80

Country	Population growth rate (%)	GNP per capita real growth rate 1970–80(%)
Benin	2.7	1.2
Cape Verde	0.9	5.5
Gambia	2.4	3.1
Ghana	3.0	− 2.6
Guinea	2.9	0.4
Guinea Bissau	n.a	n.a
Ivory Coast	5.1	1.5
Liberia	3.5	− 0.1
Mali	2.6	2.3
Mauritania	2.5	− 1.0
Niger	3.3	− 0.8
Nigeria	2.5	3.0
Senegal	2.7	− 0.4
Sierra Leone	2.6	− 1.1
Togo	2.5	0.9
Burkina Fasso (Upper Volta)	2.0	1.6

Source: The World Bank 1983 Atlas (Washington, DC: International Bank for
Reconstruction and Development).

declined from 465 million cedis to 392 million cedis, or by 16 per cent (Manu, 1983, p. 83). The important lesson from this marked decline in the performance of the economy is that it instigated both a shift in capital and the migration of skilled and unskilled labour from Ghana to Nigeria. Although there are no official statistics on the latter, we may suggest a figure of some 2 000 000 Ghanaians in Nigeria as at December 1982. This represented about 60 per cent of aliens of ECOWAS origin living in Nigeria as at that date.

Undoubtedly the oil boom in Nigeria during the 1970s was the single major factor responsible for large-scale immigration from other West African countries. As a result of the windfall in oil revenue, Nigeria embarked upon ambitious development programmes involving large outlays on physical infrastructure and overall economic development. For example, total public investment during the 1970–4 Plan period was more than ₦3 billion, or nearly 4 times the size of the previous development plan. The size of the Third National Development Plan 1975–80, was ₦30 billion, representing 10 times the planned investment in the previous plan. The size of these development plans created employment opportunities in all sectors of the economy and was responsible for inducing citizens of economically depressed countries in the community to migrate to Nigeria. Additionally, the lack of skilled labour as well as inadequate supply of highly skilled and professional categories of manpower to meet the demands occasioned by the development policies opened up opportunities for the surplus or unemployed skilled labour force of other countries especially in the ECOWAS.

Public employment in Nigeria expanded from 1.01 million in 1975 to about 2 million in 1980. A phenomenal growth was recorded in the civil services of the federation. At the federal level, for example, employment rose from 124 503 in 1977 to 264 367 in 1982, representing an increase of 112 per cent (Nigeria, 1977; 1982). Similarly, in the private sector increased industrial activity also resulted in high employment, both in the formal and informal sectors. In the former, wage employment rose from 500 000 in 1975 to 1.5 million by 1980. The industries that experienced boom and high employment include construction, textiles, services and cargo handling.

However, it must be borne in mind that these statistics on wage employment do not give the accurate picture of total wage employment mainly because government statistics cover only employers with 10 (realistically 50) workers each. But outside this loosely defined modern sector is the bulk of wage employment which, though lacking any statistical measure, can be said to represent 3 or 4 times the size of modern sector employment. Here we find the informal sector. As argued earlier, the latter is made up of two employment systems: the small-scale wage employment, generally though not always family businesses, and the self-employed people engaged as owner-operated public transporters, road-side mechanics, barbers, tailors and, of course, the road-side traders and hawkers. Again there are not statistical measures of the size of this group although it undoubtedly engages millions of income-earners in Nigeria.

The important point to note is that largely as a result of development spending the formal and informal sectors experienced unprecedented boom. This growth absorbed a large proportion of the local labour force and created labour shortages both in the unskilled, skilled and the professional categories. It might appear contradictory to argue that a labour surplus economy like Nigeria had to depend on unskilled migrant labour. This should not be so because there is still a tendency among the unemployed youth in Nigeria to gravitate toward white-collar, prestigious and better-paying jobs (Ojo *et al.*, 1985).[4] In any event, a kind of internationalisation of the labour market in the West Africa sub-region emerged from this development. As the Nigerian economy boomed it witnessed a continuous in-flow of migrants both from the rural areas and the declining economies of other West African countries seeking employment in the unprotected informal sector. This response to the boom inevitably escalated the proportion of the reserve army of labour (Southall, 1984).

ECOWAS and Labour Mobility

The movement of labour within West Africa pre-dated the colonial administration and was effectively used by the latter to solve the problem of labour shortage (Orde-Brown, 1967). According to Mabogunje (1972, p. 57), about 2 000 000 people were involved annually in pre-independence movement in West Africa. A study by the OECD (1979, p. 18) revealed that in 1975, the volume of migration within 9 West African countries was 4.4 million, or 11 per cent of the total population. The ease with which people moved from one part of the region to another was influenced mainly by the similarities in linguistic, cultural or economic characteristics even though political demarcations have tended to undermine this movement (Asante, 1983). Even then the quest for regional development, improved trade relations, and the removal of impediments to the promotion of economic integration of the West African community far outweigh political balkanisation. Indeed, it was this concern for economic integration that served as the main driving force behind the formation of the ECOWAS in 1975 (Onwuka, 1982a; Edozien and Osagie, 1982). By removal of impediments to economic integration we mean the suppression of artificial barriers between the constituent states in the region. This does not end by promoting trade within the community, evolving a common market, customs union or monetary system; it involves also the development of a policy on effective utilisation of human resources in the community.

It is undoubtedly in the spirit of this broader view of economic integration that Article 27 of the Treaty of ECOWAS confers on citizens of member-states the status of community citizenship (ECOWAS, 1981). The protocol guarantees freedom of movement and exempts community citizens from holding entry visas to member states for a maximum period of 90 days. The protocol also confers legal right to establishment, that is, the right to work and undertake commercial activities within the community. Of these 3 rights, the one central to our discussion is that relating to the right to work and engage in commercial activities.

But while the protocol may be seen as removing one of the barriers to economic integration in the community, the point is often ignored that the ECOWAS protocol is not meant to replace individual countries' immigration policies. On the contrary, the supremacy of the latter is recognised in the protocol. Justifiably perhaps, each country tends to enforce its immigration laws on in-migrants and, by so doing, exposes the conflict between these laws and the treaty on the free movement of community citizens.

First, attention seems to be focused not on the conditions in the protocol but on its general principle on free movement. This tends to ignore the point that in fact, the protocol only speaks of a 90-day free movement, after which any community citizen wishing to overstay must normalise his status under the country's immigration policy. Second, there seems to be the erroneous impression that the ECOWAS protocol, signed only in 1979, has contributed mainly to the inter-state mobility in the community. The truth of the matter is that the movement of people within the West African community is an old and ever-going process. In the case of Nigeria, for example, in-migration had been an old and continuous exercise, although as we have argued earlier, favourable economic conditions in the country since the early 1970s served to escalate the pattern. Therefore, contrary to popular opinion, the ECOWAS protocol has contributed marginally to the influx of migrant labour into the country.

Dilemma of Immigration Policies and ECOWAS

Before independence the movement of labour in West Africa was practically unhindered. Since individual countries became independent, however, international mobility within the sub-region has become increasingly difficult (Adedeji, 1970, pp. 228–9). The source of this difficulty must be traced to the economic and ideological differences among the new states which become very pronounced as each grappled with social, economic and political problems (Usoro, 1982; Mabogunje, 1972).

As a result of these difficulties, many of the West African states have resorted to harsh economic and immigration policies, culminating in embarrassing expulsion of citizens of community members. During the past two decades, nearly all the states now known as ECOWAS had employed this means in dealing with internal economic and political problems (Mabogunje, 1972).

In 1968, for example, the National Liberation Council in Ghana restricted certain areas of economic activities to Ghanaians; these included taxi service operations, small-scale businesses with less than ₵1000 operating capital, retail and wholesale trade which had annual turnover of less than ₵500 000 and ₵1 000 000 respectively (Killick, 1978; Mabogunje, 1972, p. 126). Nigeria introduced similar policy in 1972 when the Enterprises Promotion Decree came into effect. This law confines certain areas of business activities, such as retail, wholesale, light industries and agriculture to Nigerians, while the extent of non-indigenes' participation in others, particularly industrial, manufacturing, is defined by law (Nigeria, 1972; Oyediran, 1978). Although there is usually no direct connection between these economic measures and the expulsion of aliens, it is implicit that the limitation on the economic activity of non-natives is an indication of their economic burden on the host country.

In any event, these actions seem to suggest that it is a country's social and economic structures that give rise to these sorts of economic measures. It was therefore hardly a surprise when the Busia government in Ghana expelled thousands of non-natives, mostly Nigerians, in 1969. Even where there is no specific economic restructuring as has been done in Ghana and Nigeria, other countries in the ECOWAS had expelled citizens of member states at one time or another. In 1982 the Sierra Leone government expelled Ghanaian fishermen who dominated the country's fishing industry. Upper Volta had during this period expelled citizens of Benin Republic while Equatorial Guinea, whose economy had, for decades, been nurtured by Nigerian labour, expelled over 5000

Nigerian farmers in 1969 (Nigeria, 1975, pp. 17–18).

The question may well be asked how it came to be that some 2 000 000 community citizens migrated to Nigeria at a magnitude clearly exceeding the country's absorptive capacity? A simple though fundamentally important answer to this question is that the modern sector (in which the major portion of oil revenue was invested) could not, because of its high technology and consequently low demand for labour, absorb all the labour that had responded to the boom, from both the rural areas and other ECOWAS countries. Even though the monopolistic capital-intensive organisations produced a large number of dependent and secondary organisations in the informal sector, these organisations could not absorb all migrants (from rural areas and the Community) in spite of the fact that the informal sector absorbs a greater part of the country's working population.

Equally more fundamental reasons can be given. To begin, it is quite obvious that while the massive influx of community citizens was consistent with the principle of the ECOWAS protocol on free movement, it was equally a reflection of the administrative and enforcement inertia of the Nigerian immigration authority, and a clear evidence of poor planning. The immigration authority, while allowing migrants to enter the country freely, failed to ensure their prompt and orderly return to their countries after the 90 days permit.[6] The economic planning process, upon which this laxity can be justified, had been based on over-ambitious and unrealistic projections of oil output and revenue which were, in the final analysis, subject to the vicissitudes of the international economic system. Second, manifest economic mismanagement by the ruling class, later confirmed by the termination of the Shagari administration by the military on 31 December, 1983, undoubtedly confirmed the administration's desire for a scapegoat upon whom to ascribe the economic downturn.

Critics maintained that the repatriation of non-natives was nothing less than a subterfuge to draw attention away from the glaring failure of the government to provide effective and purposeful leadership. As one of these critics, Sam Aluko, put it, 'It is usual when governments have mismanaged their economies for them to find scapegoats' (*Nigerian Tribune*, 1 February 1983). It is difficult to ignore this conclusion particularly, as events turned out during the disastrous general election of 1983, that the administration was using the repatriation to distract attention from more serious economic problems, or as a means of assuring the Nigerian populace that the expulsion of aliens would revitalise the economy. Yet, while trying to give the impression that the expulsion of non-natives would promote economic recovery, the Nigerian government, as the major sponsor the ECOWAS, did not want to openly launch the first attack on the protocol on free movement.

And although the government studiously avoided the unemployment argument, it was implicit in the expulsion order that the prospect of increasing employment opportunities for the natives was a major reason. Thus, the Minister of Internal Affairs, Ali Baba, had argued that although a small proportion of aliens employed in the private sector had permission to work, the majority of those employed in the sector violated section 8.1 of the 1963 Immigration Act which prohibits employment of non-Nigerians without prior written consent of the director of immigration.[7]

With respect to the possibility that the expulsion of aliens might open up employment opportunities for natives, this was, as we shall argue presently, an illusion. First, employment patterns among aliens suggest that those affected by the expulsion performed jobs which natives were not willing to accept. Second, the expulsion was equally irrelevant since those migrant workers whose departure could have opened up employment opportunities for the natives were sheltered by the exemption clause in the order. Finally, in regard to the argument that illegal aliens, particularly those who were said to have no gainful employment and contributed to security and social problems, there is no convincing.

JOB CHARACTERISTICS OF MIGRANT WORKERS

Pattern of Employment and Unemployment

Trade union response to the employment of migrant workers can be discerned from the job characteristics of the aliens. As I have indicated, nowhere in the government repatriation order was a direct reference made to the employment of natives, although it seemed obvious that the expulsion was meant to improve the employment opportunities of natives. I shall in this and the next sections give an account of the kinds of jobs in which non-natives are mostly found and what consequences these have on the trade union movement. The argument draws heavily upon interviews with migrants, employers and trade union officials.

Available data[8] on the structure of employment in Nigeria indicates that in 1975, 27.9 million people out of the labour force of 29.2 million were gainfully employed. Modern sector employment was 1.5 million or

5.4 per cent of gainfully employed. By 1980, the number of gainfully employed had risen by 10 per cent while modern sector employment rose to 1.9 million or by 32 per cent. However, it should be noted that as at 1980, modern sector employment represented only 6 per cent of the labour force.

With respect to unemployment, registered unemployment was 256 623 in 1980 and by 1982, this had increased by 32 per cent (Table 3.2). Of the total registered as unemployed in 1982, 74 per cent were lower grade workers while primary and secondary school leavers represented 26 per cent of the unemployed. The number of job vacancies for the lower grade workers was 47 639 in 1982, which was 36 per cent higher than the 1980 figure.

These statistics must be cautiously interpreted. Firstly, unemployment figures are gathered on a voluntary basis and, as might be expected, they do not reflect the actual state of unemployment in Nigeria. Often the unemployed do not have any strong confidence in the ability of the Labour Exchanges to get them jobs. Second, registration of unemployment is, by default, confined to selected urban areas; though it is admitted that it is in these areas that open unemployment is prevalent. However, to the extent that not all urban and rural areas are covered, the aggregate data is far from reliable.

In any event there are studies that have attempted to measure and describe the characteristics of the unemployed in the urban areas. One of such studies was conducted in the Human Resources Research Unit at the University of Lagos (Fapohunda, 1974). The study revealed that unemployment was pronounced among youths (below 24 years old), accounting for 73.2 per cent of total unemployment. The unemployed

Table 3.2   Registered unemployment and vacancies in Nigeria, 1981–82

Category	1980 1	1981 2	1982 3	Percentage 1 and 3
Registered unemployment	256 623	238 352	339 231	32
Lower Grade Workers	202 519	188 438	251 130	24
Primary/Secondary School Leavers	54 104	49 914	88 101	63
Vacancies (Lower Grade Workers)	34 947	58 204	47 639	36

Source: Central Bank of Nigeria, *Annual Report and Statement of Account* (1982) p. 31.

had characteristics such as low education – secondary school or less (70.5 per cent) – and little or no skill (83 per cent). Yet 39 and 15 per cent of the unemployed wanted to work for government and statutory corporations respectively, 2 per cent preferred the armed forces and about a third wanted to work for private firms. Only 1 per cent wanted to work in education or to be self-employed. In other words, the overwhelming majority of the unemployed wanted government or white-collar jobs.

If therefore the published data is used as a measure of the scope and pattern of unemployment, and for evolving a policy on employment creation, it will be seen that mass repatriation of aliens in order to create jobs for the natives was unnecessary. All that would have been done was adopt selective repatriation of the so-called illegal aliens who were employed in the public sector as school teachers,[9] engineers, doctors, technicians, clerks, nurses and other clerical personnel. This argument is, however, unhelpful. First, illegal aliens who were employed in the public sector and who could have been subjected to selective repatriation were never affected by the expulsion order; these people were relieved of their posts only recently and obviously for a different reason.[10]

Second, the aliens who were employed in skilled jobs as technicians, artisans, fitters as well as professionals – engineers, architects, etc., in private sector were allowed to regularise their immigration status. Although there are no statistics on the proportion of aliens that were so employed, it seems that the number varied from about 10–20 per cent in the relatively big firms to 50–60 per cent in the smaller establishments, particularly in the construction industry. That this category of aliens were allowed to regularise their employment status was an open admission that migrant workers in the primary sector posed no threat to the employment prospects of the natives. To a large extent, it is also an acknowledgement of skill shortage in these occupations (see *National Development Plan*, 1981–85, p. 428). By the same token, it suggests, as we shall demonstrate presently, that the jobs that non-natives take either in the formal or informal sector labour market are jobs which natives will not accept. For example, while explaining that 2000 aliens were employed as teachers in Lagos State in 1983, the Commissioner for Education, Olawale Idris, noted that qualified Nigerians were not willing to work as teachers, especially in the rural areas (*Daily Times* 21 January 1983). Natives are unwilling to accept skilled jobs partly for lack of the required skills which in turn is a reflection of the orientation of the educational system (Ojo *et al.*, 1985). Semi-skilled and unskilled jobs have the stigma of inferior social status and low wage.

The Job Characteristics of Migrants

A distinctive characteristic of the jobs in which the overwhelming majority of non-natives are found is their concentration in the informal sector. As we have defined it, the informal sector is not just the non-wage earning class, but rather it includes those who are working for wage in the indigenous enterprises or family concerns, and the self-employed. A recent report of the OECD (1979, p. 18) on migration in 9 West African countries concluded that, 'Immigrants were employed in the lowest paid and most physically demanding activities, the mines and plantations', with a fairly significant number in higher occupations. The range of jobs in the lowest category is infinite and beyond anyone's imagination: it includes owner-operated taxi businesses and those working for wage/commission, housekeeping, i.e. houseboys/girls, maids, chauffeurs, cleaners, messengers, general labour (in factories and farms), kitchen aids, such as pounding yam in the bukateria (local canteen), road-side mechanics, carpenters, petrol and garage attendants, masonry, street hawking and roadside trading. These jobs are semi-skilled and unskilled, generally but not always attracting low wage or income. The jobs are menial, tedious and in unpleasant working environments. Those in wage-employment often have poor working conditions.

The experience of Kwami X, a Ghanaian, illustrates many of the job characteristics of the migrant worker.

Kwami migrated to Nigeria in 1978 and at the time of this interview in March 1984 he operated a *danfo* minibus for public transportation. Armed with the West African School Certificate at Grade Two he secured a clerical job with an indigenous medium-size clearing and forwarding company in Apapa in November 1978. He was paid ₦100 per month, which was below what his Nigerian counterparts were getting. Nevertheless, he was grateful to his employee for offering him a job at a period of great need.

During the week-ends throughout 1979–80, he was a freelance washerman, cleaning clothes for neighbours at the back of the house in which he rented a small room. The income from this source helped to pay his rent of ₦8 a month and bus fare to and from work. At his job, he complained that his take-home pay was little after many deductions, including contribution to the National Provident Fund which he 'never was going to get'. He also complained that he was paying 'too much' on transportation. Partly because of this he had applied for a similar job in a bigger company, so as to take advantage of the highly subsidized transport and canteen facilities but had not succeeded 'because I am not a citizen of Nigeria'.

Owing to declining business, he lost his job in May 1982 and in the 6 months following this, he drifted from one job to another: block-making, daily-paid labour at construction sites, serving as a houseboy to a rich businessman and finally, helping a Nigerian friend in his taxi business. Between 1978 and 1980 he visited his hometown near Kumasi twice. During his last visit in December 1980, he married his present wife who has born him two children. His sister in-law joined them in April 1982 to help with the children, but she was later to take up a job as a housemaid somewhere at Ikeja. His wife also began working for a small photo studio at Yaba where she earned about ₦60 a month; this varied depending on how good the business was.

By June 1982 he had gathered enough money to buy a second-hand danfo which he operated along the Yaba–Ikeja route. He confirmed with relish that his standard of living was much better than when he was a salary-earner.

I asked him what was his reaction to the quit order of January 1983 and how he managed to remain in Nigeria as at March 1984. To these questions he answered: 'I was very worried about the matter. In fact, we packed up and left Lagos for the rural area in Epe, with the assistance of my Nigerian friends. I thought if I can't operate my transport business I will just take to farming. After a while when the heat subsided I came back and we all resumed our work unmolested.' I also asked him if he planned to return to Kumasi in the foreseeable future. He said 'no' although he will definitely go back one day.

Kwami's case is corroborated by Acheampong (*West Africa*, 24 January 1983) who described his encounter with two migrants during a recent visit to Lagos:

> Kwame sells cornflakes and paper tissues along Eric Moore Road, Surulere. Thirty-six years old, he is a printer by profession and married with two children who are in Ghana. Said he, 'I came here ten months ago to work for about two years to buy some items like a sewing machine for my wife, clothes for my family and a cornmill for generating revenue when I get home.'
>
> Asked why he did not practise his profession in Lagos, Kwame said: 'The wages I was being offered were far below what a printer should earn. The highest offer I had was ₦100 per month. My in-laws, who are here, advised me to hawk rather than accept such low wage.'

Comparing his income and condition of work as self-employed hawker with a wage earner, he said: 'On the average I get ₦9 a day and I'm able to save a minimum of ₦5 a day. Moreover, when I feel tired, I just pack off and go home.'

Ekow is 29 years of age and from 8 a.m. to 2 p.m., he moves around the busy Ojota Motor Park selling meatpies. Two pies in a polythene bag cost 50 kobo and he sells 80 such bags by 2 p.m. earning a monthly commission of ₦120. After 2 p.m. he does odd jobs till 6 p.m. for a daily wage of ₦3. He spends ₦2 a day and regards his meat-pie commission as savings.

Asked what his occupation was he said: 'I am a carpenter by profession and my former employer was offering me ₦3 a day. After much pleading, it was raised to ₦4 but I felt I was being cheated so I resigned to sell meat-pies.' Asked what his future plan was, he said, 'I will go back home in April 1983. I want to acquire some personal belongings for my family and some roofing sheets.'

Employment and Wages

That many employers prefer to employ non-natives to fill certain vacancies is partly a response to the unpreparedness of natives to accept the particular jobs and partly due to the fact that non-natives can be paid sub-standard wages. These two factors are intimately related in the employment of non-natives for, in spite of their concern about the exploitative wage they get, non-natives still feel motivated to work to the satisfaction of their employers. Thus, the motivation to high productivity even at low wage is a self-sustaining mechanism which accounts for the predominance of migrant workers in the informal sector. As Mabogunje (1972, p. 134) has argued, it is the entrepreneurial and innovative attributes of the migrant workers which makes it easy for them to quickly identify areas of employment opportunities and so become dominant in certain economic activities.

With respect to wage employment, several factors, such as labour cost and the motivation of the non-native job applicant, combine to induce employers' desire to employ migrants. Although it might be difficult to disentangle one factor from the other, it is perhaps true to say that labour cost is the dominant factor. Here a host of employers who are mainly indigenous businessmen, do not, apart from paying the basic (low) wage, usually carry several of the familiar overhead costs, such as a string of benefits and entitlements. One visitor to Lagos remarked recently that, 'One peculiar thing I noticed was that Nigerian employers often preferred Ghanaians to Nigerians in mainly unskilled jobs. One confided that whereas a Nigerian would demand a monthly wage of ₦250, a desperate Ghanaian would readily accept between ₦180 and ₦200' (*West Africa*, 24 January 1981).

To shed more light on this issue, I talked to two employers. One was the owner of a small electrical appliance sales and repair shop in Ebute-Metta, Lagos who employed 14 workers, including 8 non-natives. Asked why he chose to employ non-natives, he said that he found them to be reliable, hardworking and honest. Besides, he said, 'they are our African brothers whom I am trying to help'.

With regard to compensation, except the four technicians (2 of them non-natives) who earned between ₦140 per month, none of the other workers earned up to the legal minimum wage of ₦125 per month. The businessman also acknowledged that the non-natives earned less (some 15 per cent) than their Nigerian counterparts, but that this would improve over time. He provided no fringe benefits, except that occasionally he was prepared to let anyone take a day or two off for important personal reasons. There was no provision for annual leave but any worker may take a period of non-paid leave.

I asked whether he satisfied himself that the non-natives had work permits as required by law. He said he did not bother himself because non-natives were employed 'all over the place' including government departments and schools. Also because, as he put it, 'these people were ready to work without asking for unreasonable working conditions'.

The other company I talked to was a construction firm which employed about 83 workers. Of this 80 per cent were manual labourers. A total of 42 (or 51 per cent) were non-natives. All of the latter except 11 including one woman were manual daily-paid labourers. There were 7 administrative and clerical staff, including a lady from the Republic of Benin. On compensation, the personnel officer in the company disagreed that the non-natives were paid low wages compared with their Nigerian counterparts, although he confirmed that all the unskilled migrants were daily-rated, and, as expected, they earned less than the monthly-rated employees. The wage differentials averaged about 20 per cent.

On why the company had the majority of the non-natives as daily-paid, the personnel officer said, 'it was company policy because of the nature of our work'. He added that there was a high turnover rate among non-natives. I asked if the workers were members of a union, he reluctantly answered 'no', adding that the workers 'are not interested in trade union activities'. With respect to government policy on the employment of immigrants, the officer said that although the government had itself violated the specific law or order, his company was prepared to help its worthy migrant workers to get work permits if they so desire. So far, he said, only a few, mainly the skilled workers, had asked for such assistance.

To argue that the presence of non-natives in these occupations deprived natives of their right to work, is, in the light of the experience in ECOWAS and Nigeria in particular, a highly erroneous conception. As Mabogunje (1972, pp. 142–3) has argued,

> The rights to work hard, to trade where they [migrants] like, and to accumulate wealth are not for the migrants to give. Nor can the migrants take away privileges of the indigenous people to participate in the economic activities of their country or area at a level of efficiency which they choose. One is forced to conclude that behind this statement is the mercantilist assumption that the gains of the migrants are the losses of the indigenous population.

The argument is equally misleading. When Busia expelled non-natives, mostly citizens of West African countries from Ghana in 1969, labour shortage was noticeable in the mines and cocoa farms; the expulsion of traders also created difficulties in the retail trade (*West Africa*, 31 January 1983). To take another example from Nigeria, the repatriation of non-natives left many vacancies in construction sites and in factories which were previously dependent on migrant labour. Many employers I talked to confirmed that they experienced difficulties in filling the vacancies, as there was no appreciable response from natives to take up the positions. One construction site in Lagos was closed down temporarily because of the difficulty of continuing work without adequate personnel.

In the cargo handling industry where some 7000 migrant workers were affected, difficulties were similarly experienced. The General Secretary of the Dockworkers Union, Jonas Abam, complained that natives were slow in filling the vacancies (*West Africa*, 14 February 1983). As far as househelp services were concerned, the repatriation created practically no inducement to Nigerians to take the jobs and expectedly, the average wage paid to househelps jumped by more than 30 per cent, immediately after the quit order.

In the light of the foregoing, even though the expulsion did receive popular support which was largely sentimental and understandably due to perceived prospect for employment, there were no clear indications that the expulsion opened up opportunities for the unemployed. Indeed, as a result of balance of payment difficulties which arose largely due to declining revenue from oil, the government introduced what became known as 'austerity measures' in April 1982. The policy placed severe restrictions on the importation of a wide range of household and non-consumer items. As the measures appeared to have little impact, the restrictions were extended to cover raw materials for the industrial sector with adverse consequences for employment. In the large labour-intensive textile industry, for example, more than 50 per cent of the workforce of over 200 000 people were retrenched between 1980 and 1984, the majority of the workers being relieved between 1982 and 1984.

TRADE UNION POLICIES AND MIGRANT LABOUR

The critical role of trade unions concerning international labour mobility in the ECOWAS is as complex as the issue of the protocol on free movement within the community. Hypothetically, it could be argued, *a priori*, that trade unions would strive for internationalisation of labour by ensuring solidarity on such issues as minimum acceptable standards of wages and conditions of work to be enforced on employers within the sub-region. How this objective might be achieved is however not clear nor is there any indication that the labour movements in the community have attempted any formal relationship on the problems of migrant labour.

The reason for this indifference is not far to seek. It arose primarily from the inherent weakness of the various labour movements, and the nearly insurmountable internal conflicts which individual labour movements faced, either in trying to remain as independent institutions devoid of state control or, as in some of the states in the community, to secure their legal existence (Ananaba, 1979). Other problem areas which tend to limit the geographical horizon of the labour movements in West Africa, as indeed in many parts of the developing world, are internal union factionalism, employers' resistance and domination of labour relations, financial problems and other environmental difficulties (Cohen, 1974; Damachi *et al.*, 1979).[11] Thus, primarily because of these difficulties the perspectives of trade unions tend to be confined to their limited national interests.[12] It is in this perspective that one might evaluate the response of the Nigerian labour movement to the expulsion of immigrants from that country.

There are three ways in which trade union responses can be evaluated. Firstly, unions might respond by colluding with employers to block or place obstacles to the employment of immigrants, especially where public policy was unfavourable to the employment of non-natives or where legal right to take up employment had not been given. This is a purely protectionist policy. Second, unions' response might be influenced or determined by a conscious desire to *maintain* organisational cohesion and thereby enhance their bargaining position. Policies on equal work for equal pay, union shop, through which recruits are required to join the union, and participate in trade union actions, such as the strike, are in this category. This is a solidaristic policy. Third, there might be a policy which, in the final analysis, seeks to enhance and strengthen the voice of the unions. Employment promotion policies which may be nationalistic or solidaristic, are typical.

The first alternative has neither moral nor enforcement value. To pursue it is to challenge the very root of international solidarity common to trade unions, and the potential for labour's contribution to economic integration in the community. As one commentator pointed out,

> It may be tempting for the labour movement to support the deportation orders in the false belief that Nigerian jobs would be protected. This is not the case. The deportation of the Ghanaians and others will only weaken the working class movement in Nigeria and do irreparable damage to the ECOWAS spirit. The labour movement in Nigeria should express unambigously its solidarity with the Ghanaians and others by opposing all deportations and immigration controls. (*West Africa*, 14 February 1983)

Although a few trade unionists, acting individually, did express concern about the deprivation of employment to natives there was, as far as can be determined, no official union support for this view.

With respect to its enforcement, it is inconceivable for a trade union to tell an employer whom to employ; this is neither the tradition of the labour movement nor is there any support for it in public policy. Indeed, capitalist employers as profit optimisers, would opt for the cheapest labour assuming that the marginal productivity of labour is equal to unit labour cost. If the employer is satisfied that he will get a satisfactory return on his investment by employing a foreigner at less than the official (minimum or union) wage, he will pursue this policy irrespective of any union pressure. For example, shortly after the expulsion of aliens, an employer in the block making industry was quoted as saying that he had to pay ₦12 per day to Nigerians on jobs for which he had paid aliens ₦7 (*West Africa*, 28 February 1983).

Besides, the alternative we are considering assumes that the labour market is completely organised. This is better imagined than the reality in Nigeria where the overwhelming majority of employers are not organised by trade unions. For example, during a recent interview, Sylvester Ejiofor, General Secretary of the 60 000 strong Civil Service Technical Workers Union commented on the predicament of the aliens thus:

> All that I can say is that for aliens who were employed in the informal sector where labour is disorganised, there was obviously a question of high exploitation. But what could congress [NLC] have done? These are sectors which are not in the strict sense affiliated to the Nigeria Labour Congress or members of any particular union. So there was nothing we could have done. (*West Africa*, 26 September 1983)

Even in the so-called modern (formal) sector, no industry, except perhaps the public service, has had more than 50 per cent organisation of the work-force. This is due partly to the anti-union tactics of employers, and partly to the organisational inadequacies of the unions, especially their inability to draw their net wide enough to cover their industry of jurisdiction.

In any event, having been unable to organise the easily identifiable modern sector, in spite of favourable public policy,[13] there was no conceivable way by which the unions could enter the vast informal sector so as to influence employment decisions there. Moreover, it is in this sector that migrant labour is common, and the work they do is of no interest to the unions or natives. In this perspective, the employment of migrants can hardly be seen as a threat to the employment of natives whom unions might want to guard in a protectionist policy. This is because the former are, by and large, a non-competing group and also because the unions have no organisational capability to cover the entire labour market in their jurisdiction.

The second form of response is one which in both the short and long term will enhance the credibility of the unions and which appeared to have achieved prominence in the minds of many union leaders in Nigeria. Since the focus of this alternative is on those non-natives who are employed, presumably in the modern (formal) sector, it is potentially a viable course of trade union solidaristic strategy. Traditional analysis of trade union wage policy points to a desire of unions to take 'wage out of competition' by enforcing slogans such as 'equal work for equal pay'. By ensuring that employers treat *all* workers in the same job equally, the union tries to bring the affected workers under its influence.

There are two distinct ways by which this alternative can be considered, following the dichotomy between the formal (modern) sector and the informal sector employment possibilities. On the one hand, non-natives employed in the modern sector, whether public and private are, by and large, on contract employment, which means that they hold their jobs for a specific period of time, often subject to extension. The exception are those who are permanent residents who, for this very reason, are generally no problems for trade unions, since permanency of residence implies a change in their perception of trade unionism, as well as their commitment and involvement in social institutions in the country of sojourn (Piore, 1979, p. 110; Mazumdar, 1979, pp. 5–8).

As far as those who are on a specific period of employment are concerned, this is problematic in that because they view their attachment to the job and generally the labour market as temporary they have no motivation to organise or join unions. Thus, their indifference to worker militancy stems mainly from both the lack of commitment to the labour market and their illegal status. Undoubtedly as a result of these considerations, migrant workers seem conditioned to think that they owe their loyalty not to unions, but to their employers. As such they are unprepared to make waves or do anything, such as participating in trade union protests, which might portray them as ungrateful and could, rightly or wrongly, lead to dismissal.

Unfortunately, for the labour movement, this thinking fits nicely employer's expectation of the social commitment of their migrant workers. In the teaching services which experienced unprecedented incidences of strikes over irregularity and non-payment of salaries during 1982–3, the employers, i.e. state governments, were constantly prompting non-native teachers, numbering about 60 000 in 1983, to remain working, in efforts to break the strikes. The effectiveness of these strikes, some of them lasting for a couple of weeks to 6 months, was undermined by the non-participation of non-native teachers.

When we come to consider the case of non-natives in wage-earning employment in the information sector, the problem facing trade union policy takes on an even greater signficance because of the apparent complacency of non-native workers to trade union membership. The issue of the alien's illegal residency is of a different dimension in that being outside the formal sector and not working for government (which in a sense confers on them legality of employment!) their disposition to engage in any action which might expose them was consciously recognized. Ejiofoh's comment on this issue is quite instructive. He said, 'of course, I agree entirely that in the informal petty business, a lot of them [the aliens] were used like beasts because they were illegal and of

course couldn't complain' (*West Africa*, 26 September 1983). Predictably, the employers in the sector who are mainly Nigerian indigenes and
third world entrepreneurs are fundamentally opposed to trade unions
(Damachi, 1984). It is in this sector that the problem of low wage, poor
conditions of service, marginal attachment to the labour market and
little or no trade union activity prevail. After recognising this dilemma, it
must be noted, as I have pointed out earlier, that because of their
organisational inadequacies, the unions have themselves paid little
attention to the organisation of workers, whether natives or non-
natives, in the informal sector. They are thus unable to use the dictum of
equal work for equal pay to reduce wage differentials or achieve
solidarity.

The third decision alternative for labour is one that has, expectedly,
attracted considerable debate both with respect to the xenophobia that
the expulsion created and the presumed employment opportunities it
might create for indigenous labour. The open display of support by a
section of the public, nationalists and the unemployed, was a natural
reaction grounded in the belief that once the migrants were gone, there
would be enough jobs to absorb domestic unemployment.[14] As I have
demonstrated in previous sections, this belief was no less an illusion
partly because of the complementary, non-competing nature of alien
employment and partly because of the discriminating nature of the
deportation order.

This notwithstanding, a trade union movement, conscious of the
importance of its numerical strength and its commitment to the general
improvement of the working class, may develop strategies which seek to
provide employment for the unemployed. It is indeed in the long-term
interest of a growth-conscious union to seek to increase the level of
employment in its area of operation. This responsibility is all the more
important in a society where the privileged class still describe wage
earners as a labour aristocracy simply by looking at wage earners as an
insignificant proportion of the population or the labour force (Arrighi
and Saul, 1973; Cohen, 1974).

The response of the Nigerian labour movement to this issue can, at
best, be described as pragmatic, but generally it offered no defence for
the alien workers. I shall hazard an explanation of this point later. At the
level of the Nigeria Labour Congress (NLC), all that can be ascribed to
the congress was its criticism of the manner in which the deportation
order was announced but it studiously maintained a non-commital
stance, leaving individual industrial unions to determine their position
on the issue. This was, in some respects, disappointing because being the

umbrella organisation with a better understanding of macro issues, it was expected not only to develop a cogent policy statement on the expulsion but also appreciate the impact for regional or continental labour solidarity in which the NLC plays an important role.[15]

At the level of the individual unions, very few unions commented on the employment implications of the departing aliens. In the cargo handling industry where some 7000 dock workers were affected, the Dockworkers Union of Nigeria (DUN) suprisingly embarked on a frantic though largely unsuccessful effort to recruit local labour to fill the vacancies (*West Africa*, 14 February 1983). The response of the DUN was perhaps a reflection of its organisational structure which in turn determines its financial solvency. DUN organises the relatively uneducated and unskilled employees of capitalist labour contractors whose compensation systems are characterised by irregular payment and unfavourable conditions of service. (For more on Ports trade unionism in Nigeria see Waterman, 1982). DUN's recruitment drive was therefore an attempt to stem the negative consequence which the expulsion of alien dockworkers would have on its finances rather than an open jubilation at the expulsion of alien workers.

In the textile industry where employment had been falling since 1980 due to smuggling and the recession (Fashoyin, 1984b), the union was indifferent to the relatively mundane issue of alien employment but was concerned about the fundamentally union-busting problem of declining employment in the industry. Between 1979 and 1983, for example, the union lost more than 50 per cent of its 82 000 membership (Fashoyin, 1984b). Similar problems faced the unions in the construction, petroleum, electrical products, food and beverage and paper and paperboards industries (NECA, 1984).

An Explanation

Let us at this juncture offer an explanation on why the Nigerian trade union movement offered little or no defence for the alien workers during the expulsion.

At the individual industrial union level I have noted the pragmatic outlook of the unions which arose primarily from their fight for economic and organisational survival in the face of massive decline in their membership through retrenchment. In many cases, however, retrenchment of workers was no less a deliberate design by industrialists to coerce the state to change its 'unfavourable' industrial policy. The other reason can be said to be the series of factional disputes that bedevilled the various industrial unions since their formation in 1978, but which became pronounced early in the 1980s. In spite of any hard statistics, our casual observations reveal that about two-thirds of the 42 industrial unions had had one factional dispute or another. In most of these cases, protracted litigations had followed. Big and influential unions such as the Nigerian Union of Nurses, Nigerian Union of Teachers, Nigerian Civil Service Union, Hotel and Personal Services Workers Union and the National Union of Petroleum and Natural Gas Worker (NUPENG), had had their disputes taken to court. In the case of the NUPENG, the factional dispute was made worse by employers' divisive support for a particular faction which ultimately led to the disqualification of Enas Dubre, a moderate and NUPENG President and NLC Vice-President during 1981–4, from contesting the NLC presidential election in February 1984.

Turning to the NLC which, expectedly, should play the leading role in fighting for the expelled aliens, the organisation was found wanting because it too was faced with a survival problem arising from internal and external challenges to its legitimacy and leadership. To begin with, after a brief spell of militant activity during 1978–81 when the congress, under the leadership of its outspoken and militant president, Hassan Sunmonu, suceeded in winning certain concessions (e.g. car loans and minimum wages) for workers, worsening economic conditions coupled with these challenges to which I now turn, forced the congress to move from an offensive position to one of defensive passivity. The NLC problems arose partly from the historical ideological factionalism in the labour movement which the government-sponsored restructing exercise of 1977–8 failed to remove and partly, though relatedly, to the vested interest of the state in the leadership of the NLC. Thus, when the Congress was formed in 1978, the government appeared agitated by the emergence of Hassan Sunmonu, an acclaimed Marxist and outspoken radical, as its president. Probably, government anxiety about the leftist posture of the NLC leader was attenuated by the fact that the organisation's vice-president, David Ojeli, a self-proclaimed 'democrat' but obviously more sympathetic to ruling class interest, was expected to offer a countervailing influence to Sunmonu's. Put simply, Sunmonu belonged to the 'Left' while Ojeli conveniently answered to the 'Right'.

I am however hardly enamoured by these categories which in the Nigerian situation, are little more than labels. Both men were senior civil servants and were in that respect union leaders at the pleasure of their paymasters. Throughout Ojeli remained on the payroll of government, while the latter was 'magnanimous' in granting Sunmonu a leave of absence from his post as a technical officer. My point, in other words, is that both men had been partially incorporated into the state bureaucracy, admittedly in varying degrees.

In any event, the internal opposition within the labour movement became an open issue in 1981 over the election of a new NLC president; Sunmonu and Ojeli were the two candidates. Amidst charges and counter-charges of governmental influence, Sunmonu retained not only the presidency but was also able to influence the election of other officers of the Congress, to the great discomfort of Ojeli and his sponsors. As Otobo (1981) noted, politicians and government officials were now in favour of forming a rival central labour organisation after David Ojeli, who was government-favoured candidate for the presidency, failed to win the election in February 1981.

The conflict within the labour movement which was fuelled by state intervention ultimately led to the formation by Ojeli and his group of a still-born Committee for Democratic Trade Unions. But more importantly, the division in the NLC not only undermined Congress' ability to mobilise popular support, state infiltration made it difficult for a labour movement antagonistic to government policy to coalesce. In other words, government officials were, at the slightest opportunity, quick in ridiculing the NLC as misguided and political. To take an example, the NLC-led general strike of May 1981 was denounced by politicians, while Ojeli and his group of 8 industrial unions described it as 'unfortunate and ill-timed' which was likely to 'undermine the court and place in jeopardy the industrial relations system' (Otobo, 1981, p. 76).

What is instructive from the foregoing is that during 1981–3 a considerable amount of energy and resources of the NLC leadership was devoted to wade-off attempts by the Ojeli group, politicians and government officials to remove, through legislative means, the hegemony of the NLC as the only central labour organisation in Nigeria, thereby splitting the labour movement. Whilst this effort on the part of the ruling class failed, that is, whilst the NLC remained a single body, it was heavily battered and was neither strong enough to antagonise the ruling class nor to articulate the interest of the working class, such as protesting the expulsion of alien workers from Nigeria.

SUMMARY AND CONCLUSION

This chapter has suggested that the response of trade unions to the employment consequences of migrant labour is largely a function of the nature of the labour market in the receiving country and organisational preparedness. Where migrant labour is complementary to native labour in the sense that the over-whelming majority of migrants take jobs which natives will not accept, it serves the useful purpose of preserving native jobs. Put differently, migrant labour is, by and large, a non-competing group since it is dominant in a particular labour market. Unions' response is also a function of their internal organisational preparedness. Unions that are unable to organise the relatively easier formal sector have no motivation whatsoever to dabble into the highly volatile informal sector where the peculiar characteristics of the labour market makes trade union activity highly precarious.

With respect to migrant labour in the formal sector, union efforts at achieving organisational cohesion through migrants' commitment to trade union policy is, by and large, influenced by the nature of the employment contract of the migrants. Contract employment implying a specific period of attachment offers little motivation for the migrant worker to engage in class activity. This is all the more so where the migrant worker is consciously being reminded of his disability as an illegal alien. In consequence, he becomes indifferent to class activity even when this might be advantageous in the longer-term.

When we turn to the attitude of trade unions to the expelled aliens we find that Nigerian unions were incapacitated by both internal and external pressures which made it difficult for them to fight for the aliens. Factional disputes, arising from our leadership squabbles, which were fueled by employers and state interventionist policies, introduced instability and insecurity in the labour movement. Another factor which inhibited the ability of the unions to pursue international solidaristic policy was the negative impact of the retrenchment exercise embarked upon by capitalists and the state. This policy severely undermined the organisation cohesion of the unions forcing them into a protective and defensive position.

In the final analysis, however, it seems obvious that the task before trade unions in the ECOWAS is to strive for the incorporation of migrant workers into their fold, in order to achieve a much desired solidaristic action. This will enhance the organisational cohesion of unions, especially in fighting the exploitation of migrant workers and by enforcing the policy of equal work for equal pay and conditions of service. This approach will undoubtedly strengthen the solidarity among trade unions within the Community.

Notes

1. I acknowledge the useful comments of Professor Joe Umo of the University of Lagos, Roger Southall of the University of Leicester and those of an anonymous reviewer on an earlier draft of this chapter.
2. The Economic Community of West Africa States (ECOWAS) presently has 16 members, namely: Benin, Cape Verde, Gambia, Ghana, Guinea, Guinea Bissau, Ivory Coast, Liberia, Mali, Mauritania, Niger, Nigeria, Senegal, Sierra Leone, Togo and Burkina Fasso.
3. Throughout this paper, the terms 'foreigner', 'alien' 'migrant' and 'non-native' are used interchangeably to refer to migrant workers. In the same manner, the terms 'Nigerian', 'citizen' and 'native' are used to refer to local labour.
4. Ironically, Nigerians in foreign countries are often engaged in jobs or occupations which they would not otherwise accept in their country. A good example is the case of Nigerians who migrate to developed countries of America, Britain and other parts of Europe to accept manual jobs such as dish-washing, cleaning and general factory labour.
5. It is notable that these rights are to be acquired in 3 sequential phases, each lasting for 5 years, beginning from 1979.
6. This account is not ignorant of the fact that barely after the heat of the expulsion had subsided, the migrants renewed their re-entry into Nigeria. This is a conspicuous example of the inability of the immigration department to control in-migration into the country.
7. Press Conference of the Minister of Internal Affairs, Lagos, 17 January 1983.
8. All figures from the *Third National Development Plan, 1975–80*. Lagos, Federal Ministry of Economic Development, 1975.
9. In the Ondo Central Schools Board in Ondo State 395 Ghanaians, or 39.3 per cent of all teachers in the district were employed in 1980/1. *Daily Times* 19 January 1983.
10. As a result of declining revenue and a realistic appraisal of development policies, governments at both the federal and state levels have engaged in massive retrenchment of workers, including the teaching profession where there was a large number of non-natives. Between January and December 1984 about 250 000 civil servants and teachers were affected by this purge.
11. For details of how far the state has intervened in industrial relations, including policies to strengthen the unions see Tayo Fashoyin, *Industrial Relations in Nigeria* (London, Longman) 1980, ch. 3.
12. This is not to suggest that international co-operation does not exist. The Organization of Africa Trade Union Unity (OATUU) which was formed in 1973 is a body that advances international labour solidarity in Africa. However, the efforts of the OATUU tend to be confined to continent-wide issues, such as liberation struggles and independence of trade union movements.
13. Under the Labour (Amendment) Decree No. 22 of 1978, all workers are automatically union members exception cases where there is a written note to contract out.
14. Newspaper articles and editorials during the period 20 January to end of

February were frequent in articulating this view. See, for example, *Nigerian Tribune* 20 January 1983 and the *Daily Times* of 27 January 1983.
15. The Nigeria Labour Congress (NLC) is a leading member of the continental union – Organization of African Trade Union Unity (OATUU). In January 1985 Nigeria hosted the general conference of the organisation at which the former NLC President (who was in office during the expulsion of 1983) Hassan Sunmonu was a candidate for the Presidency of OATUU. There is also an on-going move to form an organisation comprising all the labour movements in the ECOWAS.

Bibliography

Adedeji, A. (1970) 'Prospects of Regional Economic Co-operation in West Africa', *Journal of Modern African Studies*, 8, 2.
Ananaba, Wogu (1979) *The Trade Union Movement in Africa* (London: Hurst).
Arrighi, G. and J.S. Saul (1973) *Essays on the Political Economy of Africa* (New York: Monthly Review Press).
Asante, S.K.B. (1983) 'ECOWAS and the Expulsion', *West Africa* 18 April.
Bienefeld, M.M. Godfrey and H. Schmitz (1977) 'Trade Unions and the "New" Internationalization of Production' *Development and Change*, 8, 4.
Breman, J.C. (1980) *The Informal Sector in Research Theory and Practice* (Rotterdam: Erasmus University).
Bosanquet, N. and P.B. Doeringer (1973) 'Is there a Dual Labour Market in Great Britain?' *Economic Journal*, 83, 330.
Cohen, Robin (1974) *Labour and Politics in Nigeria* (London: Heinemann).
Damachi, U.G. (1984) *Industrial Relations: A Development Dilemma* (Inaugural Lecture, University of Lagos).
Damachi, U.G. *et al.* (eds) (1979) *Industrial Relations in Africa* (London: Macmillan).
Doeringer, P.B. and M.J. Piore (1971) *Internal Labor Markets and Manpower Adjustments* (Lexington, Mass, D.C.: Heath).
ECOWAS (1981) *Protocol Relating to the Free Movement of Persons* (Lagos: Economic Community of West African States).
Ewusi, Kodwo (1980) 'Scope, Structure and State of Industrialization in Ghana' in *Industrialization in the Economic Community of West African States (ECOWAS)*, V.P. Diejomaoh and M.A. Iyoha (eds) (Ibadan: Heinemann).
Fapohunda, O.J. (1978) *Characteristics of the Informal Sector* (Human Resources Research Unit, University of Lagos) Bulletin No. 78/01.
Fapohunda, O.J. (1974) *Characteristics of the Unemployed People in Lagos* (Human Resources Research Unit, University of Lagos) Research Paper No. 4.
Fashoyin, Tayo (1984a) *Internal Dynamics in Nigerian Unions: A Survey* (Department of Industrial Relations and Personnel Management, University of Lagos) Working Paper Series No. 1.
Fashoyin, Tayo (1984b) *The Impact of Economic Recession on Collective Bargaining in the Nigerian Textiles Industry* (Department of Industrial Relations and Personnel Management, University of Lagos) unpublished manuscript.
Fields, G.S. (1979) *How Segmented is the Bogota Labour Market?* (World Bank

Staff Working Paper (No. 434) Washington).
Hazelwood, A. (ed.) (1967) *African Integration and Disintegration* (London: Oxford University Press).
House, W.J. (1982) *Labour Market Segmentation: Evidence from Cyprus*, WEP, Population and Labour Policies Programme WP No. 117.
ILO (1972) *Employment, Incomes and Equality: A Strategy for Increasing Productive Employment in Kenya* (Geneva).
Killick, Tony (1978) *Development Economics in Action. A Study of Economic Policies in Ghana* (London: Heinemann).
Mabogunje, Akin L. (1972) *Regional Mobility and Resource Development in West Africa* (Montreal: Queen's University).
Manu, J.E.A. (1983) 'Performance of the Economy in the 1970s. Country Perspective – Ghana' in *Development Planning Priorities and Strategies in the Economic Community of West African States (ECOWAS)*, R.E. Ubogu et al. (eds) (Ibadan: Heinemann).
Martens, George R. (1980) *African Unions and Multination Enterprises* (Lome: Regional Economic Research and Documentation Centre).
Mazumdar, Dipak (1979) *Paradigms in the Study of Urban Labor Markets in LDCS: A Reassessment in the Light of an Empirical Survey in Bombay City* (World Bank Staff Working Paper No. 366).
Ndongko, W.A. (1977) 'A Note on Problems and Prospects of Labour Mobility within African Regional Groupings', *Nigerian Journal of Economic and Social Studies*, 19, 2.
NECA (1984) *Survey of Redundancy and Closures* (Lagos: Nigeria Employers' Consultative Association), *Annual Report of the Federal Ministry of Labour* (1960–70), *Federal Ministry of Information*, Nigeria, Federal Republic of (1975).
Nigeria, Federal Republic of (1977, 1982) *Federal Civil Service Manpower Statistics Nos. 10 and 15* (Lagos: Federal Government Printer).
Nigeria, Federal Republic of (1972) *Nigerian Enterprises Promotion Decree No. 4* (Lagos: Federal Government Printer) Gazette Vol. 59, 10.
Nigeria, Federal Republic of (1981) *Fourth National Development Plan, 1981–85* (Lagos: Federal Ministry of National Planning).
OECD (1979) *Migration in West Africa* (Paris, Development Centre).
Obregon, Quijano (1974) 'The Marginal Pole of the Economy and the Marginalised Labour Force', *Economy and Society*, 3, 4 November, 393–428.
Ojo, Falayan (1975) *Economic Integration: The Nigerian Experience since Independence* (Institute of Social Studies, Occasional Papers No. 54).
Ojo, Falayan, Adeyemo Aderinton and Tayo Fashoyin (eds) (1985) *Manpower Development and Utilization: Problems and Prospects* (Lagos: Lagos University Press).
Onwuka, R.I. (1982a) *Development and Integration in West Africa* (Ile-Ife: University of Ife Press).
Onwuka, R.I. (1982b) 'The ECOWAS Protocol on the Free Movement of Persons: A Threat to Nigerian Security', *African Affairs*, 81, 323: 193–206.
Orde-Browne, G. St. J. (1967) *The African Labourer* (London: Frank Cass).
Otobo, D. (1981) 'The Nigerian General Strike of 1981', *Review of African Political Economy*, 22.
Oyediran, O. (ed.) (1979) *Nigerian Government and Politics Under Military Rule* (London: Macmillan).

Piore, M.J. (1979) *Birds of Passage: Migrant Labor and Industrial Societies* (Cambridge: Cambridge University Press).

Sethuiaman, S.V. (1981) *The Urban Informal Sector in Developing Countries* (Geneva, ILO).

Southall, R. (1984) 'Third World Trade Unionism: Equity and Democratization in the Changing International Divison of Labour', *Canadian Journal of Development Studies*, 5, 1.

Usoro, E.J. (1982) 'Past and Present Attempts at Economic Integration in West Africa' in *Economic Integration of West Africa*, E.C. Edozien and E. Osagie (eds) (Ibadan: Ibadan University Press).

Vletter, Fion de (1978) *Migrant Labour in Swaziland: Characteristics, Attitudes and Policy Implications* (ILO, WEP, Migration for Employment Project WP) No. 22.

Waterman, P. (1982) *Division and Unity amongst Nigerian Workers. Lagos Port Unionism, 1940s–60s* (The Hague, Institute of Social Studies) Research Report Series No. 11.

Wright, M. (1981) *Transnational Corporations, Trade Unions and Industrial Relations* (Faculty of Economics, University of Sydney) Working Paper No. 10.

4 Petroleum Proletariat: Nigerian Oil Workers in Contextual and Comparative Perspective

Julius O. Ihonvbere and
Timothy M. Shaw

There is still much acute poverty in Nigeria . . . There is little evidence that Nigeria's big expenditure has made much impact on the conditions of the majority of the population. The distortions experienced by the oil exporters seem to have been repeated in Nigeria. (ILO, *First Things First,* 1981: v and 5)

Labour or the trade union movement was one of the mass organisations which experienced permanent repression throughout the duration of military dictatorship in Nigeria . . . it must be admitted that the workers and peasants in the working class have rarely, if ever, combined to mount joint class action against the bureaucratic bourgeoisie in neo-colonial Nigeria on the lines of the mass opposition to colonial rule. (Bade Onimode, *Imperialism and Underdevelopment in Nigeria,* 1982: 209 and 230)

The state acquires much technology via a triad of state comprador, Nigerian middleman and foreign supplier . . . The stakes are big, as oil revenues and an expanding bureaucracy offer extensive opportunities for patronage. The multiplication of commercial triangles can lead only to more corruption, more instability and a rapid return to military rule. (Terisa Turner, 'Nigeria: imperialism, oil technology and the comprador state', 1980: 211 and 220)

. . . oil workers have been the most understudied and misunderstood segment of the working class in oil economies, even by radical scholars. In Nigeria for instance, there has been to date no serious or comprehensive study of the 'oil proletariat' in order to determine its level of consciousness, nature of struggles, problems, union structure and struggles between and within factions/fractions of this sub-class. (Julius Ihonvbere, 'Class struggles in the oil industry', 1984b: 3)

Many people do not understand us. They just assume that we are all well paid and comfortable workers. They do not try to understand the problems and attacks we face everyday. Life is tough for all workers in Nigeria. But pressures on oil workers is higher because of the reliance on our activities by (both) the companies and government. (Elijah Okougbo, Assistant General Secretary, NUPENG, field interview, Lagos, January, 1984)

Labour, like gender, has been an almost unseen element in Nigeria's political economy; analytic attention has been focused elsewhere: on capital, commodities, energy and technology. Despite the roller-coaster of petroleum prices, regime types and economic fortunes, the emphasis has largely been on macroeconomic indicators. At best, some recognition has been extended to the lead actors in the 'triple alliance' of bourgeois fractions: state (including military?), national and transnational (comprador?) capitals (Shaw, 1984). And, notwithstanding the visible growth of inequalities, particularly of an impoverished peasantry in the countryside and the marginalised un/underemployed in the cities, minimal analysis has been extended to Nigeria's new majority: the working class. In spite of the dramatic role which oil-rent has played in the Nigerian ecomomy since the early 1970s, no study of the oil proletariat yet exists in any form. And the strategic location of these workers within the labour movement as well as in the oil-dependent economy has not been exploited by the left in Nigeria.

This chapter constitutes but one attempt to rectify this continuing neglect – political as well as intellectual – an oversight which becomes particularly important as changes in the international division of labour press upon Nigeria. The national crisis of capitalism – austerity, deflation, debt, foreign exchange and contraction – is inseparable from that at the global level; and the dramatic reduction in workers' income and influence are similarly related to external events and forces. But labour cannot itself be separated from its historical and sociological context: evolution and production generate the contradictions within which labour is situated and struggles. We turn first to an overview of these before treating contemporary and specific proletariats.

The theme of our chapter is that the position of the proletariat within Nigeria's political economy – a 'rentier' state: a distinctive 'Nigerian' mode of production? (Ihonvbere, 1984a) – is unstable because of the volatility of the national situation. Overall, however, the trend is towards marginalisation and alienation as the combination of embourgeoisement, inflation, austerity and repression make it relatively impoverished. In relation to oil workers, we argue that though they are well-placed for militant action – given the extent to which the state and companies depend on their activities – contradictions within their ranks and the relative power of state and capital have militated against effective action. To be sure, the nature of societal politicisation, linkages between labour and external radical groups, and the overall content and direction of national class struggles can determine or influence workers' action. Since oil workers in Nigeria have to date not initiated any such action with serious political goals it is essential to study them not only in comparative perspective but also to understand cleavages and contradictions within their ranks. It is only along these lines that we can comprehend intra-class struggles, forms of protest and resistance, and factors and forces conditioning the consciousness and action of the oil proletariat: why have these workers been less volatile than the energy they extract and distribute?

CONTEXT: DIALECTICS AT THE (SEMI-) PERIPHERY

Neo-Marxist analysis of Africa has been diverted all too often into rhetorical debates about supposedly non-materialist forces – race, religion, region and gender – as if class is separable from other social relations. In this chapter we take it to be axiomatic that class consciousness, conflict and cohesion are all affected by other forces, identities and values. Likewise, every class consists of a variable number of fractions based not only on relations to production but also on other social conditions. Just as the bourgeoisie is often divided into national, comprador, bureaucratic and military fractions, so labour is at times separable into skilled and unskilled, aristocratic and lumpen fractions. These distinctions should not be exaggerated, of course; they emerge out of particular struggles and situations – historical conjunctures. The identity and position of such fractions is never static but is, rather, the result of continuing struggles.

Contrarily, having excluded class from consideration for so long, on discovering or recognising it African social scientists then tended to become very structuralist: every class form identified by Marx had to be located in African political economies. This artificial, structuralist position gave rise to some hardly recognisable formulations and generated quite inappropriate predictions and expectations.

Materialist methodology means recognising not only changes in technology but also incorporating factors other than direct relationship to production. First, then, the position of workers in changing global and national divisions of labour needs to be continually reviewed. And second, forces and values other than labour power need to be recognised: race, religion, region, ethnicity and gender affect the position of the proletariat in profound ways. Together, these considerations both inform and improve, but also complicate, class analysis in Nigeria as elsewhere in the third world. As Eddie Madunagu (1982, p. 98) has insisted:

> On the level of social formulations, it is not enough to know that there are three main classes in Nigeria: the capitalists, the peasantry and the working class. It is also necessary to know that there are differentiations (often politically crucial) within each class, that the boundaries between the classes are extremely fluid, unstable and in some areas almost indeterminate.

He goes on to call for 'a concrete analysis of concrete situations' ranking Lenin's stricture on specificity higher than that on stages. For Madunagu (1982, pp. 78–9) rightly criticises 'revolutionary schematism' as being artificial and misleading because it fails to treat the particular characteristics of contradictions in contemporary Nigeria:

> Since Nigeria moved from colonialism to neocolonialism, this dogmatic schematism insists that the next stage of the revolution must be a 'national democratic' one: a stage where the working class has to ally itself with the national bourgeoisie that is patriotic, as opposed to comprador . . . This beautiful schematism fails to say explicitly in what respects the national bourgeoisie can be considered patriotic, democratic or even liberal . . . it fails to consider the state of the Nigerian working class; it fails to consider the possibility of the working class organisation moving at some subsequent period from a weak position to a leading position in a political alliance.

Such a possibility is, of course, crucial to the strength and salience of the trade union movement in Nigeria. But any reversal in the balance of forces within the progressive alliance awaits an historical conjuncture, as well as leaders able to recognise and exploit it. And any such advance is itself fraught with danger. Labour aristocrats may seek to recapture and redirect the movement away from confrontation and towards collaboration: the dialectic of success!

Leadership constitutes but one explanation for the modesty of any revolutionary pressures in Nigeria. The other major factor is the paucity and ambiguity of the indigenous working class. In a political economy dominated by commodity export, whether the 'commodity' is palm oil or fuel oil, clearly the number and status of the proletariat are limited. Despite efforts at industrialisation and indigenisation the amount of local manufacturing is still modest and the role of workers in the oil industry is, as we shall see, significantly circumscribed. Moreover, the vulnerability of labour is affected by the cyclical character of Nigeria's economy: austerity because of foreign exchange difficulties means less imported inputs for semi-industrial processing and so a dramatic decline in the demand for labour. Workers have been affected negatively everywhere by the post-Bretton Woods depression. But un- and underemployment rates have been highest in the periphery where industrial production, always problematic, has gone into further decline. In the early 1980s workers were laid off because of the pervasiveness of smuggling; subsequently they were laid off because of the demise of oil price and demand which generated economic contraction.

Two other factors erode the potential of the labour movement: the informal sector and labour migration. If workers in the formal sector constitute a minority of the population in the urban areas, their numbers are more than equalled by those in the informal sector; and, at least until the 1983 expulsions of 'aliens', the number of foreign workers again probably equalled that of employed Nigerians. The presence of both informal and migrant wage earners serve not only to keep down wage levels; they also complicate and erode the position of the natural trade union organisation. Hence the lament of Madunagu and others for the difficulties of the socialist movement in Nigeria.

According to less than reliable Nigerian data, there are at least two or three times as many workers in the informal sector as in the formal one: 7.2 million to 2.4 million respectively, according to the ILO (1981, p. 217) and national plans. The latter earn approximately double that of the former but together they earn, as 67 per cent of the population, just 21 per cent of the urban income (ILO, 1981, p. 219). Despite wage awards in the mid-1970s inflation more than equalled income improvements over the decade for most workers (ILO, 1981, p. 224). And in the 1980s, particularly in 1983, inflation was rampant. Overall, then, the OPEC decade has in relative and absolute terms hurt Nigerian labour despite growth in the national economy:

Since 1973–4, several structural changes in the economy have occurred which have resulted in a worsening of income distribution. These transformations are all directly and indirectly linked to the oil boom and have culminated in a rapid increase in the urban economy. Some manifestations of the phenomenal increase have been i) a rapid increase in urbanisation; ii) the granting of a 100 per cent wage increase to unskilled workers in 1974; and iii) a rapid increase in prices of consumer goods, especially food. (ILO, 1981, p. 220)

First Things First concludes that the number of urban poor could have doubled in the 1970s, to over 5 million households by the end of the decade boom (ILO, 1981, p. 232). It is this economic and political marginalisation which may yet radicalise the indigenous proletariat, depending on its definition of itself and on the responsiveness of bourgeois forces.

PERSPECTIVES ON THE OIL PROLETARIAT IN OTHER OIL ECONOMIES

The character of the oil proletariat varies between political economies largely depending on the class character of each state and the strength of alliances between state(s) and capital(s). Essentially, oil workers have either been incorporated, domesticated or subjected to attacks aimed at dividing them and making their unions ineffective. As a result of the relative importance of the oil sector in rentier states, orthodox studies of oil workers have tended to overlook the peculiarities of the industry and have focused instead on the relatively higher wages and better work conditions enjoyed by the oil proletariat.

A typical study, which overlooks the level of alienation and non-visible forms of protest in the oil industry is the work of Varnetta Calvin-Smith on Trinidad and Tobago. Commenting generally on the working class, Calvin-Smith (n.d., p. 203) wrote:

It is most desirable that going hand in hand with increasing control over the nation's natural resources, there should also be a positive change in the attitude of the population to work, responsibility and productivity. However, this does not obtain in Trinidad and Tobago. Instead, the society seems to be so plagued by a destructive permissiveness and general malaise in the labour sector where the guiding philosophy seems to be that indiscipline, idling, absenteeism, low productivity and disruptive labour tactics should all be rewarded with the highest possible wages.

Narrowing the criticism down to petroleum workers, she continues:

The labour unions in the petroleum industry have mastered the game of rhetorical talk, imperialist slogans and name calling. Their demands for higher wages are characterised by a sorry absence of a serious commitment to build the nation . . . The smokescreen they have deliberately erected to take the emphasis away from the more fundamental problems of the need for positive national attitudes and the development of a responsible, mature work ethic which would assist in confining the widespread carnival mentality to work and productivity to precisely where it belongs. (Calvin-Smith, n.d., p. 203)

Calvin-Smith's perspective on oil workers in Trinidad and Tobago is not an isolated case. Radical writers on the international oil sector have equally presented an over-bearing approach to labour in the industry. They all tend to assume that by working for powerful transnational corporations, using modern and complex technology, receiving relatively high wages and not mounting constant visible struggles against the state and capital, oil workers have practically 'sold out'. Thus an unmediated link is drawn between high wages and conservative even reactionary attitudes: a simplistic 'labour aristocracy' perspective.

Petter Nore (1980, p. 75), writing generally on oil and the state in the third world argues that:

Due to the peculiarities of the oil industry – with its extremely high organic composition of capital and the high rent element in the final price, it has been relatively easy for the companies to 'buy off' oil workers with high salaries and create a type of aristocracy of labour. While the history of oil workers' struggles has yet to be written, current information suggests that the labour force in the oil industry has played only a relatively minor role, specifically in demands for reorganisation through nationalisation.

Wolfgang Hein (1980, pp. 229–30), writing on petroleum workers in Venezuela, follows a similar line of argument noting that the state as rent collector has been able 'to pay oil workers well above the costs of the reproduction of their labour power in order to create a reliable labour aristocracy . . .'. Kai Bird (1980, p. 237) also contends that not only do Iranian oil workers constitute a 'strategic labour force' but also 'a worker aristocracy in the Iranian context'. Finally, Rufus Akinmoladun (1976, p. 354) has argued for the Nigerian case that oil workers 'employed by the international companies (have) become a group or class by themselves and therefore constitute a contradiction even among the Nigerian elites'.

These orthodox, structuralist radical perspectives on the class character of oil workers are misleading. There have been almost no attempts to understand cleavages and divisions within the ranks of such workers.

Since they are by no means monolithic, it means that conciousness and responses to societal (and workplace) contradictions cannot be expected to develop at an even rate. Thus, it is misleading to categorise *all* oil workers in the third world in general and Africa in particular as conservative, elitist and reactionary.

The political orientation of a rather highly-skilled, relatively well-paid and certainly 'strategic' labour force like that in the oil industry cannot be comprehended in the absence of an analysis of the relative power and position of the state and capital as well as the various methods of labour control. An understanding of these, located within the specific history of unionisation, cross-class alliances, politicisation and tendencies within the political economy would further promote an understanding of the modes of responses by workers to the control policies of state and capital. In fact, an excessive focus on *overt* indicators of consciousness and action amongst 'strategic' workers, can result in a misleading interpretation of the dynamics of contradictions and conflicts within the oil industry. Strike actions, demonstrations and other forms of open response do not exhaust all possible avenues of protest in a labour-coercive economy. Workers tend to resort to other hidden modes of protest when union leadership appears weak in the context of draconian state policies. Even at the level of overt modes of protest, oil workers all over the world *have* demonstrated a high degree of populist (if not class) consciousness.

The criticisms advanced by Calvin-Smith for instance, fail to take cognizance of the fact that absenteeism, idling, imperialist slogans and name-calling are major forms of protest against perceived grievances and contradictions arising from the unequal share of power and access to resources within and outside the workplace. Calvin-Smith fails to explain why a well-educated and highly-paid group of workers in a high-rent yielding and strategic industry like oil take a 'carnival mentality' to work. The reality of oil workers' protest in the oil industry in Trinidad and Tobago hardly supports her assertions. The Oilfield Workers' Union of Trinidad and Tobago has strong links with radical intellectuals in the country, has waged major struggles in alliance with sugar workers, has challenged the power of the state and oil companies, and has waged struggles which have articulated questions beyond 'bread and butter issues'. For instance, in a 1978 struggle against Texaco, the workers argued:

> But what is at stake in these negotiations is even larger than just the retention of wealth on our shores. Texaco is one of the biggest supporters of the wicked, evil and racist system of apartheid in South

Africa. A defeat to Texaco in Trinago is a victory for the liberation armies in Southern Africa. (Oilfield Workers' Trade Union of Trinidad and Tobago, 1980, p. 99)

The workers in this document referred to the conflict as 'a class war – the workers against the capitalists' and noted that Texaco had been exploiting the country's non-renewable resources without caring about their welfare. It is such ideas that Calvin-Smith dismisses as rhetorical talk.

Comparative critical analyses of actions by oil workers in many cases show the need to understand their 'world and culture', the sources and nature of elitist and conservative tendencies, and the extent to which all these are influenced by the nature of political and class struggles in society. In the Nigerian example, true, the oil proletariat has not yet been involved in conflicts at the level of, say, Iran nor have its statements shown any overt desire to transcend 'bread and butter issues'; but *all* of them can hardly be seen as having 'sold out'. Oil workers in Iran did not become really crucial until their unions were infiltrated, politicised and incorporated by revolutionary opposition forces. Oil workers in Trinidad and Tobago have also benefited from connections with socialist-inclined intellectuals. Thus, consciousness and action among workers – the pattern of coalition as well as contradiction – must be analysed not only in the context of the overall nature of politicisation but also in relation to efforts by state and capital to infiltrate, divide and domesticate oil workers and their unions. Analysis should recognise the political implications of any orientation as well as the genesis of class and fractional forces.

STATE, CAPITAL AND LABOUR CONTROL

Labour control is a fundamental aspect of 'industrial relations' in capitalist social formations at the semi-periphery as elsewhere (Waterman, 1982). In the oil industry the need to domesticate labour is even more pressing given the 'strategic' role the sector plays in the process of social reproduction. In (semi-) peripheral capitalist 'rentier' states, where oil constitutes the 'backbone' or 'core' of the economy as well as the basis of the relative financial autonomy of the state, there is a tendency for the latter to be extremely interventionist over, and sensitive to, industrial unrest in the oil sector. In fact, in such political economies not only does the state encourage directly or indirectly the control policies initiated by capital but oil workers are treated as a special category of the working class. As George Lenczowski (1960, p. 254) notes:

The governments have naturally had recourse to regulatory legislation. While labour laws have usually purported to affect industrial labour as a whole, they have frequently been drafted with an eye to the petroleum workers, in view of the latter's numerical and qualitative importance.

In a comparative discussion of labour control policies in Middle Eastern oil economies, Lenczowski further demonstrates how the various governments have, through rules and regulations, limited the emergence of trade unions; and when these eventually emerged they were, as in Iran, subjected to severe state control.

Ultimately, then, determinants of the success of labour control policies in peripheral oil economies include: (a) *the level of desperation of the state* and thus its readiness to invoke legislation and regulations (this, more often than not, drives the workers underground); (b) *the level of worker organisation*, mobilisation and struggle (where their struggle is part of a larger struggle, the ability to resist and violate effectively state policies is normally higher); and (c) *the existing relationship between the state and capital* (where the latter complements the efforts of the former within the industry, the ability to control workers can become more effective).

In the Nigerian case, the alliance between the state and oil companies is quite strong even if uneven and unstable. In fact, in terms of control over technology, information about the world market, etc., the state – both ministries and parastatals – is a junior participant in the industry. Yet their interest in labour control is congruent – the former is highly dependent on oil rents and the latter interested in profits from and control over the industry. Mutuality is reflected in rigorous labour policies and practices.

The oil companies in Nigeria have traditionally initiated autonomous control policies while at the same time enforcing those enacted by the state. Strategies of labour control in transnational oil corporations include 'negative' threats, victimisation, infiltration of unions, bribery, intimidation, dismissals, refusal to recognise unions or union leaders, constant use of the police and refusal to allow meetings on 'company property'. Alternative 'positive' strategies include material benefits such as the provision of housing, transportation, payment of generous allowances and high salaries as well as rigorous efforts to implement within the work place the labour control decrees and acts passed by the state. The companies equally employ training facilities at home and abroad to inculcate into the workers 'a feeling for the company and its exploitative aspirations or goals'.[1] The strategy of sending active workers or union leaders off to the rigs on the high seas is also used to control the effectiveness of unions and the participation of militant workers in union affairs (Ihonvbere, 1984a, 1984b). For company officials in Nigeria as elsewhere, the need to domesticate labour is imperative because:

> Workers who take up employment with our company automatically become obliged to obey everything we say or do. They have no right to follow union directives because the union leaders either work for us or other oil companies. We pay them, they use our buses, health centres, live in our houses and enjoy all sorts of bonus from us. If they constantly behave well and work hard, we provide sufficient material rewards which they would not find in most companies even the public sector. An oil worker, is a lucky and special worker.[2]

In line with this belief, most oil companies – depending on available resources, staff strength, 'recalcitrance' of the local union leaders, etc. – try to have an effect on workers' lives both within and outside the work place:

> There is hardly an aspect of the oil worker's life where we are not present during and after work. At work, he wears our work clothes. If he has to travel we provide an official car and free gas. If he is sick, he uses our medical facilities. His children attend our schools and he is sponsored by us to attend courses. He lives in a house built on our land by us. If he is a sportsman, we have the facilities. If he goes visiting after work, he constantly sees our petrol stations or buses on the roads. In fact, when he eats his *eba* in the evening, he might as well be consuming our *garri*.[3]

Union officials and members in Nigeria are, of course, aware of the use of such strategies. The companies attempt to use these in combination with other forms of pressure. Thus what one finds is often a combination of strategies, depending on the category of the worker and anticipated response. As the Warri Zonal Organising Secretary of the Nigerian Union of Petroleum Engineers (NUPEG) Isaac Aberare, explained:

> Management will stop at nothing to meet their goals. Infiltration of the rank and file, playing on ethnic sentiments and fabrication of lies

against vocal members have been employed. For instance, a pro-management leader is often protected by management and no one can remove him from office. He eats and dines with management. We know that these problems exist and would continue to exist. The government does it too.[4]

One might expect this realisation to compel the union to develop its own methods of resistance. However, paradoxically, what has happened generally, is that alongside increasing union–management conflicts, there has emerged a reliance on covert, individualistic and unorganised modes of conflict by most of the oil workers. An ex-NUPENG official, Mr M.G.O. Akporido, explained it thus:

When management constantly succeeds through infiltration, bribery, victimisation, the use of the police and so on to prevent workers' unity or the holding of crucial meetings especially those concerning wages and promotions, workers might begin to reduce reliance on the union. The tendency is to retreat to the use of individual strategies in order to win work-place benefits. Generally, only a handful of workers often succeed in this respect. The larger number more often than not, return to the union and sometimes become the most active members.[5]

The explanation for the variety of worker responses lies in Nigeria's recent history and current status.

The Nigerian state at political independence was unstable and its hegemony over local social forces was tenuous. It was deprived of the political power and external military and financial support which the colonial state had enjoyed. The dominant source of foreign exchange earnings – agriculture – was in the hands of rural peasant producers. Thus, lacking a bourgeoisie which accumulated from investment in agriculture, it had to rely on the preservation of inherited colonial institutions and structures to extract surpluses from peasants and the rural areas. The nascent 'bourgeoisie' was based in the import–export sector and occupied a junior and subservient role to foreign capital which dominated the commanding heights of the economy. Thus, Nigerian bourgeois elements were relegated to the role of legal advisers, local representatives, shareholders, political consultants, major or sole distributors and so on (Ihonvbere and Shaw, 1983).

The coincidence of an end to the civil war and OPEC oil price increases in the early 1970s provided the Nigerian state with the political centrality and revenue it needed to keep development projects afloat, manage class contradictions and promote the emergence of a more disciplined bourgeoisie. Gradually, but steadily, the state became dependent on the production and exportation of oil for foreign exchange. In this process, two major developments are worth highlighting.

Firstly, with the new dependence on oil, the state neglected other sources of revenue, particularly agriculture. In the process of recycling its oil rents through contacts to foreign firms, food and capital goods, imports and an extravagant foreign policy, the social formation's participation in the world capitalist system became that of a *semi-periphery* (at least until the crisis of the 1980s). Nigeria was courted by transnational corporations and foreign countries interested in taking advantage of its burgeoning internal market of near 100 million as well as its booming commercial, construction and mining sectors. This further incorporation into world capitalism, penetration by transnational interests and extreme dependence on a foreign-capital dominated source of revenue, contributed significantly to inter- and intra-class contradictions and struggles as well as to the instability of the (semi-) peripheral state.

And second, dependence on oil for up to 95 per cent of government revenue meant a direct interest in the 'maintenance of peace and harmony' in the sector. This also meant an interest in the elimination of 'all radical, militant and even communist influences from unionism in the oil industry',[6] in order to promote innovation, efficiency and continued functioning. Thus, the immediate financial interest of the state constrains its ability to move against foreign domination; or, to put it differently, forces it into an alliance with capital in order to domesticate labour. The state has passed, therefore, specific (directed at oil workers alone) and broad (directed at all workers in 'essential services', including the oil industry) labour control polices. At this 'national' level, the interests of the state and the oil companies tend to converge.

A typical example of such direct control measures is the 1975 Petroleum Production and Distribution (Anti-Sabotage) Decree No. 35. According to this, any person will be guilty of the offence of sabotage who:

(a) Wilfully does anything with intent to obstruct or prevent the production or distribution of petroleum products in any part of Nigeria; or

(b) Wilfully does anything with intent to obstruct or prevent the procurement of petroleum products from distribution in any part of Nigeria; or

(c) Wilfully does anything in respect or any vehicle of any public highway with intent to obstruct or prevent the use of that vehicle or that public highway for the distribution of petroleum products in any part of Nigeria, will be guilty of the offence of sabotage.

In addition to the above, any person who aids another person or incites, counsels or procures any other person to do any of the above, *shall whether or not that person actually does the thing in question*, be guilty of the offence of sabotage.

These provisions, while directly aimed at oil workers, including oil tanker drivers, also attempt to cover radical intellectuals who might wish to educate and/or organise oil workers. It can also be extended to cover residents of oil-producing communities who might attempt to resist oil companies over problems generated by oil production and refining. In short, Decree No. 35 covers 'any person'.

The extent to which the state was intent in enforcing this decree is evidenced in the penalties prescribed for those who violate its provisions. The mere description of such offences – even of an *intent* to encourage unrest within the industry – as *sabotage* against the state is a reflection of the seriousness with which the regime viewed the oil worker's struggle. Thus, '*any person* who commits an offence of sabotage under . . . [the] decree shall be liable on conviction to be sentenced either to *death* or to imprisonment for a term not exceeding *twenty-one years*.' Such persons were not to be tried in an ordinary court, but by a Military Tribunal consisting of 'a president who must be an officer in the Nigerian Army of or above the rank of major, or an officer in the Nigerian Navy or Air Force of or above the corresponding rank and two or four other officers, appointed by the head of state.'

The military tribunal was charged with powers to try cases under the decree to the 'exclusion of all other courts of law in Nigeria' and 'the practice and procedure applicable to proceedings before a court-martial under the Nigerian Army Act 1960 shall, with necessary modifications as may be necessary, be followed in proceedings'. The head of state was empowered to confirm such tribunal proceedings, any confirmed sentence to be executed 'by hanging the offender by the neck till he be dead or by causing him to suffer death by a *firing squad*'.

The decree defined 'petroleum products' broadly – to include motor spirits, diesel, fuel oils, aviation fuel, kerosene, liquefied petroleum gases and any lubricant – so covering practically all aspects of the industry. However, state officials deny that it was directed at the oil workers even when they concede that the latter are likely to constitute 95 per cent of those likely to violate its provisions. As one official put it:

> It is true that the decree was passed in order to protect the interests of the government and of Nigerians. You will agree with me that since our economy is reliant on crude oil sales, it makes little sense not to protect our interests in the oil sector. But the oil workers, even if the decrees affect them, most were not the main targets; the document refers to any person, even a student or newspaper man.[7]

However, labour leaders in the oil industry have been very critical of the decree, as has the Nigerian Labour Congress (NLC). Amazingly, the decree is not well-known to the rank and file in the industry; and the few who know of it are not familiar with its provisions, beyond the fact that it prescribes the death penalty for violators. This might be the result of poor worker education programmes. However, about 25 oil tanker drivers interviewed at the NNPC depot at Ore were all aware of it and the reasons why it was passed and why it has failed. As one of them put it (translation from pidgin English):

> We are drivers. We are poor people. We can die at anytime. Armed robbers can kill us if the police do(es) not shoot us to death. But we know that the government, military or civilian, is against us. They are both the same thing, its only the uniform that is different. The law which prescribes the firing squad for a protest or strike, shows how much they dislike workers. But I swear in God's name, the day they shoot one of us to death will be the last day they will produce petroleum in Nigeria. We shall all go on strike and seek alternative jobs. The government knows this, that is why the law has not been enforced.[8]

This view corresponds to those expressed by union leaders. The latter argue that the decree reflected the highest effort by the state not only to intervene in labour–capital relations on the side of capital in general, but also to promote the domestication of the working class in the oil sector in particular.

It is only in the context of such policies of labour control that we can understand the divisions within the ranks of labour, as workers collectively and individually respond to control measures, and the extent of incorporation of a fraction of the working class. This promotes our understanding of the problems and struggles of oil workers as well as enables us to situate political orientations, perceptions and aspirations amongst them. In short, it constitutes the background to the continuing debate about labour aristocracy in Nigeria.

COMPARISONS: LABOUR ARISTOCRATS OR ALIENATED LABOUR

The post-independence history of labour in Nigeria consists of a series of confrontations, co-optations and repressions, symbolised by the impressive array of strikes in 1975 and 1982, the Udoji awards of 1975–6, and the anti-labour laws and moves of successive military regimes (Ihonvbere, 1984b). At the same time, the status and income of the proletariat are threatened from below by an ever-growing pool of unemployed both inside and outside the country. Such an unpromising situation has made it difficult for the workers to establish and sustain cross-class coalitions, even with the peasantry let alone with bourgeois fraction. As Onimode (1982, p. 230) regretted in his opening citation: 'the workers and peasants in the working class have rarely, if ever, combined to mount joint class action against the bureaucratic bourgeoise in neo-colonial Nigeria'.

The seeming inability of labour to enter viable coalitions with other social forces erodes its power. The aristocractic pretensions of the proletariat are always tentative because of their sensitivity to changing economic fortunes – labour power is highest in an expanding rather than contracting period – and in the Nigerian case they are even more so because of the disinterest of related classes or fractions.

The debate about the labour aristocracy now has considerable vintage and the distinctiveness of Nigeria's political economy – semi-industrialisation, petroleum dominance and subsistence agriculture – militates against effective co-optation. Onimode (1982, p. 227) makes an attempt to treat this contradictory position of 'lumpenaristocracy':

> In times of economic squeeze or of confrontation with the bureaucratic bourgeoisie, they discover painfully that they are lumped together with the proletariat, though they may occasionally be bribed with wage increases.

> A serious problem with this working class is the existence within it of the 'labour aristocracy' of trade union leaders whose objective class positions are proletarian, but whose jobs as union officials accord them petty bourgeois life-styles. Some of them are also allegedly routinely bribed by management, especially government and MNCs in order to restrain the 'unreasonable demands' of the rank-and-file workers. In spite of that, they still objectively confront capital on the side of the working class, though their class consciousness and class allegiance cannot be taken for granted.

As we will see shortly in the case of the petroleum proletariat, in general in Nigeria there is a vestigial belief in the possibility of redistribution without revolution, especially among the leadership of the labour unions. There is also a preference for national or bureaucratic fractions rather than comprador or military. And this combination of ideology and nationalism puts labour in a somewhat contradictory position: it becomes pragmatic in seeking coalitions rather than dogmatic in opposing capitalism *per se* . . . nationalistic and economistic questions intrude on its antagonism and moderate or divert its demands. So the character of the ruling class at any time is directly related to the position and orientation of labour. And labour's status is in turn a function of the centrality and character of production in any sector. Even among the upper stratum of the rank and file, the themes of gradualism and of faith in the distorted capitalist system to correct itself are prominent.[9] Without doubt, oil workers, in the context of widespread poverty in Nigeria, are relatively privileged, particularly if this so-called privilege is measured in terms of wage levels.

Objective existential conditions show, however, that not all oil workers are so well-off. Not all workers have access to company-provided benefits such as housing, car loans, and other allowances. As we demonstrate later, the upper stratum of oil workers, i.e. those with substantial experience, some education and a level of authority particularly on the rigs, is quite conservative and elitist in orientation. The lower stratum however, i.e. those with limited or no education, some experience and little or no authority, evince a high degree of populist consciousness. The crucial 'systematic' issues – centrality and coalition as well as work-place – are important to any understanding of the political orientations of workers.

First, the issue of the 'aristocraticness' of labour is inseparable not only from the cyclical character of Nigeria's economy but also from the definition of class relations in different sectors: is the proletariat included in or excluded from the dominant class coalition which organises production in the oil and other industries? In part, this question is resolved by reference to the centrality of labour in any particular industry: construction and textiles require more workers than, say, steel or petroleum. And in part it is a function of the centrality of any industry to the political economy: labour in electrical production, beer refining or oil distribution is more crucial than that in wood production or tin mining.

And second, the definition of the ruling coalition at any time – itself interrelated with the cyclical nature of Nigeria's roller-coaster economy

– poses challenges and opportunities for workers (Falola and Ihonvbere, 1985; Shaw, 1986). One important side-debate about Nigeria's political economy is the character of the indigenous bourgeoisie. Clearly it is not homogeneous and monolithic – why, then, the coups, the policy debates, the diverse claims (Zartman (ed.), 1983). And yet it does recognise a common set of interests – hence the officers' coups on New Year's Eve in 1983 and in mid-1985 rather than any by NCOs. The mix of tension and cohesion in the Nigerian bourgeoisie – and not just over ethnicity and region but also over processes and priorities – has led to frameworks of triads or triple alliances. These usually revolve around some mix of transnational, state and local capitals. In his classic comparative study based on the example of Brazil, Peter Evans (1979, p. 313) suggests that, despite Nigeria's deficiencies as a Newly Industrialising Country (NIC), 'that the Nigerian case appears suitable to formulations of the triple alliance at all is impressive. In fact, the prospects for Nigeria moving successfully in the direction of the triple alliance seem good.' Indeed, by contrast to Turner, Evans suggests that the national fraction in Nigeria is rather resilient. Oil 'rent' might have been used to expand state rather than national capital; yet the 'indigenisation' programme, notwithstanding all its difficulties, worked to advance an embryonic national bourgeoisie:

> . . . in Nigeria as in Brazil, the local bourgeoisie has not been left out. Given the objective weakness of local private capital in Nigeria and the low likelihood of its making a significant contribution to industrialisation, it would be reasonable to expect a dualistic battle between the state and the multinationals rather than a triple alliance. But, far from being excluded, the local private sector has done extremely well for itself. Relative to its resources, it has probably done better than local capital in Brazil. (Evans, 1979, p. 299)

By contrast to Evans' eulogy for the national fraction, Turner's alternative formulation of the Nigerian 'triangle' or 'triad' (Turner, 1980, pp. 211, 217, 220) emphasises the intrusion of the 'technocrats', a sub-category within the bureaucratic bourgeoisie. Unwilling to accept the domination of international capital in the comprador state, they injected a nationalist element into the bureaucratic fraction and its state capital from the early 1970s onwards, i.e. coinciding with the first OPEC 'oil shock'. Yet rather than suggesting a trend towards indigenous capital, whether state or national, Turner (1980, p. 211) insists that the Nigerian political economy is still essentially comprador: the 'triad of state comprador, Nigerian middleman and foreign supplier'. The outcome of this intra-class tension is of considerable importance to the tactics and salience of the working class.

Tensions within the triple alliance – a distinctive element in the Nigerian mode of production – lead to the impoverishment and alienation of labour, even in its aristocratic form and mood. For the various bourgeois factions have been more concerned with their own intra-class struggles than with inter-class strategies: how to co-opt enough proletarian elements to ensure production. This myopic vision is itself a function of a rentier state: production is not as crucial as distribution or circulation (Ihonvbere and Shaw, 1983). If commodity or industrial production was crucial then dominant factions might be more concerned with placating labour; as indigenous labour is a rather modest ingredient in oil exploration and extraction so the triple alliance can be preoccupied with inter-fractional rather than inter-class disputes as well as with its own enrichment.

These dialectics, coalitions and re-alignments within the working class and triple alliance impact upon the deepening crisis within the unions as well as upon the emergence of elitist tendencies among workers. Division within the ranks of oil workers, reflective of the labour aristocracy tension, is evidenced in their perceptions and modes of struggle. Indeed, the very structure of the industry encourages aristocratic pretensions, except when general economic crisis erodes the salience of such stratification: the subdivision of workers into three distinct categories deliberately works against proletarian cohesion.

PERCEPTIONS AMONG OIL WORKERS

The three categories of oil workers discussed in this section have certain things in common. They are all members of the same union: NUPENG. Except for some Category One workers – the senior proletariat – they are not qualified for company estate accommodation, so they live in the downtown areas. Here, they are exposed to the poor conditions of social services and facilities in Nigeria, especially the lack of efficient water and electricity supplies, and the problems of noise, armed robbery and so on.

The oil companies, while initiating control measures aimed at domesticating all workers, pay special attention to Category One workers. These are workers who are highly skilled and experienced on the job; they are also very close to 'senior staff' and actual supervisory or decision-making positions. The companies' calculation, is that these senior workers command some respect among more junior Categories Two and Three workers. More importantly, being so close to senior staff positions – and the material benefits and privileges that go with them – Category One workers are more likely to respond to company incentives and benefits. For instance, the granting of allowances, access to senior staff facilities and company property (such as cars), recall to work after temporary lay-offs etc., are based on classification; and Category One workers tend to be more favoured. This category – potential aristocrats? – responds favourably to the efforts of the companies. Its members enjoy the authority which they exercise over the other two categories, especially on the rigs. They also have a more favourable or conservative disposition towards the companies and the government. This does not mean that they are often critical in general terms; but sometimes they go as far as blaming the other categories for the problems of the industry rather than capital or state.

In the administration of a 25-question open-ended questionnaire to 200 oil workers (50 Category I, 70 Category II and 80 Category III), the impact of levels of responsibility, income and opportunity for upward-mobility on political and social orientations became apparent. Interviews revealed that the oil companies have largely succeeded in using these relatively experienced and skilled workers to serve as a bridge between them and the other two categories. This category has been effective in this role because not only do they operate as company supervisors but they are also more interested in holding union positions. Though they are sometimes critical of the attitude of the companies and of government labour legislation, all those interviewed also put some blame on workers and 'individuals' within the social system rather than on the system itself. Of the fifty Category One workers interviewed, only five did not express some confidence in the union, its leaders, state institutions such as the Industrial Arbitration Panel (IAP) and belief that the military would ultimately resolve the problems of the Nigerian society.

The case of Categories Two and Three is quite different. Actually, the distinction between the two groups is not great; they have many things in common. They are usually the first to be affected by retrenchment and the first to be victimised after strike actions. They rely more on covert forms of protest and are less well paid. Their chances for upward-mobility within the company, particularly for Category Three, are very limited. These two categories are bitterly critical of the socio-economic system, the government, union leaders and the companies. They also resent the way Category One workers exercise their authority on the rigs just 'to please the big *ogas*'. They see themselves as having similar problems and struggles – they live downtown together, drink occasionally in the same places, take the same buses to work, their children attend the same company or public schools and their wives shop at the same markets. However, when it came to expressing views on social issues, especially those affecting workers, field-work revealed a lack of consensus among Category One workers on the one hand and the other two categories on the other. They differed in the emphasis with which they expressed their disaffections with current conditions and perceptions of an alternative society; the proletariat is not homogeneous either.

Respondents in Categories Two and Three supported the existence of one central labour organisation – the NLC – and one labour union in the industry – NUPENG. They also agreed that the 'only language the companies understand is strike' and that the six political parties of the Second Republic were elitist, corrupt and anti-working class in orientation. They did not believe that their poor conditions had anything to do with 'God' but everything to do with the fact that they are cheated by a corrupt government. These categories also perceived the oil companies to be full of *wayo* (trickish) people who want 'workers to work hard but don't want to pay well' and who give senior staff all the good things while others do the 'hard work'. Finally, they agreed that existing power relations were weighted against workers and that only in a society where workers and 'poor people' have 'money to talk' can workers really 'enjoy life'. The use of 'baboon' to describe the rich and 'monkey' to describe the poor was common. And they all were quite aware of their 'strategic' location within the Nigerian economy.

The responses of Category One workers to similar questions differed greatly. Of the 50 interviewed, 30 supported the existence of one central labour organisation; the remaining 20 gave various reasons for opposing a central organisation ranging from the 'radical' or 'socialist' posture of the NLC to 'the need for competition and democracy'. Interestingly, these were the same reasons advanced by politicians in Nigeria's defunct Second Republic in their attempt to split the Congress. On the question of strike, they asserted that it might be necessary but that it was not the only language management understood. Some of them emphasised negotiation – the use of IAP – with 35 of them emphasising the need to combine 'negotiation with strike threats'. Agreeing that the 6 political parties of the Second Republic were anti-working class, 28 Category

One workers noted that 'the working class voted the politicians to power' while 15 pointed out that there was 'no alternative' to the politicians. Respondents in this category felt that the other 2 categories were unjustly critical of the companies and agreed that their own position within the 'senior workers' category was earned through 'hard work', 'patience', 'good luck' and 'God's help'. All 50 respondents answered 'Yes' to the question: 'Do you enjoy your level of responsibility and do you enjoy exercising it over other lower categories?'

Differences between Category one – more conservative and aristocratic – and Categories two and three workers – more militant and 'populist' – are reflected in intra-union debates over direction, organisation and mobilisation. Despite NUPENG rhetoric, its leadership is more concerned with management than with membership. Although many union leaders live with the lower categories in the oil cities of Warri, Port Harcourt, Lagos, etc., and share their wretched conditions, they feel vulnerable: to management, police and state:

> We would like to go on strike any time against management where they try to cheat workers. But look at it this way, we have to be tactful. This is a country where management and government are in the same camp. There are several laws which can be used against us at any time. One has to handle the rank and file with care, their militancy has to be checked at times.[10]

The consciousness of the membership is itself something over which the union leadership disagrees: its character and development. In general it is a 'trade union' rather than a 'political' consciousness, with little awareness of the broader structures of either the industry or political economy. And in a post-coup, repressive period even the notion of a strike is controversial, thus constraining union education, mobilisation and impact.

Finally, then, it is clearly difficult to separate rhetoric from reality in the political views of the union leaders. At the level of rhetoric, they subscribe to 'socialism' – NUPENG's president has stated several times that he is 'anti-capitalist' – and they all condemn the political parties of the Second Republic. In reality, however, they have limited linkages with groups outside the union movement and they have not drawn up a programme of mass education and mobilisation of the rank and file. Internal divisions and diversions erode even the limited potential of the oil workers in the industry and political economy: aristocratic pretensions undermine strategic position.

PETROLEUM PROLETARIAT: POSITION IN THE RENTIER STATE

The combination of tensions within the triple alliance and ambiguities within the working class, together with the capital-intensive character of the oil industry and patterns of regional labour migration – the distinctive form of Nigeria's mode of production – have produced a petroleum proletariat which is rather marginal in both economic and political terms: externally-determined demand and price, combined with externally-sourced capital and technology make Nigerian labour rather unimportant except at occasional times of oil crisis. As the trend for the mid-term future is towards excess production rather than demand even the strategic potential of the petroleum proletariat falls away so, despite the anti-labour stance of successive Nigerian regimes and despite the transparent trend towards economic, as well as political, marginalisation, Nigeria's oil union seems intent on protracted bargaining rather than antagonistic struggle: aristocracy rather than militancy. As Ihonvbere (1984b; p.39) laments:

> Though the president of NUPENG claims to be anti-capitalist, it does not appear that the leadership understand in a clear manner the political programme required to pursue an effective anti-capitalist struggle. Though the rank and file appear opposed to capitalist exploitation and inequality, they still assume that some gains can be made through existing structures through negotiation with the state . . .

In part the weakness of the petroleum workers is organisational – there are many bits of the industry with which to deal: NNPC, multinational production and supply companies, three refineries, oil transporters and private garages, etc.[11] – but it is also structural – the nature of Nigeria's mode of production. Added to the above is the fact that petrol station attendants – numbering well over 30 000 and operating all over the country – are yet to be enrolled in the union. They would not only make it much larger: they would enable it to control production *and* distribution and to be more powerful *vis-à-vis* capital and the state. This is despite the fact that these garage workers are legally defined as part of NUPENG. Of course, as already indicated, the other problems of corruption, careerism and commitment to collective bargaining, in addition to not maximising membership have also contributed to weakening the union *vis-à-vis* the rentier state and oil companies.

To be sure the pervasiveness of these problems, the conservative
orientation of the upper stratum of the rank-and-file, and the apparent
pro-status quo orientation of the union leadership have generated a
situation where the two lower categories of workers rely more on covert
or hidden forms of protest – sabotage, abuse, theft, absenteeism,
malingering, etc. – in order to redress grievances which collective
agreements and actions cannot address. On the other hand, this
tendency to rely less on the trade union, albeit through un-coordinated
personal attacks, holds far-reaching implications not just for the future
of the union but also for the capacity of capital to domesticate and
further incorporate the leadership. On the other hand, it could also
generate the need for a form of trans-class alliance aimed at strengthen-
ing the union, even if along lines which would not pose a direct challenge
to capitalist relations of production. It is in this light that we can
comprehend not just the conservative (even reactionary) 1980 *NUPENG
Charter of Hope* but also the debates within the union hierarchy on the
possible form of cooperation with the senior staff association:
Petroleum and Natural Gas Senior Staff Association of Nigeria
(PENGASSAN).

In a rentier state characterised by comprador connections and surplus
labour rather than value, the petroleum proletariat is relatively power-
less except when oil price and demand are high: but one point in the
cycle. Otherwise, the loss of production is not *always* crucial in the short
term for either state or corporation assuming that alternative labourers
and suppliers are available. Indeed, given the costs and hassles of
production in Nigeria, some foreign companies, let alone OPEC
interest, might be just as happy if Nigeria failed to meet its quotas on
occasion. To augment their power, then, Nigerian oil workers need to
either unionise the whole industry with all its forwards and backwards
linkages and/or regulate external demand and price. As clearly the latter
strategy is impossible, particularly in a period of contraction, only the
former is feasible; and that bring it up against various competing
factions in the national bourgeoisie.

To date, the union has not done very well either in recognising and
exploiting its own 'strategic' location within the labour movement and
national economy, or in mobilising its resources against the state and/or
capital in order to establish for itself a major place in the triple alliance.
Union officials continue to pride themselves on the fact that their union
'is one of the few industrial unions that has not called a nation-wide
strike since its inception'.[12] Its suggestions for ensuring 'co-operation'
with capital in order to promote effective and mutually beneficial

industrial relations, have not been taken seriously by the companies either. This is indicated by (a) the lack of response to the Joint Industrial Council idea and (b) the continued victimisation of union leaders, e.g. Dubre at Agip and Akinlaja at African Petroleum (Ihonvbere, 1984a).

If the triple or triangular formulation is to become a reality then we might expect the workers to identify and ally with one bourgeois fraction rather than another. Not that the interests of labour and capital can ever be really compatible; but in tactical terms some reallocation *may* be useful. Given the character of the indigenous bourgeoisie and of the industry in Nigeria, any alliance with the multinational corporations is unlikely: they are foreign as well as capital. And any linkage with the national faction is equally problematic: capital even if indigenous. So the only remaining element in the triple alliance – state capital – is the most likely associate for Nigerian labour, *especially in its technocratic rather than bureaucratic or military guise.* And the technocrats have received some support from nationalist elements in the ruling class and from external interests concerned with efficiency, honesty and productivity.

However, despite some tensions within the triple alliance, such as over the Irikife inquiry and other difficulties confronting the NNPC, capital still has quite different interests from labour. And the weak position of both technocrats in particular and bureaucrats in general in the bourgeois triangle renders them unable to contain the general anti-labour inclinations of international and national capitals. If the NNPC is the weak link within the triple alliance then the technocrats are equally so within the NNPC: hardly a strong force with which labour might align itself. As Ihonvbere (1984b, p. 17) has noted:

> Being underdeveloped, the oil sector is itself dominated by trans-national oil corporations in terms of technology capital, high-level manpower and information on the local industry. To this extent the rentier state is only a junior participant in the oil sector . . . [with] very little or no influence over the world oil market.

Despite the nationalist inclinations of the Mohammed/Obasanjo period, which coincided with a strong price and demand for oil, the technocrats have never been central players in the triple alliance except perhaps at the initial stages of extending state interests into the oil industry and negotiating with the transnationals. As Turner (1980, p. 218) laments:

> On the face of it, oil technocrats resemble strata which seek to become a national bourgeoisie. But the scope and force of technocrats' oil policies are more probably symptoms of their powerlessness than

indications of their commitment to replacing foreign oil companies by an integrated state corporation.

In any event, NUPENG does not perceive much difference between NNPC and the multinationals, while NNPC sees itself as a rather benign follower of multinationals rather than the central or lead player.

In short, within the triple alliance to date, neither state nor national capital has been able to prevail against international: within the triple alliance the politics of dependence are perpetuated despite the potential of the pair of national partners (Shaw, 1984). All of which suggests that indigenous capital may have its own indigenous reasons for securing extra-bourgeois support for its position; i.e. Nigerian capital may need Nigerian labour to effect any lasting change in the balance of power within the triple alliance. As Turner (1980, p. 207) notes:

> technocrats share certain features with 'would be' national bourgeoisies, namely the command of capital and the desire to replace foreign firms, but they lack an indigenous base and are overshadowed by the comprador-middleman class.

If this is correct, then the technocrats would have to satisfy two or three major conditions for such an alliance with labour to be contemplated or initiated let alone effective. First, they would have to demonstrate to labour as a whole and not just the union leaders its distinctive interests and from those of other bourgeois fractions as well as make a commitment that such an alliance would not be against the interests of labour in the long run. In this case, the Mexican experience in the 1940s where the state allied with labour against the transnationals, but ended up domesticating unions and reversing gains, must be avoided. Second, the technocrats, should 'reach out' for labour. Essentially, the former have little or nothing to lose in such an alliance. The latter, on the other hand has a lot to lose since such an alliance is not necessarily a step towards the establishment of a proletarian state. Thus, the ability of the technocrats to initiate dialogue with labour, not necessarily clandestinely, would further demonstrate their preparedness to struggle against comprador and foreign fractions. And third, finally, whatever agenda is to be drawn up for this struggle must include programmes which not only address the interests of workers but also provide room for deepening achievements in the future. In this regard, if the initial move happens to be within the oil industry alone, the NLC must be involved in any 'dialogue' right from the beginning.

To be sure, such conditions are very problematic and difficult, even dangerous, to pursue in the face of draconian state decrees, the sensitivity of the transnationals and the desperate nature of recent military governments. But there is no reason to expect that 'democratic space' for such dialogues and alliances will expand in the future, not withstanding the human rights element in the Babangida coup. Of course, contradictions and conflicts within labour – in the oil industry as well as outside it – cannot be wished away. However, whether the petroleum proletariat and national technocrats have the ability or determination to forge such a coalition against the established triple alliance, especially in a period of military control over the rentier state, remains to be seen (Falola and Ihonvbere, 1985; Shaw, 1980). The logic of such a coalition given the Nigerian mode of production would seem to be quite compelling, but its organisation and articulation quite daunting. Perhaps the inclinations of the Babangida regime to evoke and revive a liberal military era will provide such an occasion. Alternatively, this conjuncture may yet await popular pressures outside as well as inside labour unions such as NUPENG.

Notes

1. Interview at Shell Depot, Warri, September 1983.
2. Interview with an Industrial Relations Officer with an oil major, Warri, September 1983.
3. Ibid., August 1983.
4. Interview with Isaac Aberare, NUPENG Organising Secretary, Warri Zone, Warri, September 1983.
5. Interview with M.G.O. Akporido, a retired oil worker and NUPENG official, Warri, December 1983.
6. Interview with Lawson Osagie, Assistant General Secretary (Administration) Nigerian Labour Congress (NLC), Lagos, June 1983.
7. Interview with a Senior Labour Officer, Federal Ministry of Labour, Manpower Development and Productivity, Lagos, August 1983.
8. Interview at the NNPC Headquarters, Lagos, September 1983.
9. Conclusions based on extensive interviews with about 200 oil workers of various categories and national and local officials of NUPENG, May 1983–July 1984.
10. Interview with J.I. Akinjala, NUPENG Headquarters, Lagos, February 1984.
11. Interviews with NUPENG and NLC officials, Lagos, 7 June 1984.
12. NUPENG files, NUPENG Headquarters, Lagos.

Bibliography

Akinmoladun, Rufus O. (1976) 'Oil and Development: a study in political economy of development', unpublished PhD thesis, Howard University.

Bird, Kai (1980) 'Iranian Oil Workers and Revolution (1979–1980)' in *America's Energy* edited by Robert Engler (New York: Pantheon).

Calvin-Smith, Vernetta (n.d.) 'The Legal Regulations of Foreign Investment in the Petroleum Industry of Trinidad and Tobago', unpublished MSc thesis, University of the West Indies.

Evans, Peter (1979) *Dependent Development: the alliance of multinational, state and local capital in Brazil* (Princeton: Princeton University Press).

Falola, Toyin and Julius O. Ihonvbere (1985) *The Rise and Fall of Nigeria's Second Republic, 1979–84* (London: Zed).

Hein, Wolfgang (1980) 'Oil and the Venezuelan State' in *Oil and Class Struggle*, edited by Petter Nore and Terisa Turner (London: Zed) 224–51.

Ihonvbere, Julius O. (1984a) 'Labour, Transnational Corporations and the State in Nigeria's Oil Inudstry', unpublished PhD thesis, University of Toronto.

—— (1984b) 'Class Struggles in the Oil Industry: the 'rentier' state and labour control in Nigeria', *Canadian Association of African Studies Conference*, Antigonish, May.

—— and Timothy M. Shaw (1983) 'Nigeria: oil production, class formation and social contradictions in a (semi-)peripheral capitalist society', *Canadian Association of African Studies*, conference at Laval, May.

International Labour Office (1981) *First Things First: meeting the basic needs of the people of Nigeria* (Addis Ababa: JASPA).

Lenczowski, George (1960) *Oil and State in the Middle East* (Ithaca: Cornell University Press).

Madunagu, Eddi (1982) *Problems of Socialism: the Nigerian challenge* (London: Zed).

Nore, Petter (1980) 'Oil and the State: a study of nationalisation in the oil industry' in *Oil and Class Struggle*, edited by Petter Nore and Terisa Turner (London: Zed) 69–88.

—— and Terisa Turner (eds) (1980) *Oil and Class Struggle* (London: Zed).

Oilfield Workers' Trade Union of Trinidad and Tobago (1980) 'In Defence of our Members and the People of Trinago against Global Texaco – exploiter of our labour and our natural resources' in *Oil and Class Struggle*, edited by Petter Nore and Terisa Turner (London: Zed) 99–118.

Onimode, Bade (1982) *Imperialism and Underdevelopment in Nigeria* (London: Zed).

Shaw, Timothy M. (1984) 'The State of Nigeria: oil crises, power bases and foreign policy', *Canadian Journal of African Studies* 18:393–405.

Shaw, Timothy M., and Julius O. Ihonvbere (1986) *Nigeria: Africa's great power?* (Boulder: Westview).

Turner, Terisa (1980) 'Nigeria; imperialism, oil technology and the comprador state' in *Oil and Class Struggle*, edited by Petter Nore and Terisa Turner (London: Zed) 199–223.

Waterman, Peter (1982) *Division and Unity among Nigerian Workers: Lagos Port Unionism, 1940s–1960s* (The Hague: Institute of Social Studies)

Research Report No. 11.

Zartman, I. William (ed.) (1983) *The Political Economy of Nigeria* (New York: Praeger).

5 The Structure of the Indian Working Class and Conventional Unionism

Jaganath Pathy

Till recently, most Indian Marxists shared the optimistic belief that in the long run the differences between the various sectors of the economy and within the labour force would be homogenised by the objective laws of historical development. Homogenisation of workers as a cultural and political collectivity would eventually emerge with the natural triumph of monopoly capital (Desai, 1948; Mukherjee, 1984; Dutt, 1949; Dange, 1952). The logic of commodity production would lead to imminent de-peasantisation and consequent proletarianisation of rural workers (Katovsky, 1964; Harris, 1972; Choudhuri, 1975; Gough, 1980; Gupta, 1980; Thorner, 1980), and the whole of the unorganised and informal sector would merge into the large-scale, organised sector. This oversimplified teleological notion of historical transition being treated almost as a maxim forbade any logical discussion or empirical scrutiny. A few excerpts from the writings of Marx and Engels were thought sufficient to buttress the expected process of change.

CONVENTIONAL WISDOM

In the historic *Communist Manifesto* of 1848, Marx and Engels wrote:

> Of all the classes that stand face to face with the bourgeoisie to-day, the proletariat alone is a really revolutionary class. The other classes decay and finally disappear in the face of modern industry, the proletariat is its special and essential product. (1973, p. 117)

They thought that once the structure of the capitalist mode of production is introduced in a society, it would impose its own logic of development, breaking down all pre-capitalist structures and the multiple forms of development.

The more developed the capitalist mode of production the less it would be adulterated and amalgamated with the survivals of pre-capitalist systems (Marx, 1971, p. 172). Modern industry achieves economic domination by subordinating and then destroying domestic industry and manufacture in town and countryside, and capturing the entire home market for itself (Marx, 1970, vol. I, ch. 13). Lenin too predicted the necessary dissolution of pre-capitalist structures with the universalising tendencies of capitalism (1960, vol. III).

For Marx, peasants, artisans, small manufacturers and shopkeepers are the inevitable victims of progress from feudalism to capitalism. It means that in order for the capitalist mode of production to be dominant the peasants have to be separated from their means of production or peasant labour has to be freed of its principal condition of production (Marx, 1970, vol. I, p. 714). In other words, the dissociation of the peasants from their means of production is 'the basis of the capitalist mode of production' (ibid., p. 768). And once this separation is achieved, the commodity status of labour power dictates the manner in which capitalist society reproduces itself. Lenin (1960) also expected a similar process of de-peasantisation and rural proletarianisation. The pertinent issue thus is to find the extent of pauperisation of peasantry and of labour power becoming a 'freely' saleable commodity in the labour market (Mukherji and Chattopadhyay, 1981).

Although Marx characterised capitalism to be universalistic in its urges, and even considered imperialism as an agency of reproducing capitalistic relationships on an international scale, his analysis is tied to many significant considerations of structures and processes. He cautioned any mechanical application of his propositions in *Capital* to historical experiences outside Western Europe. In *German Ideology*, for instance, Marx and Engels wrote:

> Viewed apart from real history, these abstractions have in themselves no value whatsoever. They can only serve to facilitate the arrangement of historical material, to indicate the sequence of its separate strata. But they by no means afford a recipe or scheme, as does philosophy for neatly trimming the epochs of history. (1945a, p. 15)

Later, in his famous letters to Schmidt, Bloch, Mehring and Starkenburg, Engels stressed the need to avoid any predilection for a deterministic economic interpretation of history (Marx and Engels, 1945b, pp. 417–25, 447–50, 453–5).

CONTOURS OF THE DEBATE

In spite of these clear remarks, there was little questioning to the general proposition of capitalist transformation in the Indian Marxist studies. The Dobb-Sweezy controversy of the 1950s on the correct Marxist explanation of transition from feudalism to capitalism in the light of the European experience (Hilton, 1976) too had no immediate impact. It is only since the early 1970s, followed by an unprecedented economic crisis with severe food shortage, industrial stagnation, massive inflation, devaluation of currency, increased urban unemployment, and the revolutionary peasant struggles organised by the Communist Party of India (Marxist–Leninist) that there has been a rethinking on the classical assumption of capitalism integrating and homogenising different sectors and modes, and transforming use value producers into 'free' wage earners. This debate began around the fact that the development of capitalism in India, instead of dissolving pre-capitalist structures, appears to conserve them and subordinate them to its needs. The theories of dependence and of articulation have provided the intellectual support to the debate. None the less, it may be stressed that the dogmatic assertion is still in circulation, although increasingly less widely supported.

Dependency theory visualises all pervasive penetration of the capitalist world market, creating worldwide hierarchical unity of the capitalist system, and offers the image of a unified system with a centre and a periphery. The dependency theorists justified their position by taking Marx's assumption of universalising tendencies of capitalism to the extreme (Frank, 1969, 1973). It is argued that because of external links and dependence, there develops a local bourgeoisie in the periphery whose interests are subservient to those of the foreign 'metropoles'. Free labour is not an essential characteristic of the 'world system'. In fact, given the diverse eco-demographic features, different systems of labour control are best suited. Free labour in the core countries and forced labour in the periphery points to an important feature of world capitalism and its colonial exploits (Wallerstein, 1974, p. 350). However, according to Brenner (1977) this whole approach is trade-centred techno-determism and offers no insight into the production relations within these 'satellite' countries; and in India, there are very few takers of this theory (Mitra, 1977) to explain the persistence and growth of pre-capitalist sectors and unorganised labour.

A much more convincing and plausible explanation to the present context comes from the theorists of articulation of modes of production. But before that it may be recalled that Marx distinguised two forms of 'subsumption of labour' under capital. The first form is 'formal', where capital subordinates labour on the basis of the same technical conditions of production within which labour has hitherto been formed. In other words, this does not alter the labour process itself. The second form is 'real' which is linked with large-scale industry and relative surplus value. This indicates the maturity of capitalism. Accordingly, some have argued that the so-called pre-capitalist relations represent 'formal subsumption of labour under capital', and therefore exist within the wider capitalist system (Gupta, 1980). But this tautological argument is as weak as dependency theory, precisely because the domination of capitalism is taken as axiomatic and then all pre-capitalist forms and relations are described as falling under 'formal subsumption'. In a slightly different way, theorists of a colonial mode of production have argued that the present indissoluble unity between capitalism and pre-capitalism is expressed in the fact that both unfree and free labour 'share a common condition – *viz.* that of dependence, a personal dependence, on their master, a condition that is not static but is contingent and vulnerable' (Alavi, 1975, p. 1249). Such a hierarchical structural relationship, representing the character of formal subsumption of labour by capital is the colonial mode of production (Alavi, 1981). Presently, however, the very proponents of this analysis have drastically changed their own position.

In addition, as early as 1913 Luxemburg (1963) argued that capitalist penetration means both destruction and preservation of 'natural' economies. Reproduction of capital is possible with the existence of non-capitalist strata and regions; for the extension of market, means of production and labour power require the very same conditions. Preservation of non-capitalist sectors and strata, however, does not mean that they remain unaffected. In fact, capitalist penetration violently attacks and brings them under formal or marginal subsumption. She also argued that accumulation and hence the realisation of surplus value is impossible within a closed capitalist sector. Realisation and capitalisation of surplus value produced within the capitalist sector necessarily entails an assimilation of the pre-capitalist sector (see also Sweezy, 1942, pp. 202–5). This is of course the chief inspiration for the dependency and world systems theorists. But the articulation theorists emphasise the ongoing process of use-value production. They insist that there is an ongoing primitive accumulation in the third world by which non-capitalist and structurally heterogeneous spheres are being trapped for extraction of surplus labour and surplus product. This primitive accumulation does not necessarily precede the process of capital accumulation. In other words, it is not an aberration of the capitalist accumulation process which will disappear with 'mature' capitalism but is a necessary pre-condition and result of the present type of capitalist development in the third world. The unorganised, informal sector and artisans, peasants and petty-traders bound by traditional leadership are not withering away, instead they are highly interdependent with the formal capital sector, though subordinated to it. Thus there is a coexistence and interpenetration of capitalist with pre-capitalist modes of production (Laclau, 1971).

It is increasingly recognised now in India that the simultaneous existence of various structures is not necessarily a transient phenomenon (Bettleheim, 1977). They are relatively stable. The large masses of semi-pauperised peasants and urban underemployed poor are not going to be absorbed into the formal wage labour proper. The severity of the phenomenon can hardly be explained in terms of what Marx called 'reserve army of labour' as an inherent feature of capitalist society. In fact, further development of capitalism is not going to lead to their proletarianisation. Unorganised informal labour is crucial and integral to the very structure of capitalism in India (Mies, 1980, pp. 2–14). The pre-capitalist social relations of production are found advantageous to the expansion of capital in India, and hence there is no linear tendency for the peasantry to disappear and the unorganised to be dissolved (Bagchi, 1982, p. 159; Chattopadhyay, 1972). Some have given different roles to capital. They hold that its universalising role leads to:

a differential impact on pre-capitalist structures – sometimes destroying them, sometimes modifying them to fit in with the new demands of surplus extraction and the new procedures of governance, and at other times keeping in fact, perhaps bolstering, pre-existing productive systems and local organisations of power, while merely establishing a suitable extraction mechanism. (Chatterjee, 1983, pp. 347–8)

While there is an interpenetration and integration of pre-capitalist and capitalist relations, where even the landless households are not proletarian or semi-proletarian (Lin, 1980; Saith and Tankha, 1972, pp. 1069–76), the pre-capitalist agrarian relationship act as a fetter upon capitalist development and have retarded the development of capitalism (Bhaduri, 1973; Sau, 1975; Chandra, 1975; Patnaik, 1976; Chattopadhyay, 1980; Lin, 1980; Omvedt, 1981). Besides, imperialism too, contributed to the arrest of capitalist development (Sengupta, 1977). Hence a replacement in totality of one mode of production by another is considered as a divorce from reality (Sharma, 1983).

These perspectives, especially the articulation of modes of production approach, through questioning the classical wisdom of eventual homogenisation and proletarianisation, have not extended the debate amongst Indian Marxists beyond a reconsideration of nature and role of Indian agriculture. Indeed, there is hardly any literature directed to the urban industrial sector, and its divisions and interconnections.

ECONOMIC PROCESS

Few analysts now adhere to the classical Marxist projection of proletarianisation and homogenisation of economy. Its most serious error rested in the inability to comprehend the nature and process of capital formation in India, as distinct from that of the West European countries. The fact that unlike the Western experience, capitalism in India grew not by destroying feudalism but by adjusting to it, and associating with imperialism, was either ignored or deliberately undermined. It needs a mention here that several of the most important initial investors of Indian capital were the despotic feudal princes, landlords, moneylenders, and comprador merchants (Parsees, Banias, Marwaris) having close links with feudal potentates (Timberg, 1978). Unlike Europe, the dispossessed artisans and craftsmen were compelled to depend on village economy and earn their livelihood as landless peasant and agricultural labourers. Thus Indian labour lacked the proletarian tradition of the West (Sen, 1977, p. 27; Roy, 1973). Besides, agriculture became encapsulated by colonial capital without any profound transformation taking place in the forces of production (Pavlov, 1975). This has imposed a 'dual disjunction' between the growth of agriculture and the growth of industry inhibiting the possibilities of growth of subeconomies in which the two could stimulate each other (Bagchi, 1976, pp. 28–33).

Even after three and a half decades of Independence, Indian capital has not been able to divorce itself from the bindings of imperialism and pre-capitalist social forces. One simple proof is the inability of the state to successfully implement land reforms and liberate agriculture from its overall backwardness. Feudal relations with various forms of tenancy, permanent labour, excessive importance of land rent, consumption loans to workers at exorbitant rates on enslaving terms, payment of wages in kind, widespread extra-economic compulsions, personal subservience of the immediate producers to the overlords, a highly skewed pattern of land control and the like are naturally a great hindrance to the growth of home market; and consequently to normal development of commodity production and industrial development. Hence, knowing well the significance of land reforms for the stimulation of Indian industry, the Indian bourgeoisie have for long been one of the strongest advocates of land reforms (Pathy, 1982, p. 21). Soon after Independence, through legislative means, attempts were made to abolish the intermediary tenures. Although this did eliminate or conceal various medieval feudal forms of oppression and extortion, and perceptibly curbed the social domination of some of the outlived princes and absentee landlords, it remained broadly as a reform of revenue administration (Myrdal, 1971, p. 1309). None the less the success of this major anti-feudal reform to date can be attributed to the ideological alienation of a parasitic class of big feudal lords on account of their identification with colonialism, and the urgent need to pacify prevailing widespread peasant struggles in different parts of the country.

The second major factor has been the abolition of tenancy by providing rights of ownership to the tenants on payment of compensation to landlords, which although challenging the feudal mode, benefited only a small section of upper tenants, the tenants-in-chief, who already had stable rights. At the same time the conditions of the large masses of unprotected cropsharers and sub-tenants were worsened by large-scale evictions, high rent, and harsher terms and conditions of work (Vyas, 1970). The official data on the decline of tenancy and sharecropping is more than misleading. For instance, the Agriculture census (1970–1) estimated that there were about half a million sharecroppers in the state of West Bengal; however, the state government in its efforts to legalise sharecropping under its scheme of 'Operation Barga' could register over 1.4 million sharecroppers between 1977 and 1982.

The most crucial test, however, was the fixing of a ceiling on land ownership and distribution of surplus land to the small peasants and landless labourers with special preference to the 'backward' communities. But curiously when 10 per cent of the landowners control 53 per cent of cultivable land (Table 5.1), the declared ceiling land is as little as 0.7 per cent of the net cropped area, and less than half of that has been redistributed to the 'weaker sections' (Planning Commission, 1978, pp. 11–12). This is an adequate testimony not simply of the bankrupt policy but primarily to the weakness of the Indian bourgeosie 'to exercise hegemony over the state apparatus and often their interest appears complementary with that of the semi-feudal interest' (Pathy, 1982, p. 24).

Failures of these reforms are striking. It is estimated that every year 12.5 million hectares of cultivable land, i.e. above 8 per cent of total sown area, is left fallow. While food production has increased considera-

Table 5.1   Operational land holdings in India (in percentages)

Size (hectares)	Holdings	Area
Below 1	54.6	10.9
1–5	35.8	40.3
5–20	9.0	38.6
20 and above	0.6	9.6

Source: H. Ezekiel (ed.) 1984, p. 32.

bly, the per capita availability of food grains, low as it is, has actually declined from 469 gm per day in 1971 to 454 gm in 1982 (Govt. of India, *Economic Survey* 1982–3, p. 90). Meanwhile, the market for industrial consumer products is relatively shrinking over the years (Sau, 1982). Thus the first objective of land reforms in increasing agricultural production and expanding home market for industrial goods has been little accomplished. Notwithstanding the so-called 'green revolution' in certain parts of India, the semi-feudal production relations remain unaltered, albeit concealed in large areas. This strangulates the growth of productive forces and acts as the mainstay of imperialist domination (for e.g. Bettleheim, 1977, pp. 20–42).

Regarding imperialist ties one only needs to note that both direct investment and official loan capital into the country has increased phenomenally since the time of Independence. In 1948, total foreign private investment was just Re 2.6 billion (US$1 = approx. Re 12) but by 1981, it had increased to Re 25 billion. The transnational corporations have also increased their number of branches, subsidiaries and joint ventures in collaboration with the Indian bourgeoisie. From 1957–84, as many as 8624 foreign collaborations have been approved. In 1983 and 1984, 673 and 752 collaborations were approved whereas as recently as in the second half of the 1970s, the number of collaboration agreements used to average no more than 275 per annum. During 1981–2 alone, foreign investment involved through collaborations amounted to Re 737 million. This is however an underestimation of power of foreign capital as technology supplied by them gives effective control of joint ventures without majority ownership or legal control of the board. Out of the 591 and 673 foreign collaborations approved in 1982 and 1983, 477 and 443 collaborations, respectively are for technological imports. The recent spurt in the collaboration agreements in automobiles, electronics, synthetic textiles, synthetic drugs, inorganic fertilisers, tobacco products and electrical equipment is an instance of how foreign technology imports makes the country permanently dependent (Chaudhuri, 1978, ch. 4). This has enhanced the need for more loans and grants to tide over balance of payment problems (Patnaik, 1972). India's outstanding debt on government account alone in 1981 was over Re 140 billion and the debt servicing payments over Re 9 billion. The IMF loan of US$5.8 billion has enchanced the liability further. Annual interest charges for this particular loan will be Re 5 billion (see also Table 5.2). In this context, India's increasing trade deficit from Re 10.9 billion in 1978–9 to Re 58.7 billion in 1981–2 is alarming. The trade deficit has increased ten times since 1966. This is precisely because while the value of exports increased four fold, the value of imports increased eight fold during 1970 to 1980 (see Table 5.3).

Growing control of foreign capital over major sectors of economy, the escalating foreign debt, the increasing dependence upon trade with the imperialist powers, export oriented industrialisation, and the type of

Table 5.2   External debt and debt service of India (US$million)

Year	Debt	Debt service
1973	10 543	652
1975	12 344	753
1977	14 725	818
1979	15 911	1033
1781	18 150	1025
1982	19 813	1157

Source: World Debt Tables: External Debt of Developing Countries (The World Bank: Washington) 1984.

Table 5.3   Trends in India's foreign trade (Re billion)

Year	Exports (+)	Imports (−)	Balance of trade
1971–72	16.08	18.25	− 2.17
1975–76	40.43	52.65	−12.22
1979–80	64.59	89.08	−24.49
1982–83	86.38	140.47	− 54.10

Source: H. Ezekiel (ed.) 1984, p. 131.

planning pursued by the State, have constricted genuine development and created a surplus population which cannot be absorbed either in agriculture or in industry. Industrial growth was about 7 per cent per annum during 1951–65, but has fallen quite significantly and the average is just over 4 per cent per annum since then. The profit rate in Indian industry has been maintained evidently by pushing down the real wage rate (Sau, 1981, p. 81). Since the mid-1960s, the rate of demand for industrial goods declined. Green revolution, plan holiday (1966–9), the devaluation of rupee and satisfactory harvests in the recent years have not been able to resolve the market problem of private industry, precisely because of narrowness of home market and inability of the Indian bourgeoisie to compete in the world market, thereby stunting the growth of Indian capital, and enabling foreign capital and transnational corporations, including local collaborators, to make huge profits (Dagchi, 1982, p. 235).

Indian capital is obviously dependent on foreign capital. Take for instance, the two biggest houses of the Indian bourgeoisie – the Birlas and Tatas. Whilst 28 per cent of capital invested in the former's firms is foreign owned, the Tatas have an even closer link with imperialist capital – USA, West Germany and Britain (for details see Reddy, 1978, pp. 280–5). Because of this close link and dependence, contradictions between the interests of foreign capital have rarely induced the Indian bourgeoisie to make common cause with the ordinary people in fighting the imperialist expansion (Bagchi, 1973a; Patnaik, 1972).

In short, the Indian bourgeosie is incapable of transforming production relations so as to get rid of bondage and usury, and has also equally failed to use the state apparatus to effectively counter the power of foreign capital. Thus it cannot determine its own course except within very narrow limits (Bagchi, 1982, pp. 140–1). Small wonder, then, that the extrapolations and trajectory of a mechanistic transformation of Indian society has been negated by the present day Indian political economy. But this does not mean that further penetration of imperialist interests would further strengthen the semi-feudal base. It only holds that capitalism is not developing and cannot develop in India in the way it developed in the metropolitan Western countries, and that the various segments of the Indian working class are impoverished without being able to shatter the pre-capitalist relations.

STRUCTURE OF THE LABOUR FORCE

With nearly 80 million wage earners, India has a major contingent of the world's working class. There is also a rapidly rising number of unemployed and seasonally underemployed. Registered unemployment also has jumped from 1.6 million in 1966 to nearly 24 million today. Chronic unemployment in 1980 was 35 million and the daily status unemployment, including seasonal and part-time employment, was 60 million (Ezekiel, 1984, p.182). The enormous volume and nature of unemployment does not exactly correspond to a classical capitalist 'reserve army of labour' in that it contributes to the increase of labour productivity at the given level of technology whilst remaining politically quiescent (Maddison 1971, p. 95). Disguised unemployment is also formidable. For instance, there are over two million peons, guards and bearers, etc., under the central government alone, whose labour is grossly under-utilised. One estimate suggests that on an average they are usefully employed for just 12 minutes a day. Taking all these factors into consideration, the estimated labour force in India is 268 million, out of which only 23 million, i.e. less than 9 per cent, belong to the organised sector. The factory sector proper accommodates around eight million which means 3 per cent of the total labour force. Even when all the regular wage employment, irrespective of legal status, is considered organised, then also only 15.8 per cent of the workforce seem to be involved in the organised sector.

From 1961 to 1971, the unorganised sector absorbed nearly 33 million workers – of which agriculture accommodated 29 million – while the workforce in the organised sector recorded an addition of only seven million. In fact, the number of workers employed in the organised segment of mining and quarrying decreased by over half a million. The annual rate of increase of employment in the organised sector has fallen from 5.5 per cent during 1961–5 to 2.4 per cent during 1966–82. The decline is sharper in the private sector, decelerating from 4.7 per cent to 0.7 per cent for the same period. In the public sector however, it decreased only from 6.2 per cent to 3.4 per cent and thereby increased its share of employment from 26 per cent in 1961 to 86 per cent in 1982 (see also Table 5.4). The trend in recent years indicates that only about 12 per cent of the increase in labour force is absorbed in the organised sector. Suffice here to reiterate that, of necessity, this has entailed the rapid expansion of the informal and unorganised sector.

Ironically, the more highly developed regions and sectors have increasingly contributed to the expansion of the informal sector. Spontaneous transitory movements of poor peasants, tenants and labourers of dry regions to irrigated parts have been happening for several decades. But what is striking today is the seasonal recruitment of such labour in the so-called green-revolution belt through the contract

Table 5.4   Labour in organised sector in India (in millions)

Year	Public sector	Private sector	Total
1961	7.05	5.04	12.09
1966	9.38	6.81	16.19
1971	10.73	6.76	17.49
1976	13.36	6.84	20.20
1981	15.48	7.39	22.87

Source: H. Ezekiel (ed.) 1984, pp. 176–7.

system. This is a relatively novel device to extract cheap labour under an unusual kind of bondage, for the intermediary labour contractors enforce some sort of bonding by means of real or fictitious indebtedness. Every year, it is estimated that over one million workers from South Bihar, Western Orissa, Eastern Madhya Pradesh and Eastern Uttar Pradesh are taken to the North-West region for wheat and paddy harvests alone. Likewise every year the sugar factories of Maharashtra recruit 400 000 migrant and contract labourers as sugarcane cutters and carriers. Thus in the green revolution belt, capitalism in agriculture has led to the replacement of paternalistic relations between employers and workers by formal annual contracts as against the expected freeing of wage labour (Bhalla, 1976).

The widespread recruitment of migrant contract labour is largely due to the persistence of backward agricultural regions (Barik, 1984, pp. 39–50). In spite of the over-publicised green revolution, there remain large areas which raise crops primarily for subsistence whilst institutions like sharecropping, tenancy and diverse forms of bondage continue to survive.

Not only the capitalist enclaves of agriculture but also industrial enterprises, including public sector projects, mines, steel and fertiliser plants, ports, railways, etc., recruit millions of contract labourers. In 1982, for the ASIAD constructions in Delhi, there were 300 000 contract workers (Lin and Patnaik, 1982, p. 23). Contract labour is also employed in regular processes such as nickel polishing, textile processing industries, woollen and carpet manufacturing, irrigation projects, breweries and salt manufacturing. At least 20 per cent of the labour force in these spheres are contract labourers. This clearly indicates that the development of capitalism, instead of dissolving pre-capitalist institutions and relations, has conserved and subordinated them to its needs.

They are reproducers of cheap migrant labour power for employment in capitalist enterprises.

The major reason for the recruitment of migrant contract labour as against locally available labour is that the former can easily be dominated and rendered cheap. They accept lower wages and harsh working and living conditions than the local labourers (Pradeep and Das, 1979; Pathy *et al.*, 1983). Besides, this means shifting the full cost of reproduction of labour to the migrants' home areas (Breman, 1979, p. 181). The workers are therefore tied both to their underdeveloped home areas and to a system which consistently returns them to work in the harvest campaigns. Further, the ability of the workers to continue working at extremely low wages depends to a considerable extent on the existence of tiny plots of land in their native place (Ramaswamy, 1977). In fact, nearly half of the rural wage workers have small plots of land, reflecting the indissoluble link of the capitalist sector with pre-capitalism. Insecurity of employment compels the migrant labourers to preserve their uneconomic holdings at any cost. Thus the notion that with the logic of commodity production, there would be an eventual de-peasantisation and proletarianisation of workers does not bear empirical scrutiny. Also, given the fact that the most developed capitalist regions and sectors impose mostly contractual relations and thereby employ cheap labour, one can discern the type of imperialist directed Indian capitalist development that forcibly and unevenly integrates the economy and society.

The high percentage of agricultural workers and its increase from 47 to 54 millions between 1971 and 1981 is obviously not the result of a capitalist agriculture but simply an evidence of agricultural overpopulation. Among them, there are at least 2.7 million bonded labourers (Sarma, 1981; Alexander, 1979). Though it constitutes a severe indictment of Indian society, it does not adequately convey the grave dimensions of feudal atrocity and the domination of usury (Bagchi, 1973b). Every year half a million people are pushed below the poverty line. Rural indebtedness, according to government estimate, has increased by nearly 17 per cent during 1965–75, when the average debt of an agricultural labour household increased from Re 148 to Re 387. Moneylenders accounted for nearly 48 per cent of the total rural credit. Though the system of bonded labour was belatedly abolished by law in 1976, this archaic and inhuman system has none the less penetrated into a large number of modern industries in a different contractual form, as well as in the informal sector of mines, small industries and construction in the urban sector.

Factory organised labour constitutes a small fragment of the entire work force, and the capacity to absorb labour has steadily declined in the organised industrial sector. It has been observed that the sex-ratio of Bombay and Calcutta metropolises is roughly 600 women to 1000 men, which bespeaks the reproduction of the industrial workforce being carried out in the countryside. Cotton mills of Bombay, synthetic textiles of Surat, jute mills of Calcutta and the engineering industry of Jamshedpur, to mention only a few, recruit nearly 80 per cent of their workers from far off places in the country. As much as 45 per cent of urban employment in Bombay, Calcutta and Ahmedabad is in the 'irregular' and informal sector. In fact, taking all cities together, more than half of the working population is engaged in unorganised, capital-scarce and low technology production systems, where there are neither wage nor work hour regulations. And this sector is expanding faster than the urban population. Most of the 16.5 million child workers, accounting for one-third of the world's total working children, work in this petty-commodity production (Sahoo, 1981). In Delhi, there are 20 000 children employed by wealthier citizens as domestics alone (Das et al., 1984, p. 13). Over 90 per cent of women workers are employed in this sector (Banerjee, 1979). Survival of this sector is linked with the unemployment of large masses of people, built-in disunity in the recruitment of labour and open flouting of labour laws, and very low wages. Besides the handloom industry with over 10 million workers, the construction industry with 10 million workers, sericulture with 3 million, handicrafts with 2 million, bidi (Indian cigarette) making and coir industry with one million workers each, have still worse conditions of existence (South Gujarat University, 1984).

TRANSCENDENCE OF DICHOTOMIES

Though the labour market appears to be fragmented it does not exist as separate compartments, nor is there a trend towards homogenisation of the various sectors and work force. Rather there is an interpenetration of sectors and workers. As capitalism is imposed from outside, it has the effect of 'conservation-dissolution' of pre-capitalist institutions and relations. The persistence of both types and relations of capitalism and pre-capitalism denotes a 'retarded capitalist development' (Bagchi, 1982, p. 167).

In academic circles, however, there is an overwhelming tendency to treat the rural–agricultural sector as an unstructured backward entity which is forcibly engaged in an unequal exchange with the urban industrial sector. This is an oversimplification. Migration and remittances express not only the interconnections between rural–agricultural and urban–industrial sector but also the interrelationship among the workers of two widely separate places of production (Breman, 1976). The importance of migration for capitalist production and survival of semi-proletarians has already been mentioned. Besides, the rural market for industrial goods is nearly three times that of the urban market for the same. About 10 per cent of the rural population produces two-thirds of the rural marketable surplus and consumes one-third of the total industrial goods sold to the ruralities (Davey, 1975, pp. 114–16). Agro-based industries constitute about one-third of all organised industries and contribute two-thirds of the foreign exchange earnings. The operation of unequal exchange is normally facilitated by the articulation of the interest of the superior economic classes through the dominant and reactionary sections of the rural society; wherein both stand to gain, though unequally, at the expense of the producing masses (Pathy, 1984). In other words pre-capitalist, capitalist and imperialist relations of exploitation overlap and intertwine with one another. The present crisis while widening the gulf between the exploiters and the toiling people is also leading to the greater integration of the ruling classes. This implies that the strategy for class struggle cannot but inevitably include all sections of the oppressed masses.

Likewise the dichotomy between small and monopoly capital is not as sharp as it appears to be. The State is said to be committed to protecting financially weaker sections of the bourgeoisie. Reformist policies like promotion of intermediary technology, tax concessions, export orientation, loans and subsidies have in fact contributed to the strength of monopoly capital and transnational corporations, and bridged the workers with global accumulation. Big industrial houses manufacture several reserved items for the small-scale sector. They have openly established small-scale units, either directly under their control or indirectly operated through middleman and market (Basu, 1977a, 1977b; Subrahmanian, 1976). They split their processes in different places and establish satellite ancillary units as separate enterprises (Kurian, 1978; Banerjee, 1981; Streefkerk, 1981). Greater seems to be the circumvention of legal provisions with increased facilities and protections for the small-scale sector! Such a decentralisation generates super profits from the work force and helps the owners to tide over any challenge from the organised working class. It needs a special mention here that foreign capital and multinational corporations have not spared the so-called small-scale sector.

The existence of large industrial houses and multinational corporations in the small-scale sectors promotes an unfair and grossly unequal competition in all aspects of industry to the detriment of genuine small-scale units. The small units are either dependent on the larger units or wholesale traders (Singh, 1981). The rate of profit in small units is not only lower than that of the bigger companies, but it is also more volatile. In a labour surplus diverse economy, large and small firms face different market conditions. The first in terms of market, capital and technology while the latter with the cheap labour. This asymmetry makes it possible for small firms to coexist with large ones.

Subcontracting is by now common to several industries dominated by both transnational and monopoly capital or the public sector. They employ thousands of intermediary contractors (Banerji, 1978; Lal, 1980; Harris, 1982; Goyal *et al.*, 1984). As the big units control both product and input markets, and the small units with their obsolete technology produce lower level of goods and market through a chain of parasitic intermediaries, they indulge in primitive expropriation of surplus and blatantly violate labour legislations. But this does not mean that there is a clear antagonistic contradiction between small and monopoly capital. In fact, although non-monopoly capital is the most reactionary sector, it articulates monopoly interests against the organised unity and struggle of the working class. Though both sectors have unequal relations, their existence is complementary (Acharya, 1983; Pathy *et al.*, 1983). True, the inherent contradictions can be utilised by the working class, but only in specific cases and moments, and not as a general principle.

Given the above, the division of workers into those working in the formal and informal sectors is analytically inadequate and leads to inappropriate working class strategy. The informal sector subsumes considerable heterogeneity and thus its analytical value is highly restricted. In addition, the formal sector recruits labour on a regular basis along with its permanent work force. Exceptions apart, there is no principled difference between the working conditions or a large portion of the workers in the factory sector and those in the non-factories. Not only workers belonging to the same family work in different sectors, but also the same worker in his life time may move from one to the other sector, either way.

In sum, what is argued here is that the classical Marxist projections of the direction of change in the political economy, specially the nature of the work force have been far from substantiated. So also the sectoral divisions and dichotomies are found to be oversimplified exaggerations (Breman, 1978–9). Instead, there is the interpenetration of different production systems, albeit with necessary and inevitable contradictions but where none of the ruling classes has the strength or objective to destroy the other. Working class politics cannot ignore this.

CONVENTIONAL TRADE UNIONISM

Trade unions originated as an organised challenge to capitalist control of society. In India, the first ever workers' strike over wage rates was organised at the Empress Mills of Nagpur in 1877 (Dutt, 1949, p. 375). And in 1920, 64 trade unions with a membership of 140 854 formed the All India Trade Union Congress (AITUC) under the chairmanship of Lala Lajpatrai. Soon the British administration was forced to pass the Trade Unions Act of 1926, which regularised the trade union movement in India. Soon in 1929, the 'moderates' separated from AITUC and formed the Indian Trade Union Federation, and again, within two years, the Communists divided the remaining AITUC and established the Red Trade Union Congress. While all unions joined together under AITUC in 1940, it was short lived, for the split re-appeared the very next year. In 1947, the Indian National Trade Union Congress (INTUC) was formed with Gandhian ideology. The Hind Mazdur Sabha (HMS) was established by the Socialist Party in 1948. Today, every political party, irrespective of ideology, has its own Union. Congress has INTUC with 1163 affiliated unions and 1.3 million members in 1968, the Communist Party of India's AITUC with 1005 affiliated unions had a membership of 600 000 in 1968, the Socialist Party's HMS with 274 unions had a membership of 463 000, the RSP's United Trade Union Congress (UTUC) with 216 affiliated unions had 126 000 members in 1968, and likewise, the Communist Party of India (Marxist) has the Centre of Indian Trade Unions (CITU), the Communist Party of India (Marxist–Leninist) has their IFTU, even the religious organisations have their trade union wings like CFTU, NFITU and BMS.

Not only are the trade unions patronised by all sorts of national, regional and communal parties but also their leadership has belonged to classes other than the working class. The main leaders of the past were Mahatma Gandhi, N.M. Joshi, S.A. Dange, V.V. Giri, Muzaffar Ahmad, R.R. Gokhale, Diwan Chamanlal, M.N. Roy and B.P. Wadia. Right from the beginning, trade union leadership has been largely in the hands of petty-bourgeois intellectuals, and the outlook of these leaders as philanthropists, nationalists, liberals and reformists has dominated the labour scene since its inception (Sen, 1977, p. 144). Such a leadership has not infrequently preferred to satisfy management rather than the needs of the workers (see, for example, Mamkoottam, 1982). Very often the leadership is 'bought off' and well 'pampered and sheltered' (Rudra, 1975, 9; Bannerjee, 1983).

All these unions have concentrated their organisational efforts on the so-called formal sector. But it is wrong to presume the formal sector of wage employment is synonymous with the organised working class. In 1961, for instance, there were 12 million workers in the formal sector but only some 4 million workers were unionised. Today, total membership of the trade unions account for only less than half the number of factory workers and less than 30 per cent of the formal sector work force (Michael, 1984, p. 144). It may also be mentioned that in 1927, though there were only 29 unions, average membership was 3594, which declined to 1026 at the time of Independence when there were 2766 unions. Within three decades, the figure of registered unions increased to an all-time high, 31 781. But only 7755 submitted returns showing an average membership of 736. Density would decline sharply when all unions are taken into account, as normally the smaller ones fail to submit returns (Table 5.5). Hence not only have unions failed to cover the workers of the organised sectors, but their average membership has declined considerably over the years, whilst their efforts have had little demonstrable effect on wages and working conditions, etc.

Of course, in the context of excruciating poverty and vast unemployment, the living conditions of the organised industrial workers in urban enclaves may appear advantageous in that their average wage is twice that of the rural unorganised workers; that they enjoy job security,

Table 5.5   Growth of trade unions during 1951–78

Year	Trade unions submitting returns		Average membership
	No.	Membership in '000s	
1951	2556	1996	781
1956	4006	2275	568
1961	7087	3977	561
1966	7244	4392	606
1971	9029	5470	606
1976 (P)	9102	6182	635
1978 (P)	7755	5702	736

Note: (P) is provisional and incomplete.
Source: H. Ezekiel (ed.) 1984, p. 191; see also V.B. Karnick, 1982, p. 25.

medical benefits, paid leave, overtime allowance, bonus, dearness allowance, provident fund, house-rent allowance, etc., which are flatly denied to more than 90 per cent of the work force (Dandekar, 1978), and that most of the Acts passed by the government for the welfare of the workers relate to this sector – Factories Act, 1948; Wage Acts, 1936; Employees' State Insurance; Employers' Provident Funds; Death Relief and Pension; Industrial Disputes Act, 1947, and the like. However, the real earnings of organised workers have failed to show any significant growth over the last several decades (Venkatramaiah, 1978). During 1961–75, when per capita income increased by 18 per cent in the country, the same for the organised workers was just 3 per cent (Sau, 1977). In fact, the share of wages in industrial value added has fallen considerably since the 1950s (Shetty, 1973). The organised workers' better living is only in relation to the large masses of unemployed and underemployed, and more as a result of the specific division of capital than on the strength of trade union struggles.

Certainly, piecemeal economic struggles of the unions are occasionally met with small concessions, but when the movements are not prepared to accept those, repression is let loose. The central thrust of government policy is to control the unions so as to ensure that the unions abstain from politics and confine their demands and activities to wages and conditions of work at the point of production. This position also gets support from within the trade unions themselves. None the less while the number of workers involved in industrial disputes has not shown any increase, the man-days lost have increased considerably (Table 5.6), although study of industrial disputes through 1961–79 reveals that hardly 30 per cent of them were somewhat successful (Michael, 1984, p. 50). Multiplicity, undue party control, fluctuating membership, lack of

Table 5.6 Industrial disputes and man-days lost

Year	Number of disputes	No. of workers involved in '000s	No. of man-days lost in millions
1961	1357	512	4.9
1966	2556	1410	13.8
1971	2752	1615	16.5
1976	1459	736	12.7
1981	1926	1183	22.6

Source: H. Ezekiel (ed.) 1984, p. 187.

suitable leadership and internal dissensions all render unions ineffective as an instrument of challenge to the domination of capital. Further, the unions have remained unconcerned with the toils and tribulations of unorganised labour, peasants, women, and minorities. During the Emergency (1975–7), INTUC supported the regime, AITUC collaborated, and CITU remained a silent spectator (Selbourne, 1979). Of course, the trade unions had a few important movements like the 110-day strike of 20 000 Delhi textile workers in 1972, 20-day railway strike of 2 million railwaymen in 1974, and more significantly, the two-year (1982–4) textile strike in Bombay with 250 000 workers from 60 textile mills under the militant leader Dr Datta Samant (Bhattacherjee, this volume). However, these movements could not have been possible without the support of the rural people. But, curiously, in the longest strike of textile workers of Bombay, only 17 per cent of workers of the city participated. It was only in 1974 that there was an all-India solidarity strike of the working class to support the railwaymen's strike. But this was without parallel. There is evidence of more acts of solidarity by non-workers with workers than vice-versa (Waterman, 1982, p. 480).

In short, the national trade unions have been created in capitalist form and culture from above by all sorts of political parties. These unions fight amongst themselves even on non-controversial trade-union issues (Mamkootam, 1977). When their party rules, they remain silent if they do not openly oppose the movement of other unions. White collar union leaderships tend in particular to be careerist and opportunist (Breman, 1980). The unions are further divided by caste, religion, region, language and other primordial grounds (Bettleheim, 1977, p. 99). Such a superimposed leadership, as well as endemic corruption within a highly authoritarian and opportunist power structure, works heavily against their potentiality to challenge the power of the capital. Almost always the general workers think that they are being cheated through a series of compromises and traditionally corrupt leadership. Apathy is hence common (Pathy, 1983, pp. 74–9), there is the clear lack of political education and class consciousness is obstructed while a bureaucratic ethos and bourgeois practices penetrate the working class.

NEW UNIONS

Fortunately, traditional unions and leadership are increasingly being challenged by new militant leaders like A.K. Roy, Sankar Neogy, Datta Samant and the like, who break through the legal niceties and traditional forms (Waterman, 1982). Some independent, radical but politically autonomous, geographically limited, popular unions have thus emerged, uniting different sections of labourers and peasantry. Widespread discontent among the masses and their spontaneous resistance has given strength to these movements. Shramik Sanghathan of Dhulia district in Maharashtra (Omvedt, 1980), Bhoomi Sena in Thane district of Maharashtra (Da Silva *et al.*, 1979), Chattra Yuva Sanghurah Vahini in Bodh Gaya of Bihar, Jharkhand Mukti Morcha (JMM) of the Jharkhand region, Chattishgarh Mines Shramik Sangh (CMSS) of Chattishgarh, Bihar Colliery Kamgar Union (BCKU) of Dhanbad in Bihar are but a few of the radical unions to mention.

Most of these trade unions have arisen since the mid-1960s. Unlike those of the traditional trade unionists who assume that the proletariat alone would be playing a messianic role or has promethean qualities, the shared proposition of these unions is that the only way to transform the present unjust order is to awaken the critical consciousness of all the oppressed people, not simply the proletariat (Sethi, 1984, pp. 27–44). These unions hence concentrate on local issues of oppression and injustice, and with their notion of accountability to the masses display a greater degree of involvement with the issues of daily concern. For instance Neogy's CMSS is involved with the issues of health care, child recreation, adult education and alcoholism, etc., and similarly, Roy's BCKU joins hands with JMM which fights on issues of deforestation, regional development and tribal problems, etc., these being treated as important as wage and bonus issues (Pradeep and Das, 1979, pp. 240–55; Pardeshi, 1980; Dhar, 1980). They have given a political approach to may spheres of life which rarely excite the attention of the conventional trade unions. The most important contribution however is their ability to articulate the interest of the organised with those of the unorganised workers, not only on economic issues but also on socio-political matters.

These militant political unions are the most vulnerable to state's repressive actions. As their movements do not focus on broader objectives and are often isolated from fraternal organisations, they themselves tend to decline with the declining wave of militancy. The problem is how to increase their strength in alignment with that of progressive political parties. Also, how to curb the tendency of the organisations becoming cults around individuals. None the less, the major point is that while the official trade unions have failed to build the unity of the working class as a whole and intervene in political matters outside the self-imposed boundary of their work place, the militant unions have shown remarkable success in the very same spheres. That means the objective conditions are not unsuitable for building the unity of all the sections of working people.

Marx said that although trade unions should defend the daily interests of workers, they must act consciously for the emancipation of the entire working class, by organising and protecting the interest of the less organised, low paid workers and by participating and supporting every important socio-political movement. The Marxist–Leninists in India have also been rightly asserting that the urban proletariat cannot emancipate itself without bringing about the emancipation of the entire exploited people.

Though this chapter suggests structural linkages, it would however be mechanical to propose the commonality of interests of all strata of working class, specially when schisms are increasingly manipulated by capital. Stratification rooted in different positions in the social labour process has been reinforced by deep seated ethnic and linguistic divisions, castes and sub-castes and other contradictions within the working class. This ultimately dilutes working class power as a living and dynamic entity. But in spite of all this, poverty and degradation being the main overall feature of even the better strata of the working force, material differences are quantitative rather than qualitative. In the face of the entire complex of dissatisfaction of the workers in both pre-capitalist and capitalist production systems, and their desire to take actions expressed in their constant oppositions, talks and moods, it may not be too difficult to formulate appropriate strategies of uniting all the toiling people. The objective conditions for such a development are already present.

However, for proletarian organisations to unite the segmentalised labour force they have to address themselves to the problems of all the labouring people including small peasants, agricultural labourers, share-croppers, artisans and the unemployed. They have to participate also in non-economic social movements like the movements of women, minorities, 'untouchables', and ecological protection. This means they have to break away from the traditional equation of factory worker-proletariat-working class (or working-class core). The strategy of alliance of all sections of workers and the peasants however requires detailed programming. Besides unionising the non-unionised workers, all attempts ought to be made to bring the militant trade unions together on a common platform. And with regard to the existing official unions, there is an urgent need to expose and replace the despotic and corrupt union bosses and democratise the structure and make them genuinely responsive to the working people.

Note

1. I am grateful to the editor and Suguna Paul for helpful comments on an earlier version of this chapter. However, I of course remain solely responsible for its shortcomings.

Bibliography

Acharya, Sarthi (1983) 'The Informal Sector in Developing Countries', *Journal of Contemporary Asia*, XIII (4): 432–45.
Alavi, Hamza (1975) 'India and the Colonial Mode of Production', *Economic and Political Weekly* (Bombay), Special No: 1235–62.
—— (1981) 'Structure of Colonial Formations', *Economic and Political Weekly* (Bombay) XVI(10–12): 475–86.
Alexander, K.C. (1979) 'Bonded Labour System: Government Measures for its Abolition', *Man in India* (Ranchi, India), 59(2): 153–70.
Bagchi, A.K. (1973a) 'Foreign Capital and Economic Development in India', in K. Gough and H.P. Sharma (eds), *Imperialism and Revolution in South Asia* (New York Monthly Review Press): 43–76.
—— (1973b) 'Some Implications of Unemployment in Rural Areas' *Economic and Political Weekly*, Special No., August: 1501–10.
—— (1976) 'Reflections on Patterns of Regional Growth in India during the Period of British Rule', *Bengal Past and Present* (Calcutta) XCV(1), No. 180. 28–33.
—— (1982) *The Political Economy of Underdevelopment* (Cambridge: Cambridge University Press).
Banerjee, Nirmala (1978) 'Women Workers and Development', *Social Scientist* (Trivandrum, India), No. 68.
—— (1979) 'Indian Women in the Urban Labour market', *Labour, Capital and Society*, XII(2).
—— (1981) 'Is Small Beautiful?' in A. Bagchi and N. Banerjee (eds), *Change and Choice in Indian Industries* (Calcutta: K.P. Bagchi & Co).
Bannerjee, S. (1983) 'Where are the Workers of Yester Year', *Economic and Political Weekly*, Dec. 17–24: 2157–60, 2207–11.
Barik, B.C. (1984) 'Rural–Urban Migration and Economic Development', *Man and Development*, I(3): 39–50.
Basu, Timir (1977a) 'Calcutta's Sandal Makers', *Economic and Political Weekly*, August 6: 1262.
—— (1977b) 'Hosiery Workers of Calcutta', *Economic and Political Weekly*, Dec. 17: 2089–90.
Battleheim, Charles (1977) *India Independent* (Delhi: Khosla & Co).
Bhaduri, Amit (1973) 'An Analysis of Semi-Feudalism in East Indian Agriculture', *Frontier* (Calcutta), Sept. 29: 11–15.
Bhalla, S. (1976) 'New Relations of Production in Haryana Agriculture', *Economic and Political Weekly*, No. 27: A23–30.
Bhattacherjee, Debashish 'Unions, State and Capital in Western India: Structural Determinants of the 1982 Bombay Textile Strike', in this volume.
Breman (Jan. 1976). 'A Dualistic Labour System', *Economic and Political Weekly*, Nov. 27, Dec. 4 and 11: 870–6, 1905–8, 1939–44.

132 *Structure of the Indian Working Class and Conventional Unionism*

—— (1978–9) 'Seasonal Migration and Cooperative Capitalism: the Crushing of Cane and Labour by the Sugar Factories of Bardoli, South Gujarat', *The Journal of Peasant Studies*, VI(1): 41–70; and VI(2): 168–209.

—— (1980) *The Informal Sector in Research: Theory and Practice* (Rotterdam: Erasmus University).

Brenner, Robert (1977) 'The Origins of Capitalist Development: a Critique of Neo-Smithian Marxism', *New Left Review*, No. 104.

Chandra, N.K. (1975) 'Agrarian Transition in India', *Frontier* (Calcutta), VII(28–30): 3–9.

Chatterjee, Parth (1980) 'More on Modes of Power and the Peasantry', in Ranjit Guha (ed.), *Subaltern Studies II* (Delhi: Oxford University Press).

Chattopadhyay, Paresh (1972) 'Mode of Production in Indian Agriculture', *Economic and Political Weekly*, VII(13): A39–46.

—— (1980) 'Mode of Production in Indian Agriculture', *Economic and Political Weekly*, XV: A85–8.

Chaudhuri, P. (1978) *The Indian Economy: Poverty and Development* (Delhi: Vikas).

Choudhuri, B.B. (1975) 'The Process of De-peasantisation in Bengal and Bihar', *Indian Historical Review* (Delhi).

Dandekar, V.M. (1978) 'Nature of Class Conflict in Indian Society', *Artha Vijnan*, XX(2): 102–24.

Dange, S.A. (1952) *On the Indian Trade Union Movement* (Bombay: CPI Publication).

Das, A.N. *et al.* (1984) *The Worker and the Working Class* (New Delhi: Public Enterprises Centre for Continuing Education).

Da Silva, G.V.S. *et al*, (1979) 'Bhoomi Sena: A Struggle for Peoples' Power', *Development Dialogue*, No. 2: 3–70.

Davey, Brian (1975) *The Economic Development of India* (Bristol: Spokesman Books).

Desai, A.R. (1984) *Social Background of Indian Nationalism* (Bombay: Popular Prakashan).

Dhar, Hiranmay (1980) 'Split in Jharkhand Mukti Morcha', *Economic and Political Weekly*, 15(31): 1299–1300.

Dutt, R.P. (1949) *India To-day* (Bombay: Peoples' Publication).

Ezekiel, Hannan (ed.) (1984) *The Economic Times: Statistical Survey of the Indian Economy* (New Delhi: Vikas Publishing House Pvt. Ltd).

Frank, A.G. (1969) *Capitalism and Underdevelopment in Latin America* (New York: Monthly Review Press).

—— (1973) 'Reflections on Green, Red and White Revolutions in India', *Economic and Political Weekly*, VIII(3): 199–24.

Gough, Kathleen (1980) 'Modes of Production in Southern India', *Economic and Political Weekly*, XV(5–7): 337–64.

Goyal, S.K. *et al.* (1984) 'Small Scale Sector and Big Business', *Business Standard*, February.

Gupta, Dipankar (1980) 'Formal and Real Subsumption of Labour Under Capital', *Economic and Political Weekly*, XV(39): A98–106.

Harris, John (1982) 'Characteristics of an Urban Economy', *Economic and Political Weekly*, XVII(23–4): 945–54, 993–1002.

Harris, Nigel (1972) 'The Marxist Left in India', *International Socialism*, No. 53: 23–39.

Hilton, R.H. (ed.) (1976) *The Transition from Feudalism to Capitalism* (London: New Left Books).

Kalpagam, U. (1981) 'Labour in Small Industry: Case of Export Garments Industry in Madras', *Economic and Political Weekly*, Nov. 28: 1957–68.

Karnik, V.B. (1982) *Trade Union Movement and Industrial Relations* (Bombay: Somaiya Publications Pvt. Ltd).

Katovsky, G. (1964) *Agrarian Reform in India* (Moscow: Progress Publishers).

Kurian, C.T. (1978) 'Small Sector in New Industrial Policy', *Economic and Political Weekly*, March 9: 455–61.

Laclau, E. (1971) 'Feudalism and Capitalism in Latin America', *New Left Review*, No. 67: 19–38.

Lal, Sanjay (1980) 'Vertical Inter-Firm Linkages in LDCs: an Empirical Study', *Oxford Bulletin of Economics and Statistics*, 42(3).

Lenin, V.I. (1960) 'The Development of Capitalism in Russia', *Collected Works*, III (Moscow: Progress Publishers): 21–607.

Lin, S.G. (1980) 'Theory of a Dual Mode of Production in Post-Colonial India', *Economic and Political Weekly*, xv (10–11): 516–29, 556–73.

Lin, S.G. and N. Patnaik (1982) 'Migrant Labour at ASIAD 82: Construction Sites in New Delhi', *Bulletin of Concerned Asian Scholars*, xiv (3): 23–31.

Luxemburg, Rosa (1963) *The Accumulation of Capital* (London: Routledge & Kegan Paul).

Maddison, Angus (1971) *Class Structure and Economic Growth: India and Pakistan Since the Mughals* (London).

Mamkootam, K. (1977) 'Factionalism and Power in Trade Unions', *Indian Journal of Industrial Relations*, 15(2): 167–90.

—— (1982) *Trade Unionism: Myth and Reality* (Delhi: Oxford University Press).

Marx, Karl (1970) *Capital* I (New York: International Publishers).

—— (1971) *Capital* III (Moscow: Progress Publishers).

Marx, K. and Engels (1945a) *The German Ideology* (New York: International Publishers).

—— (1973) *Selected Works*, I (Moscow: Progress Publishers).

Michael, V.P. (1984) *Industrial Relations in India and Workers' Involvement in Management* (Bombay: Himalaya Publishing House).

Mies, Maria (1980) 'Capitalist Development and Subsistence Reproduction', *Bulletin of Concerned Asian Scholars*, xii (1): 2–14.

Mitra, Ashok (1977) *Terms of Trade and Class Relations* (London: Frank Cass).

Mukherji, P.N. and M. Chattopadhyay (1981) 'Agrarian Structure, and Proletarianization and Social Mobilization', *Sociological Bulletin*, 30(2): 137–62.

Mukherji, R.K. (1948) *The Indian Working Class* (Bombay: Popular Prakashan).

Myrdal, Gunnar (1971) *Asian Drama: an Enquiry into the Poverty of Nations* (London: Penguin Books).

Omvedt, Gail (1980) *We will Smash this Prison: Indian Women in Struggle* (New Delhi: Orient Longman).

—— (1981) 'Capitalist Agriculture and Rural Classes in India', *Economic and Political Weekly*, xvi (52): A 140–59.

Pardeshi, Ghanshyam (1980) 'Jharkhand', *Mainstream* (New Delhi), 18 (47–50): 6–9, 25–7, 29–31.

Pathy, Jaganath (1982) 'Land Reforms in India: Imperatives and Potentials', in

S.K. Lal (ed.), *Sociological Perspectives of Land Reforms* (New Delhi: Agricole Publishing House): 19–28.
—— (1983) 'Trade Unionism and Class Struggle in The Third World', *The Journal of Sociological Studies*, II: 74–9.
—— (1984) *Tribal Peasantry: Dynamics of Development* (New Delhi: Inter-India Publishers).
Pathy, Jaganath, *et al.* (1983) 'Oriya Labourers in Surat Textile Industries', *Vision* (BBSR, India), II (3): 55–61.
Patnaik, Prasant (1972) 'Imperialism and the Growth of Indian Capitalism', in R. Owen and B. Sutcliffe (eds), *Studies in the Theory of Imperialism* (London: Longman): 210–29.
Patnaik, Utsa (1976) 'Class Differentiation Within the Peasantry', *Economic and Political Weekly*, July: A82–101.
Pavlov, V. (1975) 'India's Socio-Economic Structure from the 18th to Mid-20th Century', in V. Pavlov *et al.* (eds), *India: Social and Economic Development* (Moscow: Progress Publishers): 7–92.
Pendse, Sandeep (1981) 'Labour: The Datta Samant Phenomenon', *Economic and Political Weekly* XVI: 695–99, 745–49.
Planning Commission (1978) *Draft Five Year Plan 1978–83* (New Delhi: Government of India Press).
Pradeep, Prem and A.N. Das (1979) 'Organization of the Future? A Case Study of the Bihar Colliery Kamgar Union', *Human Organization*, II (3): 240–55.
Pradhan, P.H. (1974) 'Reactionary Role of Usurers' Capital in Rural India', *Economic and Political Weekly*, IX (32–34): 1305–8.
—— (1979) 'Semi-Feudalism: the Basic Constraint of Indian Agriculture' in A.N. Das and V. Nilkant (eds) *Agrarian Relations in India* (New Delhi: Manohar Publications): 33–49.
Ramaswamy, E.A. (1977) *The Worker and His Union* (New Delhi: Allied Publishers).
Reddy, T.N. (1978) *Indian Mortgaged* (Anantapuram: TNR Memorial Trust).
Roy, M.N. (1943) *India: Labour and Post War Reconstruction* (Calcutta: Renaissance Publishers).
Rudra, Ashok (1975) 'White Collar Workers', *Frontier* (Calcutta), VIII (2): 8–10.
Sahoo, U.C. (1981) *Child Labour, A Sociological Study*, M.Phil dissertation, S.G. University, Surat (India).
Saith, Ashwani and A. Tanakha (1972) 'Agrarian Transition and the Differentiation of the Peasantry', *Economic and Political Weekly*, VII (14); 712–23.
Sarma, Marla (1981) *Bonded Labour in India* (New Delhi: Biblia Impex Pvt. Ltd).
Sau, Ranjit (1975) 'Farm Efficiency Under Semi-Feudalism', *Economic and Political Weekly*, X (13): A.18–21.
—— (1977) 'Share of Wages', *Economic and Political Weekly*, 25 June: 1020–1.
—— (1981) *India's Economic Development* (Calcutta: Orient Longman).
—— (1982) 'Development of Capitalism in India', *Economic and Political Weekly*, 19(30) PE. 73–80.
Selbourne, David (1979) *An Eye to India: The Unmasking of a Tyranny* (London: Penguin).
Sen, Sukomal (1977) *Working Class of India* (Calcutta: K.P. Bagchi & Co).
Sengupta, Nirmal (1977) 'Further on the Mode of Production in Agriculture',

Economic and Political Weekly, XII (26): A55–63.

Sethi, Harsh (1984) 'Undesired Aliens: Elements from a Collective Autobiography', *Lokayan* (India), II (1): 27–44.

Sharma, K.L. (1983) 'Agrarian Stratification', *Economic and Political Weekly*, XVIII (42–3): 1796–1802, 1851–5.

Shetty, S.L. (1973) 'Trends in Wages, Salaries and Profits of the Private Corporate Sector', *Economic and Political Weekly*, October, 13: 1864–90.

Singh, Baljit (1981) *The Economics of Small Scale Industries* (Bombay: Asia Publishing House).

South Gujarat University (1984) *Working and Living Conditions of the Surat Textile Workers* (Mimeo), Surat (India).

Streefkerk, H. (1981) 'Too Little to Live on, Too much to Die on: Employment in Small Scale Industries in Rural South Gujarat', *Economic and Political Weekly*, 11, 18, and 25 April: 659–68, 721–8, 769–86.

Subrahmanian, K.K. (1976) 'Linkages of Small Scale Industry: Implications for Employment Generation', *Indian Journal of Labour Economics*, XIX (3–4).

Sweezy, P.M. (1942) *The Theory of Capitalist Development* (New York: Monthly Review Press).

Thorner, Daniel (1980) *The Shaping of Modern India* (New Delhi: Allied).

Timberg, T.A. (1978) *The Marwaris: From Traders to Industrialists* (New Delhi: Vikas Publishing House).

Vyas, V.S. (1970) 'Tenancy in a Dynamic Setting', *Economic and Political Weekly*, V (26): A73–80.

Venkatramaiah, P. (1978) 'Nature of Class Conflict in Indian Society', *Artha Vijnan*, XX (2): 135–42.

Wallerstein, Immanuel (1974) *The Modern World System* (London: Academic Press).

Waterman, Peter (1982) 'Seeing the Straws: Riding the Whirlwind: Reflections on Unions and Popular Movements in India', *Journal of Contemporary Asia*, XII (4): 464–83.

6 Between Capital and Labour: Trade Unionism in Malaysia[1]

Leslie O'Brien

INTRODUCTION

In capitalist societies, relations between capital and labour are the key social and central political issues. An understanding of the nature of the relationship between these two major groups and their agents, e.g. trade unions, employer organisations, the state, is prerequisite to an understanding of the structure of any any capitalist social formation. This chapter will examine the dynamics of the relationship between capital, labour and the state in peninsular Malaysia.[2]

TRADE UNIONS

A trade union is

> A voluntary association of wage earners organised to further or maintain their rights and interests through collective bargaining with the employer, esp. for improving wages, hours and conditions of employment. Originally, trade unions were organised by craftsmen strictly by crafts . . . they have come to be organised also vertically through an industry . . . and some include unskilled agricultural and white collar workers. (*Webster's New Collegiate Dictionary*, 1956, p. 901)

How effective are trade unions as a means for representing the interests of workers *vis-à-vis* employers? To what extent do unions generally represent the interests of their members, union leaders, non-unionised workers in similar/the same occupations or industries? To what extent do, or can, trade unions represent the interests of the working classes *vis-à-vis* the capitalist class and/or the state?

According to Marx (n.d., p. 26), wages are a component of the cost of production in capitalist societies, and wages for workers and profits

136

for capitalists stand in inverse ratio to each other; profits rise as wages fall, or the reverse. Wages must be sufficient to cover the cost of the reproduction of labour power, but 'high' wages mean less profit. Capitalists and workers, therefore, are engaged in constant struggle; the one group trying to keep wages down, the other seeking to maintain their real wages and improve their conditions of work. To the extent that trade unions do represent the collective interests of the working classes then, given the nature of the class relations of capitalism, we might expect to find unions embroiled in some degree of conflict, not only with employers and their organisations but also with the various institutions which together represent the state (e.g. the government, the administration, the judiciary, the military and paramilitary organisations) (see Miliband, 1969, for discussion) and which collectively aid in the reproduction of the class relations of capitalist societies. What are the implications of such conflicts for the stability or otherwise of the capitalist order? Can revolutionary structural and/or ideological change be introduced through the medium of trade unionism? We will examine these questions by reference to the historical instance of Malaysia.

TRADE UNIONISM IN MALAYA

In the eighteenth century, the Malay peninsula was drawn into the orbit of the expanding capitalist world economy through the medium of British colonialism. Capitalist penetration was both diverse and restricted. At the political level, this unevenness was manifest in the differential rates of incorporations of the social formation into a colonial state which, until the 1940s, comprised a bewildering array of politico-administrative units: the Straits Settlements of Penang, Malacca and Singapore, the Federated Malay States of the west coast of the peninsula, the Unfederated Malay States of the north and east. Later, these diverse units came to be known as the Federation of Malaya and the Crown Colony of Singapore. In 1957, the colonies gained political independence from Britain. In 1963, they joined, together with the Borneo states of Sabah and Arawak, into the Federation of Malaysia. In 1966, Singapore left the Federation and is now an island republic. (For a more complete history and discussion see Gullick, 1958; Emerson, 1964; Jomo, 1977.) European style trade unionism in this region is largely a post-Second World War phenomenon although, as will be discussed below, certain categories of labour were associated in organisations which represented their interests *vis-à-vis* employers and the wider society. The very nature of the labour force in the region, however, meant that few of these organisations were such as to draw in anything other than segments of the working class; the Malayan labour movement was, from its inception, characterised by a very high degree of fragmentation.

In the early years of colonial rule, the majority of the population of the Malay peninsula, the indigenous Malays, were tied to the land. They worked as peasant farmers or fishermen and entered the wage labour force only on the most intermittent basis. In addition to this local population there were, at the beginning of the colonial period, sizeable numbers of Chinese in the region. Some Chinese (as well as Indians, Arabs and others) had come to the peninsula to engage in trade. Chinese were also involved in the mining of alluvial tin, later the plantation production of spices and rubber. By the late nineteenth century, British interests had become involved in tin mining and in the production of such tropical crops as spices, tapioca and coffee. Early in the twentieth century, British capital began the large scale cultivation of rubber. In support of these expanding mining and plantation industries, immigrant labour was introduced into the country in large numbers. At first, Chinese were brought in to work the tin mines. Later, so as to avoid the possibility of an overconcentration of workers of one ethnic group in the work force, the colonial government adopted a policy of assisting the immigration of workers from India into the then expanding plantation sector of the economy (Jackson, 1961; Singh, 1969; Halim, 1982).

The early Chinese workers came into the colony as indentured or contract labour. Many were little better than slaves, having literally 'sold' themselves to a labour contractor. Both the supply of this labour and its organisation once in the peninsula was controlled by secret 'triad' societies. These were, according to Purcell (1965, p. 272):

> Originally religious or benevolent 'self help' associations which assumed a political or anti-dynastic character at the time of the Manchu conquest, and later degenerated into organizations of criminals for exploiting and intimidating the community.

Indian immigrant workers entered the colonies in the early years of the twentieth century. Many were brought in through the medium of 'kangany' recruiters:

> The 'kangany' was a labourer of some standing or influence in his own village in India who was provided by the Malayan employer with a free passage to India plus a commission for each labourer recruited. (Stenson, 1970, p. 2)

The 'kangany' was often able to obtain the labour he sought in the subcontinent not just because conditions of the home were so poor but also because many potential immigrants to Malaya, or their families, were in debt to the 'kangany' and thus obliged to follow his wishes (see Stenson, 1970, 1980 for further details). Many immigrant workers from China and India were never really 'free' wage labourers the entire time they were in Malaya. They were not free of debt. They were not free to leave a harsh or unjust employer and find another job so long as they were bound by a contract, and many employers were both harsh and unfair. The contractor or the employer specified where they were to work and under what conditions. Neither were issues the immigrant labourer was in any position to bargain about. Most of these early workers were provided with accommodation and food in lieu of wages. Wages were often withheld until the end of the labour contract, the sum finally paid 'less debts and deductions', meaning the labourer might see little cash return for years of toil (Jackson, 1961; Stenson, 1970, 1980; Jomo, 1977; Halim, 1982).

The introduction of foreign workers to meet the needs of the bourgeoning mining and plantation sectors (as well as the labour requirements of some sectors of the state apparatus itself) was due, in part, to the reluctance of the Malays to enter the wage labour force. The peasants, of course, could have been forcibly expelled from their land. This tactic was not, however, adopted by the colonial powers, rather the reverse (i.e. the Malays were more or less contained to the small-holder agricultural sector. For details of the various policies and practices used to attain this end see, amongst others, Roff, 1967; Jomo, 1977; Lim, 1977; O'Brien, 1982). In leaving the Malays on the land, the British were at once able to ensure some local contribution to the food supply, promote the idea that traditional Malay society had been little disturbed by capitalist penetration and colonial intervention whilst, at the same time, fostering the development of a labour force so divided by ethnicity, language, religion and other aspects of culture as to maximise the potential for its control. What is more, the possibility of the importation of ever more immigrant workers from China and India at that time functioned as a 'non-resident' reserve army of labour which served to depress the wages and added even more to the potential for control of workers already in the country.

THE MOVE TOWARDS THE FORMATION OF LABOUR ASSOCIATIONS AND LABOUR UNREST

The years prior to the Second World War were, in Malaya, an era of

140 *Trade Unionism in Malaysia*

laissez-faire bourgeois capitalism, marked by a very limited degree of state intervention. Such mediation as did occur generally took the form of legislation designed to regulate the flow of labour into the colonies and to ensure that certain minimum standards were followed as regards the treatment of all, but most especially mining and plantation workers.[3] Some of this legislation reflected, amongst other things, liberal and humanitarian ideals which had developed in the imperial homeland, i.e. Britain. The colonial state thus played a somewhat contradictory role *vis-à-vis* capital in the colony at that time, enforcing the often reluctant compliance of employers to standards they neither formulated nor wanted as regards the treatment of labour. Although the state did in this way act, to a certain extent, as the champion of labour, it would be wrong to believe that this was not within the context of a situation the state ultimately and closely controlled on behalf of the general interests of capital. So as to maintain this control the state did not encourage, indeed it discouraged, the formation of such workers' organisations as might post any real threat to the status quo.

As noted above, Chinese workers were brought into Malaya through the medium of the secret 'triad' societies. Once in the colony, most were soon absorbed into craft or trade guilds that were often under the control of the triads. The Societies Ordinance, passed in the Straits Settlements in 1889, the Federated Malay States in 1895, made triads illegal. Such secret societies, of course, still persisted but due to the determination of the state in this regard, the hold of the triads over the immigrant workforce declined. Membership of trade guilds, by comparison, grew. Trade guilds had existed in China for centuries. Their membership was rather like that of the craft guilds of medieval Europe, and included master craftsmen, journeymen and apprentices. In Malaya, the guilds were usually formed by people who came from the same province or village in China and who were engaged in the same trade. The guilds aimed to protect the interests of their members *vis-à-vis* the outside world as well as providing some welfare services. They were also a forum for the regulation of relations between members. The majority of the guilds had a membership of both employers and employees. They were governed by committees which drew on both these elements, although employers were the stronger power in the coalition, so they used the guilds to exercise control over their work forces. The guilds dealt with such matters as wages, conditions of work and holidays and as such they can be seen as an early and indigenous form of trade unionism (for further discusssion of trade guilds in the region, see amongst others Awbery and Dalley, 1948; Gamba, 1962; Purcell, 1965; Stenson, 1970).

Chinese workers in Malaya were the first to organise themselves into associations which in any way approximated modern trade unions. Their acts of association had their roots in China and, in the Malay peninsula, were linked to their ethnic status. As the twentieth century unfolded, the association of Chinese workers in Malaya continued to be linked to social changes in China. Following the 1911 Revolution there, branches of the Guomindang (GMD, i.e. the Chinese Nationalist Party) were established amongst overseas Chinese in communities such as existed in Malaya and Singapore. These branches of the GMD were at once the means for the support of and solidarity with the Chinese revolution, as well as serving as a way of regenerating all 'things Chinese' (especially language and literacy, which was promoted in schools that were established as a consequence of this upsurge in national pride). The left wing of the GMD put considerable emphasis upon working class issues and stressed not only nationalism but also the dignity of labour. Those influenced by the left wing of the party began to establish secret, illegal and unregistered labour unions in the region. By the 1920s, the Chinese Communist Party (CCP) too was actively involved with the overseas Chinese. They established The Nanyang (Southseas) Communist Party and a Nanyang General Labour Union (GLU) in Singapore in 1925. A GLU was established in Malaya one year later. Like the GMD, the communists organised workers into illegal unions. Both used existing trade guilds as a mean towards the end of organising the Malayan and Singaporean work forces. Both also established associations which transcended the more divisory lines of the guilds but these were essentially restricted to the Chinese members of the population (Stenson, 1970).

As for the non-Chinese workers in the peninsula: the majority of the immigrant workers from India were employed in the plantation agricultural sector, the rest worked in government service. These people did not establish their own workers associations or combinations until much later in the twentieth century. Nor was there, at that time, an Indian nationalist or other political association intent upon organising Indian workers in Malaya in the way that the nationalists and the communists were organising Chinese workers.[4] As regards the Malays, in the 1920s – and indeed until the 1970s – most Malays were involved in small-holder agricultural activities. Those engaged in wage labouring generally only worked on an intermittent or seasonal basis.[5] There was thus little reason for a union or similar organisation to represent the interests of Malay workers, especially as the interests of the Malays generally were supposedly being cared for by the traditional Malay aristocracy and the colonial state (see Roff, 1967, for elaboration). What we might term 'trade unionism' in Malaya at that time was, therefore, very much a Chinese phenomenon. The historical roots of such workers' organisations as did exist in the region were planted in or emigrated from China. Although combination was not entirely a consequence of external forces (there seems to have been some degree of association of workers as a consequence of the development of worker consciousness) the general *rate* of association of workers seems largely to have been linked to external political considerations,[6] especially to the nationalist struggle in China.

By the 1920s, more and more workers in Malaya – mainly Chinese – were organised. With the demise of the indenture system and a gradual increase in the number of workers born in the colony, workers were becoming more familiar with the structures within which they were located. As the economy expanded, workers began at least to react to the low rates of pay and poor conditions of work that characterised their employment. They began to engage in some form of protest. There were sporadic outbreaks of strike action and go slows in different parts of the country, some due to communist agitation, some a consequence of developing class consciousness. For whatever reason, workers in Malaya had begun to show evidence that they were not quite the docile and submissive components of production employers had enjoyed in the past. This outbreak of industrial unrest was neither expected nor well received by capital or the state but as the world demand for tin and rubber was such as to require the continuation of production, some concessions were granted to labour. As association and activism came to be recognised as effective means towards the end of improving wages and conditions of work, ever more workers came to join the struggle of organised labour.

When the colonial government realised that there was a definite trend towards the formation of workers' combinations, and that these organisations posed a threat – if not to their rule, then at least to the ease with which capital could be accumulated and to the semblance of order – it acted in a way designed to maximise the potential for state control of the situation. In 1928, a decision was taken to override the earlier policy of refusing to register trade guilds under the Societies Ordinance because 'they were universally suspected of subversive tendencies' (Stenson, 170, p. 9). After that time, such workers' associations as existed, or those wanting to be formed, had now to obtain the state seal of legitimacy, i.e. registration, albeit as societies not as trade unions. The extent to which registration represented an effective state weapon became apparent at the end of the decade: as the 1920s drew to a close there was an even greater upsurge of industrial unrest in the colonies. The governments of the day acted by deregistering those societies involved (and thus making them illegal associations), refusing the registration of others and imprisoning or deporting the leaders of guilds and other worker's organisations identified as the main cause of the 'trouble'. On the whole these were the guilds established or infiltrated by the communists. Not all workers' associations were disbanded but between 1928 and 1931 the communist or communist controlled General Labour Unions, i.e. those with the greatest potential for uniting the working class, were all but eliminated by the colonial state (see Gamba, 1962; Stenson, 1970 for further details).

After 1929, there was a general collapse of the capitalist world economy. There was a downturn in the demand for, and the price of, all major commodities. In Malaya, depending as it did upon rubber and tin, this downturn in demand resulted in a major socio-economic crisis. Unemployment became widespread. Those workers in employment had their wages reduced. This was a period of hardship for those in and out of employment. Although the colonial government had sought to eliminate the challenge that organised labour presented to the stability of their order by deregistering the General Labour Unions, there were still a great many people in the colony sympathetic to the cause of labour and the aims of communism. As wages and living conditions declined in the early 1930s, therefore, communist activists had little difficulty in reorganising labour. A Malayan Communist Party (MCP) was established, as well as a number of front organisations (e.g. the Malayan General Labour Union). As in the 1920s, the communists again infiltrated existing workers' organisations, as well as setting up new groups (especially, as in the case of the GLUs, ones designed to maximise the potential for the unification of the working class). Neither the MCP or the GLUs were given legal recognition. Although severely restricted by law, colonial policies and practices, labour was once again organised and active, spurred on as much by the severe hardships experienced by the working class as by communist activism. At that time, however, organised labour was able to do little or nothing to alleviate the low rates of pay and widespread unemployment experienced by the working class, because these conditions were so closely linked to wider global processes rather than the decisions of individual employers in the colony.

During the Depression, the first restrictions were imposed on the importation of immigrant labour into Malaya. This measure was designed to avoid an even greater escalation of the already significant problem of unemployment in the colony and thus the potential for even further destabilisation of the society. As Stenson (1970) notes, the action of the colonial government at that time typified the attitude of the state towards labour: turn on the immigration tap when labour is needed, turn it off when workers are no longer required. The flow of immigrants from China and India came to a halt but by the mid-1930s the capitalist world economy was moving towards recovery. There was again a demand for primary commodities, especially tin and rubber. Mining and plantation capital in Malaya sought to expand the scale of their production. Now, however, with labour in short supply, at least some sections were fairly well organised and thus in a better position to bargain for the restoration of wages to previous levels, as well as for improvements to be made in conditions of work. After the mid-1930s, industrial action undertaken by organised labour met with considerable success (Stenson, 1970).

The extent to which workers in Malaya were organised and active at that time was linked, as in the past, to a combination of internal factors (the socio-economic conditions in the colony) and external events (particularly the political situation in China). The Japanese invasion of Manchuria in 1937, for instance, resulted in heightening of nationalist sentiments amongst the Chinese in Malaya. An alliance was formed between the GMD and the CCP–differences were put aside in the interests of unity against a common foe. In Malaya this had the effect of making it easier for the MCP to organise those workers who were GMD sympathisers. The majority of workers already organised, or who joined workers' associations as a consequence of this new push were, as in the past, ethnically Chinese. The MCP had a policy of encouraging the association and collaboration of workers of all ethnic backgrounds, necessary if they were to achieve their end of establishing a Malayan republic. Due to the nature of the division of labour in the colony, however, and the overtly 'Chinese' appearance of the Party, they met with very little success amongst Malay or Indian workers. By the late 1930s, however, Indian workers had begun to form their own associations. Earlier in the decade, urban-based Indian elites had begun to form associations arising out of the nationalist struggle in India. In 1937, Nehru visited Malaya and spoke of the need for trade unions. His speeches stirred working-class Indians and this led to the formation of the first working-class Indian associations in the country (Stenson, 1970, 1980). In 1938, the government of India put a stop to assisted immigration of Indians to Malaya, in an attempt to boost the wages of Indians already in the country. This added to the labour shortage in the colony and further increased the relative power of the working class. In 1938 and 1939, industrial unrest became even more widespread than it had been in the past. The majority of stoppages and go slows involved Chinese workers but now, for the first time, Indian plantation labour and Indian and even Malay workers in certain government facilities were involved (Stenson, 1970, 1980; Halim, 1982).

At the end of the 1930s, industrial unrest was widespread, involved many different categories of workers and was closely linked to factors other than 'outside agitation'. The colonial government was under considerable pressure to develop some mechanism for regulating the relationship between this mass of increasingly dissatisfied labour and their employers. The first step taken in this direction was one of repression: in September, 1939, Emergency Regulations were gazetted. These banned strikes in essential services and industries. This legislation was effective but it was clearly not a long-term solution to industrial relations in the country. Workers were organised in guilds and associations which approximated trade unions but these organisations were either unrecognised or registered under the Societies Ordinance. No collective bargaining machinery existed. The colonial government began to prepare draft trade union legislation, then in 1940 the Colonial Development and Welfare Act was passed by the British Parliament. Under this Act, Britain was to give long-term aid to her colonies, providing they had laws allowing and protecting trade unions, requiring fair wages and banning the employment of children. The draft legislation, then under consideration, was amended so as to take into account the wishes of the (then a Labour) government of England. In 1940, a Trade Unions Ordinance was passed in the Straits Settlements and also in the Federated Malay States. These enactments were quite restrictive, specifying for instance that trade union funds were not to be used for political purposes (and thus preventing union funds being used to finance a party that could challenge the government on its own terms). The legislation almost made it difficult for workers in government service to join a trade union. When the law was passed, it was condemned by both capital and labour. The one because it gave recognition to organised labour at all, the other because it was seen as a copy of British legislation 'without any of its better features'. Altogether it was considered quite unsuited to conditions in Malaya (Awbery and Dalley, 1948; Gamba, 1962; Stenson, 1970). As it was, the legislation was not implemented at that time due to the Japanese invasion and occupation of Malaya and Singapore.

THE OCCUPATION AND THE EMERGENCY

The Occupation lasted from late 1941 until 1945. During this period the British were effectively driven out of the region. The MCP, comprised as it was of people who had been born in the region, went underground. Two new communist organisations were formed, the Malayan People's Anti Japanese Army (the MPAJA, the military wing of the MCP) and the Malayan People's Anti Japanese Union (the MPAJU, the administrative arm of the communist party). The aim of the MCP at that time was to drive out the Japanese and work towards the establishment of a Malayan republic. The British, for their part, sought to expel the Japanese so as to be able to regain control of their strategic and profitable colony. During the Occupation, for their different reasons, the MCP and the British worked in collaboration with each other. The British army was unable to work in the region but they were able to supply arms to the MCP. The MPAJA and the MPAJU worked from the jungle, or underground amongst the civilian population of the towns and cities. In military terms, the MPAJA posed only a limited threat to the Japanese. The MCP organisations were, however, able to achieve a great deal in ideological terms. They represented a non-European challenge to an often cruel invading army. The MCP obtained considerable support, not only from the traditional base of Chinese workers and small farmers but also from many Indian estate workers and certain sectors of the Malay peasantry. In some areas, MCP authority rivalled that of the Japanese (for further discussion of the Occupation and the nature of the co-operation between the British and the MCP see, amongst others, Hanrahan, 1954; Short, 1975; Stenson, 1970).[7]

During the Occupation, the interests of both the MCP and the British were best served by a united effort against the Japanese. In late 1945, the British returned to the region, not as conquering heroes but as a consequence of the Americans dropping an atomic bomb on Japan (Stenson, 1970). They were, none the less, determined to re-exert control. In the immediate post-war years, however, neither the colonial state apparatus nor the capitalist class were fully organised. The British had to achieve their aims in an environment in which a popular communist party—which, due to its war efforts was tolerated as a more or less legal entity—was equally determined to put an end to colonial rule. Soon after the Japanese surrender, the communists began to establish institutions designed to assist them mobilise the working class and establish a people's republic. A General Labour Union opened office in Singapore. General Labour Unions soon appeared in all the major towns in the peninsula. Workers, willing to organise, and suffering the hardships of the post-war period, were called out on strike. The concerted efforts of the MCP in combination with food shortages and high inflation saw a massive movement of labour into worker's combinations and a major outbreak of industrial unrest (Stenson, 1970). The working class had not yet become a class for itself; ethnicity, religion, occupational differences, regional loyalties, etc., were very strong. The rate of association and the extent of the labour unrest was such however, as to create conditions so unsettled that the rule of the colonial state could be challenged. In 1946 the government intervened. The Trade Union Ordinance of 1940, originally designed to cover the Federated Malay States was amended so as to apply to the entire peninsula. A Registrar of Trade Unions was appointed. All associations functioning as trade unions were required to register, this designed to allow a distinction to be made between legal and illegal associations. It provided those so recognised with the right to enter into collective agreements with employers on behalf of their members. It also provided the state with the legal means of close control. The compulsory registration of trade unions did not, of course, lead to any easing of the industrial unrest. The Trade Union Enactment was, therefore, amended so as to restrict trade unionism to those engaged in a similar trade, occupation or industry. General Labour Unions, the main instruments of the MCP, were made illegal. Lacking legal outlets, the MCP went back into the jungle and began a guerrilla war against the capitalist class and the colonial state. In 1948, the Communist Party was made illegal, a State of Emergency was declared and nearly half the trade unions in the country were de-registered. (The succession of processes leading up to the declaration of an Emergency was far more complex than the brief outline presented above. The main aim in this instance is to note how effective a challenge the MCP, its front organisations in particular and organised labour in general presented to colonial rule. For full details of this period, see Gamba, 1962; Stenson, 1970.)

LABOUR UNDER CONTROL – TRADE UNIONISM AFTER 1948

During the Emergency, the state had two aims. The first was to win the battle against the communists. The second was to gain the support of the mass of the people. A necessary first step towards this latter end was to give some form of recognition to organised labour. Before this could be done, the state had first to encourage workers in the country to reorganise, because the labour movement as it had stood had more or less collapsed following the events of 1948. At Stenson notes:

> The realisation that the M.C.P. guerillas could not be beaten by force alone, and the eventual acceptance of General Templer's dictum that the battle was one for the 'hearts and minds' of the local population, gradually convinced leading employers and officials that unionism was not a luxury promoted by a socialist Labour Government but a necessity, at least in the major industries and government departments. (Stenson, 1970, p. 237)

In 1950, the Malayan Trades Union Council (MTUC, now the Malaysian Trades Union Congress) was established on the basis of such unions as had not been infiltrated by the MCP and thus not de-registered (e.g. the railwaymen's union, various estate worker's unions). 'Responsible' new unions were allowed to register and affiliate with the MTUC. 'Responsible' men, i.e. those seen as likely to work with the government in its attempt to foster the development of a moderate labour movement, were chosen to head this instrumentality. The MTUC draws its membership from trade unions of workers in a variety of trades, occupations and industries. It thus has the potential of acting on behalf of the entire working class. So as to limit this potential, the MTUC was registered as a society, not a federation of trade unions, hence it did not enjoy the right to bargain for its members although it could 'speak out' on behalf of labour. In 1954, mainly Indian estate workers amalgamated their various unions into the National Union of Plantation Workers (NUPW). The NUPW affiliated with the MTUC. In 1957, government employees were co-ordinated into a Congress of Unions of Employees in the Public and Civil Services (CUEPACS). (The MTUC is supposed to represent unions in the private sector, CUEPACS to represent public sector unions. They were, for a time, combined but this association ended in 1980.) By 1957, the year the colonies obtained formal independence from Britain, more workers in Malaya were unionised than at the peak of the MCP activism. As opposed to the situation that pertained in the 1920s, 30s and 40s, however, in 1957 nearly half of all those unionised were ethnically Indian, a representation far in excess of their ten or so per cent share of the population; one third of all unionists were government employees, the remainder were in small, often in-house unions. Chinese workers in the private sector, whether self employed as petty traders, semi- or skilled tradesmen or employees in services and industry were more or less prevented from unionising.

Outside the agricultural sector, Chinese comprised the majority of wage labourers. Hence a very substantial proportion of the workforce was denied any representation, or a voice in the emerging industrial relations machinery of the country (for labour force statistics, see Malaya, Del Tufo, 1949; Fell, 1960. For discussion, see Stenson, 1970; Jomo, 1977; Hing, 1984).

THE SPREAD OF WAGE LABOURING

Malaya gained independence from Britain during the Emergency. By 1960, it was felt that the communist 'problem' had been sufficiently contained as to allow for the lifting of the Emergency Regulations. The post colonial government was able to direct its attention to other issues. The economy at the time of independence was highly dependent upon the sale of rubber and tin, and the price obtained for these primary commodities was subject to marked fluctuations. The majority of the population of working age were in the agricultural sector, working either as small-holder producers or as employees in agricultural industry. Despite the large numbers of people whose energies were directed towards agricultural production, Malaya did not produce sufficient food for its own needs. Food had to be imported. Most consumer goods had to be imported (as in most colonial economies, the manufacturing sector had been neglected. Malaya represented not only a source of raw materials for British industry but a small but not insignificant market for goods manufactured in the 'motherland'.) The ex-colony was marked by poverty, unemployment and uneven development (for discussion see Wheelwright, 1965; Jomo, 1977).

The first development plans put forward by the post colonial government did not address the issues of foreign ownership or inequalities of class, rather they aimed to develop the society by way of the development of infrastructure (roads, railways, harbours) and the diversification of agriculture (new types of tropical crops were encouraged, new tacts of land were opened). Some attention was now given to the development of a manufacturing sector, particularly one capable of producing as wide a range of consumer goods as possible (i.e. 'import substitution' manufacturing industry, aimed at reducing foreign spending and at creating job opportunities for the rapidly expanding population. For further discussion, see amongst others Wheelwright, 1965; Lim, 1967; Lim, 1973; Hoffman and Tan, 1980).

The 1960s were a period of relatively stable commodity prices.

Malaysia was able to attain an economic growth rate of 6-8 per cent per annum (although the benefits of this prosperity were not spread throughout the population). Rubber and tin remained the mainstays of the economy but palm oil began to make a substantial contribution to this growth. The development of agricultural industry led to the creation of more employment opportunities on the estates but the importance of the agricultural sector as regards employment began to decline as people began to leave their agricultural small-holdings and the countryside and move to the towns in search of a cash income. In the period 1957-70, the agricultural labour force declined from 59 per cent of the population of working age to just under 53 per cent. Manufacturing grew somewhat in importance; by 1970 the manufacturing sector was contributing 13 per cent to GDP and the proportion of the labour force engaged in manufacturing jobs had moved from 6 per cent in 1957 to 9 per cent in 1970. Employment opportunities generated by 'import substitution' manufacturing, however, was little more than the population growth rate. As people moved from farms to towns and as the population expanded, unemployment became even more widespread. (For statistical details, see Malaya, Fell, 1960; Malaysia, 1971; Malaysia, Chander, 1977. See also Hoffman and Tan, 1980.) The tendency towards the contraction of small-holder agriculture and the expansion of agricultural and manufacturing industry continued in the period after 1970 but within the context of a radically different society.

THE NEW ECONOMIC POLICY AND THE PROLETARIANISATION OF THE MALAYS

Malaysia is an ethnically heterogeneous society. In 1980, Malays and other indigenous people comprised 54 per cent of the population of Peninsular Malaysia, those of Chinese ethnic origin comprised 35 per cent, Indians approximately 11 per cent (Malaysia, 1981, Table 12-2, p. 219). The Malaysian economy has long been characterised by a high degree of foreign ownership and control. The highest local share of ownership of the corporate economy has rested and still rests in Chinese hands. Malaysia too has long been characterised by a pronounced fusion of ethnicity and economic function. The Malay aristocracy were the traditional rulers. Today they are the symbolic but wealthy remnants of the past. Malays today dominate government, the upper levels of the administration as well as the entire military and paramilitary arms of the state. The bulk of the Malays have been peasant farmers and fishermen.

Poverty has been more widespread amongst the Malays, as an ethnic group, than the other groups in society. The Chinese, as an ethnic group, have been spread throughout the class structure and the division of labour. There are Chinese poor but this group have significant ownership of the means of production. Their ownership gives them power but they have lacked access to effective parliamentary or bureaucratic authority. The Chinese are well represented in the professions. Chinese have predominated in retail trade, transport and commerce. Chinese are found in large numbers amongst the artisans, craftsmen and small farmers in the country. Chinese poverty is less apparent than the Chinese stronghold on the urban economy. There is some Indian ownership of the corporate economy and Indians are over-represented in the professions. The majority of the Indians in the population have been confined to the low pay estate agricultural sector or the lower levels of government service (Malaya, Del Tufo, 1949; Fell, 1960; Malaysia, 1971, 1976; Malaysia, Chander, 1977; Malaysia, 1981). Malaysia is characterised by what can be expressed theoretically as an 'articulation' (i.e. a co-existence) of class and ethnic structure and ideology (see O'Brien, 1984b, for further discussion). This fusion of class and ethnicity has been used, since colonial times, to aid in the control of the society. Sporadic outbursts of class/ethnic violence have long occurred between the Malays and the Chinese because they occupy different locations within the class relations of capitalism. In May 1969, widespread dissatisfaction amongst the Malays (due to their disadvantaged class position) and unrest amongst the Chinese (due, amongst other causes, to their limited access to formal social power) erupted in communal rioting up and down the peninsula. After these events, the government of the time embarked upon a New Economic Policy (NEP) as a means towards restructuring Malaysian society.

The NEP was introduced and implemented under the Second Malaysia Plan, 1971–5 (Malaysia, 1971). The NEP is to run until 1990. It aims, amongst other things, to eradicate poverty and to reduce and eventually eliminate the identification of 'race' with economic function. A major means towards these ends has involved the state bringing Malays into ownership and control of the corporate economy. Malays have long been sponsored in education. Under the NEP this sponsorship continues and is expanded. Under the NEP, Malays are also given preference in the labour market. Both government departments and the private sector are under instruction to employ Malays in all industries and at every level of the various occupational hierarchies until they are proportionately represented throughout the division of labour.[8] The

NEP seeks to move the Malays out of the villages and into the mainstream of Malaysian society.

The attainment of the NEP goals depends not only upon their implementation by the state and their acceptance by the people but is also contingent upon a buoyant and diverse economy. Linked as it is to the wider capitalist world economy, a certain amount of fluctuation in fortune is beyond the control of any of the individual social formations which together comprise the greater entity. Within these constraints, the NEP attempts to develop and restructure the economy and the society. Emphasis continues to be given to the modernisation and diversification of agriculture. This is not a new development strategy. It is a tactic adopted by all the previous post-colonial governments of Malaysia. What is new is the degree of emphasis given to the development of the manufacturing sector, both as a source of economic growth and of job creation. If the Malays are to be lured from the farms, they must be provided with some means of earning a living, and not all the Malays have the educational prerequisites for employment as white collar workers in the commercial and service sectors. Many have limited education and few skills. Under the NEP, import substitution manufacturing continues to be encouraged. In the period after 1970, this form of industry has grown, although the rate of expansion is slow (and hence its employment creation value is limited) because the local market is small and there is a marked consumer preference for imported goods. Under the NEP, considerable emphasis has been placed upon the further exploitation of Malaysia's natural resources. Industries such as those processing natural rubber and the manufacture of rubber products, the extraction of oils and fats (from tropical palms and nuts), sawn timber, the manufacture of plywood and veneer – all of which are aimed at the local, regional and world markets – are promoted by way of a variety of incentives. In the period after 1970, such industries began to make a substantial contribution to value added in the manufacturing sector and to employment creation. In addition to the 'import substitution' and 'resource based' export oriented industry noted above, under the NEP considerable attention has been directed towards the development of 'light' export oriented manufacturing industries, linked to foreign capital and foreign technology and generally located in special industrial enclaves known as Free Trade Zones. (For details of the different types of incentives available to different categories of investment in the manufacturing sector, see Malaysian Industrial Development Authority, 1984.)[9] This 'export oriented' industrialisation involves, in particular, the production of electrical machinery including electronics, textiles and the manufacture of scientific instruments. This form of production makes only a small contribution to value added in the manufacturing sector, a substantial contribution to manufactured exports (the real value of which is diminished by the amount of manufactured imports used in the industry) and to job creation. Inputs from these different types of manufacturing industries in the decade 1970–80 were such as to see the manufacturing sector share of GDP rise from 13 per cent to 21 per cent. In the same period, agriculture, forestry and fisheries expanded considerably but this sector's share of GDP fell from 31 per cent in 1970 to 22 per cent in 1980 (Malaysia, 1981, pp. 9–11). These and other changes in the economy are related to the formation of a very different labour force in Malaysia.

By 1980, the highest percentage of the labour force was still to be found in the agricultural sector but the relative significance of agricultural occupations continued the downward decline that began in the post-war years. In 1970, just over 50 per cent of the labour force worked in the agricultural sector, by 1980 this number had declined to 37 per cent. By comparison, manufacturing, building, construction and the service sector labour forces grew. These changes are detailed in Table 6.1.

The NEP involves a radical break with the previously held and near sacrosanct idea that 'Malay' has, does and should mean 'kampong' (i.e. village). Under the NEP, the sons and daughters of Malay farmers and fishermen are being lured from the villages and into the factories and

Table 6.1   Peninsular Malaysia: percentage distribution of experienced labour force aged 10 years and above by sector of employment

Sector	1970	1980	% change
Agriculture	50	37	− 13
Mining and quarrying	2	1	− 1
Manufacturing	9	16	+ 7
Construction	2	5	+ 3
Transport, storage and communication	4	4	
Electricity, gas, water and sanitation	1	1	
Commerce	10	12	+ 2
Services	17	22	+ 5
Not adequately classified	5	2	+ 5
Totals = 100%			

Source: Malaysia (1984) Table 5.6: 50.

offices of the 'modern', 'urban' and 'industrialising' society. The expansion of the parameters of education in recent years, the preferential employment of Malays in many occupations and the decline in the economic and cultural attractiveness of small-holder agriculture is 'pushing' these young people into the towns and cities. Under the NEP, the change from an essentially rural, agricultural-based labour force to an urban commercial and industrial labour force has, therefore, involved a substantial change in the ethnic division of labour in Malaysian society. Some of these changes are outlined in Table 6.2.

The proportion of Malays, Chinese and Indians in the agricultural sector remained the same throughout the decade. What is very different is that Malays are leaving the small-holder agricultural sector in great numbers. Many are moving into the estate agricultural sector (the proportion of Malays amongst estate workers increased from 27 per cent in 1970 to 38 per cent in 1980. The Chinese share of this sector declined from 31 per cent to 14 per cent, the Indian share increased from 42 per cent to 48 per cent, Malaysia, 1984, Table 5–7, p. 51). Others are moving from the villages to town and city; from farm and fishing hamlet to urban office or factory. Malay migrants from the rural areas are joining the Chinese and Indians in the factories, offices and shops throughout the country. Malay men and women from small-holder agriculture (i.e. self-employment; the peasantry) family backgrounds are entering the wage labour force and thus the working class. Some have entered the 'traditional' (i.e. industrial manufacturing) working class. Some are the sellers of mental and/or highly skilled labour power. Some work in the rural areas, others in the urban regions. That so much of the post-1970 proletarianisation in Malaysia has involved people who are ethnically Malay has major implications for both class relations and the future direction of industrial relations in the country.

THE TRADE UNION MOVEMENT TODAY

In 1980, there were some 4 million people in the labour force in Peninsular Malaysia. There were 276 trade unions with a membership of 532 428 people, i.e. approximately 13 per cent of the labour force was unionised (this figure includes a small number of people in employer unions). In ethnic terms, 51 per cent of all unionised workers were Malay, 22 per cent were Chinese, 27 per cent were Indian. This contrasts markedly with the situation that pertained at Independence, when the majority of union members were ethnically Indian. Now, the number of

Table 6.2   Peninsular Malaysia: percentage distribution of the labour force in selected sectors, 1970 and 1980, by ethnicity

Sector	Malays 1970	Malays 1980	Chinese 1970	Chinese 1980	Indians 1970	Indians 1980
Agriculture	68	67	22	20	10	11
Manufacturing	29	40	65	50	5	10
Commerce	23	30	65	61	11	9
Services	47	62	37	26	14	11

Source: Malaysia, 1984. Table 5–6: 50.

Malays in unions correlates with their participation in the wage labour force, Indians are still over-represented but their share is declining. As has been the case since 1948, Chinese workers are denied a voice in the industrial relations machinery of the country relative to their share of the proletariat (calculated from Malaysia, 1984, Table 3–3, p. 39; Table 5–11, p. 54; Table 11–1, p. 171; Diagram 11–2, p. 174 and Table 11–10, p. 180).

More than half (52 per cent) of those unionised worked in the private sector but they represented only 8 per cent of the private sector labour force; 48 per cent of all trade union members were employees in government service, statutory bodies or local authorities. More than half (52 per cent) the public sector labour force was unionised (calculated from Malaysia, 1984, Table 3–3, p. 39; Table 5–11, p. 54; Table 11–1, p. 171; Table 11–10, p. 180). Private sector workers were much less likely to be unionised than their public sector counterparts. Amongst those private sector workers who did belong to a union, nearly half (46 per cent) worked in the plantation agriculture sector. In 1980, 56 per cent of all plantation labour was unionised. There were 48 unions to represent the interests of workers in the manufacturing sector. These unions had a combined membership of just over 87 000 people, i.e approximately 29 per cent of all unionised workers in the private sector and 15 per cent of the manufacturing labour force. The majority of workers in foreign capital owned, export oriented factories located in Free Trade Zones were not unionised. The remaining 25 per cent of those private sector workers covered by a union were mainly service sector employees (especially employees in banks, insurance companies and other financial institutions, etc.–hotel, restaurant, cinema workers and the like are not unionised) or transport and communication workers (calculated from Malaysia, 1984, p. 116; Table 5–17, p. 57; Table 11–1, p. 117; Table 11–10, p. 180 and data supplied by Electrical Industries Workers' Unions and Textile and Garment Workers' Unions, Malaysia).

The wages and conditons of work of employees in the public sector, i.e. those most likely to fall under the union umbrella, are covered by General Orders and are subject to not infrequent review by specially appointed Commissions of Inquiry which are subject to considerable public scrutiny. These workers were the most likely to be unionised but, as we shall see, the state exercises very tight control over the activities of organised labour in this sector. As for workers in the private sector, i.e. those least likely to be unionised, the Employment Act 1955 (Act 265, Revised 1981), sets down certain standards as regards the terms and conditions of employment. The Act specifies, for instance, that the regular work day should not exceed 8 hours, the regular work week should not exceed 48 hours; it requires the payment of wages for work performed and that payment should be made in legal tender. The Act, however, covers only those employees in the private sector who earn M$750 or more per month. A large number of workers, therefore, (e.g. domestic servants, contract and part time workers) fall outside the scope of the Act. Nor does the Act require the payment of a basic or minimum wage for workers in the private sector (the implication being that market forces alone should determine the wage rate). The Act also allows for the dismissal of employees, without notice, on the ground of 'misconduct' (and 'misconduct' is subject to very discretionary interpretation). The wages and conditions of work of approximately 9 per cent of the private sector labour force are determined by way of collective bargaining between (generally weak) unions and (generally stronger) employers. The wages at least and many of the conditions of work of the majority of employees in the private sector labour force depend largely upon the good will or otherwise of individual employers.[10]

As the above data shows, the majority of workers in Malaysia lack an official voice, lack any representation in the industrial bargaining machinery in the country. Even those workers who are unionised are members of combinations that have extremely limited legal or effective power. If workers combinations per se, i.e. trade unions, present a potential challenge to capitalism, resting as it does upon a divided and hence more controllable labour force, in Malaysia, the historical association of organised labour with an armed and active communist movement meant that from its inception, the new (i.e. the post 1948) labour movement, was subject to a very high degree of state control. In the first instance, there was legislation designed to prevent the new union movement being infiltrated or used by the MCP. As time went on and the 'threat of communism' subsided, a trend towards the more 'normal' control of labour as an aid towards capital accumulation became discernible.

The first pieces of trade union legislation, the Trade Unions Enactment of 1940 and the Trade Unions (Amendment) Act of 1946 were restrictive. The latter specified that only those workers engaged in a similar trade, occupation or industry were able to form a union. No general labour unions, capable of uniting the working class, were to be allowed. No union funds were to be used for political purposes, i.e. the legal channels wherein a trade union movement might develop into a political voice for the working class, in the manner suggested by Marx, were closed. This tendency towards legal control continued to develop in the post independence period. For example, Articles 149 and 150 of the Merdeka (i.e. Independence) Constitution, allow for the declaration of an Emergency and the suspension of Parliamentary rule whenever it is considered necessary. In 1959, the newly independent Government of Malaya passed a Trade Union Ordinance which allowed Emergency regulations to be enforced after the Emergency was over. Under this Ordinance, the power of the Registrar of Trade Unions was increased so as to allow him to reject an application for a potential union, deregister individual union members (a means used to 'weed out' undesirable elements such as Chinese workers considered to be communist sympathisers) and to register unions in such a way as to promote weak sectoral units: General labour unions were already disallowed. Now began a tendency to disallow peninsula wide registration of workers in the same trade, occupation or industry if such a nation-wide organisation was deemed to pose any threat to the status quo. In those instances where unions of workers in the manufacturing sector, i.e. unions of the 'traditional' industrial proletariat, have been allowed, most have been registered on a state by state or regional rather than on a national basis. Regional concentrations of power in the hands of organised labour have also been prevented by way of arbitrary registration of workers in small, weak unions that bear little apparent relationship to their trade or industry. (For instance, the Metal Industries Workers' Union organised a factory that makes metal clothes pins, hair pins. The addition of these workers would have made for an even stronger Metal Industries Workers Union. The Registrar, however, ruled that these workers should belong to a haberdashery union. Another example: the Electrical Industries Workers' Union organised a factory making calculators. The

Registrar of Trade Unions ruled that these workers should belong to the less powerful Machinery Workers' Union.) In recent years, even this level of organisation of labour is under threat because the present government is promoting the development of in-house rather than state, regional or national unions. In-house unions are not a new mode of organising labour in Malaya/sia. Some of the earliest associations of workers were in in-house unions. The present focus on in-house unions is partly a consequence of an early 1980s government policy to 'Look East', emulate the Japanese model of social organisation, industrialisation and cultural values and thus enable Malaysia to work towards the same level of economic development as Japan. In addition, however, it would seem that the Malaysian Government is promoting in-house unions as an aid to the control of the developing wage labour force and for reasons related ethnically-based political considerations.

As noted, there has been a massive influx of people into the wage labour force in Malaysia in the years after 1970. To deny these people union representation would be to court trouble, if not now then in the long run. The aim of the state, then, is to ensure that this new labour force is organised in such a manner as to maximise the potential for state control over the labour movement. In-house unions represent the ultimate fragmentation of the labour movement and of the working class, and thus offer the highest likelihood of control. In addition, and as also noted above, a very high proportion of the recent entrants into the wage labour force, in the plantation sector, in commerce and in import substitution, resource based and light export oriented manufacturing industries, are people who are ethnically Malay. The maintenance of the dominant position of at least the parliamentary wing of the essentially-Malay state depends upon the continued loyalty of the Malay masses. It is dependent upon the bulk of the Malays continuing to think and act – especially vote – along ethnic lines, rather than in terms of the class position they share with members of other ethnic groups. By insisting upon the formation of in-house unions, and via his power of the discretionary deregistration of union members, the Registrar of Trade Unions can and does work towards developing in-house unions of Malay workers, whose leaders too are ethnically Malay.[11] This is but one more instance of ethnicity being used as ideology to divide and rule and aid in the reproduction of the present class relations of capitalism within the Malaysian social formation. In 1980, nearly half of all unions (46 per cent) and a quarter of all unionised workers were members of an in-house union (Malaysia, 1984, Table 11–9, p. 179). An increase in this direction, as is indicated by both government policy and practices, presages the ultimate fragmentation of organised labour in Malaysia. The question this raises is: Is the organisation of workers in fragmented units better than no organisation, no representation at all? We would suggest that this is a research topic of considerable pertinence at present.

The trade union movement in Malaysia therefore, is, as in many other places, highly fragmented. There are also a great many legal and other restrictions on the type of actions trade unionists are able to undertake. In 1949, during the Emergency, a Trades Dispute Ordinance was passed which placed limits on the rights of workers in essential services to strike. The first Emergency ended in 1960. A second 'State of Emergency' was declared from 1963 to 1965 during 'Confrontation' with Indonesia. Once again limits were placed on the workers in essential services to strike. Nearly everything (including pineapple canning) was declared 'essential'. During the 1960s, despite the tight control of labour by capital and the state, there were several fairly major industrial disputes involving such public sector employees as railway, postal and firefighting workers. This oubreak of industrial unrest led in time to the passing of the Industrial Relations Act, 1967. Under this Act, earlier 'Emergency' prohibitions on the right of workers in essential services to strike were made permanent. Some of the earlier, more extreme definitions of 'essential' were removed. Workers in those services designated 'essential' – nearly all departments in the public sector and much of the private sector – were now required to give their employer 42 days' notice, in writing, of their intention to strike. No strike is permitted within 21 days of such notice being given or else the strike can be deemed illegal. Under the Industrial Relations Act, 1967, Part I, what constitutes a strike is very broadly defined:

> 'Strike' means the cessation of work by a body of workmen acting in combination, or a concerted refusal or a refusal under a common understanding of a number of workmen to continue to work or to accept employment; and includes any act of omission by a body of workmen acting in combination or under a common understanding, which is intended to or does result in any limitation, restriction, reduction or cessation of or dilatoriness in the performance or execution of the whole or any part of the duties connected with their employment.

This means that any concerted action, any go-slow can be deemed a strike, and, if the correct procedures have not been followed, such action can be declared illegal.

The state in Malaysia has aimed to control the labour movement, not just because of the association of trade unionism with communism but also because a controlled labour force is needed to attain a high rate of capital accumulation. For instance, and as noted above, The Employment Act, 1955 gives permission to an employer to dismiss a worker on the ground of misconduct. The Industrial Relations Act, 1967 states that the approval of the Minister of Labour is required for any collective agreement between management and workers in any 'Pioneer' industry which contains terms or conditions more favourable to workers than those contained in the Employment Act, 1955 (an Act 12 years old in 1967, 30 years old today).

In May 1969, following the outbreak of violence between the Malays and Chinese in Malaysia, a 'State of Emergency' was imposed for the third time. In October of that year, the Industrial Relations Act was amended to further limit the rights of organised labour. Under these new Amendments, workers lost the right to negotiate with management as regards such issues as dismissals and transfers. In 1971, parliament resumed (although the Emergency has not, as of 1985, been declared to be over). The above mentioned Amendments to the Industrial Relations Act were incorporated into comprehensive new legislation. Management powers were further strengthened (e.g. employers no longer had to give any reason for the dismissal of workers). More issues (e.g. union recognition) became non-strikeable. Under the 1969 legislation, union officials are prohibited from holding key positions in political parties (i.e. further severing the possibility of any link between trade unionism and the politicisation of the working class). (For discussion of the legislation to 1970, see Mills, 1971; Dunkley, 1982; Wu, 1982. See also *Suara Buruh*, monthly newspaper of the Malaysian Trades Union Congress, various issues.)

The period after 1970 was the period of the implementation of the New Economic Policy (NEP). By that time, capitalism was clearly the mode in dominance in the articulation of modes of production that pertained in Malaysia. After that date, capitalist relations of production began to emerge as a major mode of extraction. The state, through the medium of a complexity of institutions which together comprised its reality, acted ultimately to control labour on behalf of local, regional and/or international capital. After 1970, the state itself entered into considerable acquisition of ownership and control of various sectors of the corporate economy, on behalf of the Malay and other indigenous people, the supposed beneficiaries of the NEP. (See Malaysia, 1971, 1975, 1981 for details of increases in state ownership of the means of production.) The interests of plantation, merchants and manufacturing capital (import substitution, resource based and 'light' export oriented industries) had all to be safeguarded. Malaysia had to be and be seen to be a politically stable environment so as to attract the foreign capital and technology deemed necessary to aid its development and thus have the economic wherewithal to attain the goals aimed for under the NEP. 'Political stability' excludes the possibility of industrial unrest. Despite the then considerable legislation on the statute books designed to regulate and control labour, the 1970s were a period of considerable labour unrest. High rates of growth, as measured by GDP, were attained but there was a great deal of sectoral poverty that the NEP seemed unable to address. What is more, although highly controlled, the expanding labour force was becoming much more self-conscious; aware of its location within the class relations of capitalism. This growth in self-consciousness was due to a number of factors: gradual increases in the level of education of the labour force and hence exposure to wider ideas about the world; the spread of mass communication, bringing the people in Malaysia at least some information about the radicalism and worker/ student alliances in the advanced capitalist societies and elsewhere (e.g. neighbouring Thailand) at that time; inputs from visiting academics and trade unionists, travel abroad by local counterparts. This combination of material conditions and inputs of ideology from abroad was related to increases in industrial action in Malaysia. There were a great many go-slows; picketing became more widespread; despite the legal difficulties involved, there was an increase in the rate of strike activity in the country: In 1975 there were 64 strikes, in 1976 there were 70, in 1977 there were 40, in 1978, 36 (Malaysia, 1984, Table 11–16, p. 185). In 1978/ 79, Airlines Employees Union members, working for the national carrier Malaysian Airlines System (MAS) went on strike. They received support from unionists abroad (Australian unionists, for example, grounded an MAS plane at Sydney airport). The case received extensive media coverage in the South Pacific region. This was considered particularly bad publicity for a country in the act of selling itself as a stable economic environment with a disciplined labour force. The government of the time responded to this strike by gaoling union leaders, de-registering the Airlines Employees' Union and establishing an in-house union for MAS employees only. The following year, legislation was enacted which effectively neutralises the last vestiges of the power of organised labour in Malaysia.

Two pieces of legislation were enacted in 1980: The Industrial Relations (Amendment) Act, 1980 and the Trade Union (Amendment) Act, 1980. These Acts give workers and unionists certain rights and enshrine the notion of industrial relations through the mechanism of collective agreements, industrial dispute settlement via conciliation and arbitration. The law as it now stands, however, presents a number of almost insurmountable obstacles for organised labour. For instance: Part II (4) of the Industrial Relations Act, 1967 and as Amended 1980 specifies that no person shall interfere with, restrain or coerce a workman or employer who wants to form or join a trade union. Despite legal prohibitions to the contrary, a great many employers and manufacturers do discourage, or actively prevent, their workers from unionising. Given that the Employment Act, 1955 and subsequent Amendments allow for the dismissal of workers without any need to give a reason, a worker who attempts to organise his/her colleagues (i.e. a person seen by many employers or managers to be a 'trouble maker') can be easily contained. Besides outright dismissal of such organisers, other tactics employed in Malaysia to prevent unionisation include transfers of key workers or promotion (i.e. co-optation). The state colludes in this practice of inhibiting unionisation. For example, manufacturing companies accorded 'Pioneer' status are promised that their first five years of operation will be 'union free' (and given the discretionary power of the Registrar of Trade Unions as regards registration or non-registration, this can be attained with little difficulty).

Section 27 of the Trades Union Ordinance, as Amended in 1980, places further limits on unionisation and union activities in the public sector, i.e. the sector most likely to be unionised. No police officers, prison personnel, armed forces personnel or any officers engaged in a confidential, security, managerial or professional capacity in government service or a statutory body are able to join or form a trade union. No trade union, whose membership is confined to persons employed by a statutory authority, is allowed to affiliate with any other trade union or federation of trade unions whose membership is in any way different from their own (which limits any across the board associations which might unify the working class).

The Registrar of Trade Unions has long had wide ranging powers as regards the registration or non-registration of unions. Under the Trade Union (Amendment) Act, the Registrar is given the absolute power to de-register any union alleged to have done something contrary to the national interest. The Act empowers him to refuse to register any application for a union without his having to give a reason (and unionists claim the ministry often delays a decision for so long that potential members of the union pending registration lose interest, change jobs or have been dismissed. As strikes are illegal while a decision is pending as regards registration, the implication is that delays may be deliberate. See Dunkley, 1982, p. 433 for further discussion of this issue.) Before 1969, appeals against the Registrar's decision on any matter could be referred to the Industrial Court. After 1969, appeals were directed to the Minister of Labour, i.e. as long ago as 1969 there was the beginning of a trend for the transfer of legal decision making from the judiciary to the bureaucracy. The 1980 Amendments to the Trades Union Ordinance enhances this trend. Now the Registrar and the Minister of Labour have been given the right to assume the role of trial judges: the Registrar is empowered to conduct prosecutions, monitor union funds and investments, call witnesses to inform on union activities, obtain court orders to enter union premises and seize articles or documents when he has reason to believe some illegality may have been committed.

The Industrial Relations Act, 1967 as Amended 1980 gives yet more power to employers. Under Part IV of the Amendment Act, more things have become 'non-negotiable' in the process of drawing up collective agreements between trade unions and employers: promotions, transfers, employment, termination, dismissals, reinstatements, assignments or allocation of duties are issues no longer open to discussion and thus no longer legitimate reasons for collective action. Even if workers want to undertake collective action, it is very difficult for them to do so. For instance, and as noted above, no worker in an 'essential service' can go on strike without giving his/her employer 42 days' notice of intention to strike. No workers, whether in essential services or not, are permitted to go on strike pending the settlement of a trades dispute, once the matter has been referred to the state machinery. Any workman who goes on an illegal strike, or stays on one, is liable to a maximum of one year's jail, a fine of $1000 ringgit (US $412 and at least two months' pay for an unskilled or semi-skilled worker) or both. Under Section 25A(1) of the Trade Unions Ordinance, before a union of workmen are permitted to call a strike, or a member of a trade union of workmen can go on strike, they must first hold a secret ballot, two thirds of the members must agree to the strike and the results of the ballot must then be submitted to the Registrar, who will then rule whether the proposed strike is legal, or whether it would contravene the Ordinance and is, therefore, not permitted. Contravention of these regulations, or the conduct of an illegal strike, renders every member of the executive committee of the union concerned liable to fine of $2000 ringgit (approximately US $825), a maximum of one year's jail or both. Given the very broad definition of what constitutes a strike, the ease with which any concerted action can be deemed a strike – and, if the correct procedures for its conduct have not been followed – and declared illegal, the threat of legal action hangs closely over the heads of union leaders in Malaysia, encouraging them to hold their members in check. If the Trade Union (Amendment) Act and the Industrial Relations (Amendment) Act are insufficient to intimidate union leaders and their rank and file, the state can always apply the Internal Security Act (introduced onto the statute books by the British during the first State of Emergency, 1948–60) which allows for the indefinite detention, without trial, of anyone considered to pose a threat to the security of the nation, this generally interpreted as anyone who challenges the combined power of capital and the state.

CONCLUSION

What can we conclude as regards the extent to which trade unions in Malaysia can or do represent the interests of workers *vis-à-vis* employers? What can we conclude as regards the extent to which trade unions in Malaysia can or do represent the interests of the entire working class? Despite the enormous number and wide variety of types of constraints placed upon organised labour, neither the individual trade unions, nor the federations of unions (e.g. MTUC or CUEPACS) are entirely ineffective. As regards the individual unions, whether national, state or in-house: most union energies seem to be spent not on industrial action but on recruiting members, organising factories and keeping such members as are recruited. The remainder of time and effort is spent preparing for and engaging in collective bargaining with employers, or their representatives, in attempts to obtain concessions from capital as regards wages and conditions of work. Strikes and go slows are uncommon, although picketing is not infrequently used as a means of expressing dissatisfaction. Although trade unions are weak, unionised workers – especially in the private sector where market forces are more apparent – do seem to enjoy slightly higher rates of pay and better conditions of work than their non-unionised counterparts. Thus we must conclude that in economic terms, unions have some effect. Only a small section of the labour force of Malaysia is, however, unionised, thus such economic concessions as are obtained by the different trade unions flow to only a small number of workers, rather than the entire working class. Second, given the combination of external constraints and the high degree of fragmentation of the union movement, there is very little likelihood that the working class will be politicised; will become a class 'for itself' through the medium of any of the existing unions.

As regards the federations of unions: The MTUC speaks on behalf of the interests of the private sector section of the working class in Malaysia, CUEPACS speaks on behalf of the public sector. Although there has been some consideration given to the unification of CUEPACS and the MTUC, the mass media at least suggests very strained relationships between the leaders of these two federations, thus only a limited likelihood of their unifying and even less chance of their uniting to speak on behalf of the entire working class in Malaysia.

The MTUC has both a 'Youth' and a 'Women's' section, showing that the leadership recognises the special needs of these categories of workers. CUEPACS does not have these divisions. The MTUC seems to make no distinction on the basis of ethnicity, i.e. there is a marked tendency for issues to be argued in terms of the 'needs of workers' (the working class?) rather than ethnic lines. Although 'moderate', the leadership of the MTUC has been consistently vocal, much more so than the leadership of CUEPACS. The MTUC literally bombards the government and the press with a stream of statements, memoranda and letters of protest which do seem to have served to bring about some rethinking, some modification of some of the more harsh policies and practices of capital and the state towards labour and the labour movement. Losses, however, seem to far outweigh victories in this regard. The MTUC is only a society, it is not a trade union. It cannot enter directly into collective bargaining with employers or their representatives as regards particular groups of workers, although MTUC representatives do sit on different, overarching tripartite bodies of government officials, employers and unions. Although the MTUC might informally encourage the leaders of some of its member unions to call their rank and file out on strike, it cannot directly enter into industrial action and, because of the limited number of unions affiliated with this federation, it would have only limited success in attempting to bring about a general strike.

The MTUC engages in regular and wide ranging education of the labour force on trade union issues, as do most of the individual unions. CUEPACS seems less involved with this type of activity. The MTUC has set up a 'Worker's Bank', which we might see as a business enterprise which represents an attempt to establish the means to fight capital and the state on their own terms. This bank, however, is only one small effort, nor is it meeting with the level of success that had been hoped for. The MTUC and the labour movement generally is constrained legally, limited financially and lacks a military or paramilitary wing. It is highly fragmented. Most 'battles' between trade unions and capital/the state take the form of ideological warfare (e.g. collective bargaining, memoranda to the government; i.e. words). The power of capital and the state to refute the challenge posed by organised labour lies not in their control of the mass media in particular and a great deal of culture but in the structure of ownership of Malaysian society. We might conclude, therefore, that the individual trade unions, the MTUC or CUEPACS – no matter how dedicated their leadership, and this is not always the case – present only the most limited threat to the status quo.

Notes

1. This paper forms part of a wider study of foreign investment, industrialisation and development in Malysia, funded by the Australian Research Grants Scheme and carried out with the assistance and co-operation of the Centre for Policy Research, Universiti Sains Malaysia, Penang. The author is indebted to a number of people for discussions on the issues which are the subject of this paper. In particular, thanks are due to Lim Teck Ghee, University of Malaya; Chan Lean Heng, Universiti Sains Malaysia, Penang; Trisha Todd, University of Malaya and Chandra Muzaffar, Aliran, Penang. Of course the usual disclaimers apply.
2. Malaysia is a national entity comprising the Malay peninsula and the Borneo states of Sabah and Sarawak. These latter states are known as East Malaysia. This essay deals only with Peninsular or West Malaysia.
3. In the late 1870s, a Protector of Chinese was appointed. In 1880, a law on indebtedness was passed, making it illegal to bring in immigrant workers via indebtedness higher than the amount of their passage to Malaya. In the late 1890s, triads were made illegal. In 1910, the indenture system was made illegal. The 1912 Labour Code specified that all labour contracts were to end by 1914. For details see Jackson, 1961; Stenson, 1970, 1980. For discussion, see Jomo, 1977; Halim, 1982.
4. In 1923, however, the Government of India did appoint an Agent in Malaya to investigate labourers' complaints.
5. The subject of the rate and nature of the involvement of Malays in wage labouring in the colonial period is clearly of great importance for our understanding of the dynamics of ethnic relations in the first half of the twentieth century. As yet this matter has only been partially researched.
6. The concepts 'internal' and 'external' in this instance are matters of degree.
7. Not all Malays, however, supported the MCP. Many collaborated with the Japanese (a fact that led to even greater animosity between the Malays and Chinese both during and after the Occupation). Further, the Indian National Congress in India decided not to co-operate with the British war effort, believing that the enemy of their enemy was their friend. Many

Indians in Malaya, following the lead of their countrymen at home, formed associations which lent support to the Japanese. After 1945, these associations were disbanded and their members were the object of a considerable backlash by those who had suffered under the Japanese. For details, see Stenson, 1970, 1980.

8. The NEP thus adopts a 'racial' solution to what is essentially a problem of class. This inherent limitation of the Policy, plus some degree of mismanagement, has served to increase the wealth of the already well-to-do Malays, made some but not enough improvements in the standard of living of the mass of the Malays and has heightened, rather than eliminated, the 'racial' tension it sets out to contain. For elaboration, see O'Brien, 1984b.

9. From the late 1960s onwards, Malaysia began to receive substantial inputs of foreign capital, especially from the USA and Japan, which have been invested in export oriented manufacturing industry. Manufacturers in the advanced capitalist countries, faced with rising labour costs, labour unrest and falling profits at home, began to locate some or all of their production processes 'off shore' in such lesser developed countries as Malaysia. The creation of this 'global production line' was made possible by a near revolution in transport and technology, and involves only certain industries, most notable amongst them being electrical machinery including electronics, textiles, scientific instruments and the like. Factories have been established in Malaysia and elsewhere. Cheaper local labour is employed to produce these highly transportable goods, meant for sale on the world market. (For further discussion of the 'global production line', the emergence of a new international division of labour and the socio-economic implications of these processes for countries like Malaysia, see Grossman, 1978; Frobel, Heinrichs and Kreye, 1980; O'Brien, 1981, 1985).

10. Not all workers in the private sector are employees. A substantial number are self-employed or unpaid family workers. Data in this regard from the 1980 Census of Population is not yet available. In 1970, however, 33 per cent of the labour force was self-employed, 17 per cent were unpaid family workers, i.e. a total of 50 per cent of the labour force were not wage earners. We might expect that the majority of these people were private sector workers. Even given the enormous movement of workers into the wage labouring sector in the years 1970 to 1980, we might expect that a substantial number of people are still 'in' the labour force but not in receipt of a wage. (Calculated from Malaysia, Chander, 1977, Table 7–8, p. 426.)

11. There are a number of reasons for believing that present government policy is to disallow the re-registration of quite a number of existing occupation or industry based trade unions so as to make the legal 'space' necessary for a Malay-dominated in-house union.

Bibliography

Awbery, S.S. and Dalley, F.W. (1948) *Labour and Trade Union Organization in the Federation of Malaya and Singapore* (Government Press, Kuala Lumpur).
Braverman, H. (1974) *Labor and Monopoly Capital* (Monthly Review Press, New York).

Burawoy, M. (1979) *Manufacturing Consent: Changes in the Labour Process Under Monopoly Capitalism* (Chicago University Press, Chicago).

Dunkley, G. (1982) 'Industrial Relations and Labour in Malaysia' in *The Journal of Industrial Relations*, September: 424–42.

Edwards, H.W. (1978) *Labor Aristocracy: Mass Base of Social Democracy* (Stockholm).

Emerson, R. (1964) *Malaysia: A Study of Direct and Indirect Rule* (Oxford Univeristy Press, Kuala Lumpur).

Engels, F. (1968) *The Conditions of the Working Class in England*, translated and edited by W.O. Henderson and W.H. Chaloner (Stanford University Press, Stanford).

Frobel, F., Heinrichs, J. and Kreye, O. (1980) *The New International Division of Labour* (Cambridge University Press, London).

Gamba, C. (1962) *The Origins of Trade Unionism in Malaya. A Study in Colonial Labour Unrest* (Singapore: Oxford University Press).

Grossman, R. (1978) 'Women's Place in the Integrated Circuit', *Pacific Research*, 9 (5–6): 2–26.

Gullick, J.M. (1958) *The Indigenous Political Systems of Western Malaya* (The Athlone Press, London).

Halim, F. (1982) 'Capital, Labour and the State: The West Malaysian Case', *Journal of Contemporary Asia*, 12 (3): 259–80.

Hanrahan, G.Z. (1954) *The Communist Struggle in Malaya* (New York: Institute of Pacific Relations).

Hing, A.Y. (1984) 'The Development and Transformation of Wage Labour in West Malaysia' in I. Norlund, P. Wad and V. Brun (eds), *Industrialization and the Labour Process in Southeast Asia* (Institute of Cultural Sociology, University of Copenhagen).

Hoffman, L. and Tan, S.E. (1980) *Industrial Growth, Employment and Foreign Investment in Peninsular Malaysia* (Oxford University Press, Kuala Lumpur).

Hyman, R. (1971) *Marxism and the Sociology of Trade Unionism* (London, Pluto).

—— (1975) *Industrial Relations: A Marxist Introduction* (Macmillan, London and Basingstoke).

Jackson, R.M. (1961) *Immigrant Labour and the Development of Malaya, 1786–1920* (Government Printer, Kuala Lumpur).

Jomo, K.S. (1977) *Class Formation in Malaya: Capital, The State and Uneven Development* (Ph.D. diss. Harvard University).

Lenin, V.I. (1984) *What is to be done?* (International Publishers, New York).

Lim, C.Y. (1967) *The Economic Development of Modern Malaya* (Kuala Lumpur: Oxford University Press).

Lim, D. (1973) *Economic Growth and Development in West Malaysia, 1947–1970* (Kuala Lumpur, Oxford University Press).

Lim, T.G. (1977) *Peasants and Their Agricultural Economy in Colonial Malaya, 1874–1941* (Oxford University Press, Kuala Lumpur).

Littler, C.R. (1982) *The Development of the Labour Process in Capitalist Societies* (London: Heinemann Educational Books).

——(1984) *Class at Work* (London: Batsford).

Malaya, Federation of (1949) M.V. Del Tufo, *Malaya. A Report on the 1947 Census of Population* (Crown Agents for the Colonies: London).

——(1960) H. Fell, *1957 Population Census of the Federation of Malaya*, Report No. 14, Department of Statistics, Kuala Lumpur.

Malaysia, Federation of (1971) Economic Planning Unit, Prime Minister's Department, *Second Malaysia Plan, 1971–1975* (Government Printer, Kuala Lumpur).

—— (1976) Economic Planning Unit, Prime Minister's Department, *Third Malaysia Plan, 1976–1980* (Government Printer, Kuala Lumpur).

—— (1977) R. Chander, *General Report on the Population Census of Malaysia, 1970*, vol, 1, (Department of Statistics, Government Printer, Kuala Lumpur).

—— (1981) Economic Planning Unit, Prime Minister's Department, *Fourth Malaysia Plan, 1981–1985* (Government Printer, Kuala Lumpur).

—— (1984) Kementerian Buroh, *Labour and Manpower Report, 1981/82* (Ministry of Labour, Kuala Lumpur).

—— (1984) Malaysian Industrial Development Authority, *Investment Incentives Act, 1968 (Revised 1978) Incorporating all Amendments up to 1st September, 1980* (Malaysian Industrial Development Authority, Kuala Lumpur).

Marx, K. (1976) *Capital*, vol. 1 (Penguin, Harmondsworth).

(n.d.) (a) 'Wage Labour and Capital' in K. Marx, *Selected Works* (International Publishers: New York)

(n.d.) (b) 'Value, Price and Profit', in K. Marx, *Selected Works* (International Publishers: New York).

Marx, K. and Engels, F. (1983) *The Communist Manifesto* (International Publishers: New York).

Miliband, R. (1969) *The State in Capitalist Society* (Weidenfeld and Nicolson: London).

Mills, C.P. (1971) *Industrial Disputes Law in Malaysia* (Singapore).

O'Brien, L.N. (1981) 'Asian Women and the New International Division of Labour', paper presented to Asian Studies Association of Australia 'Women in Asia' Workshop, University of New South Wales, Sydney. A revised version of this paper, 'Malaysian Women and the New International Division of Labour' appears in L. Manderson and G. Pearson (eds), *Class, Ideology and Women in Asian Societies* (Asian Research Service, Hong Kong, 1985).

—— (1982) 'Divide and Rule: Education in Colonial Malaya', in Centre for Development Studies *Education and Development*, Discussion Paper No. 4 (The Flinders University of South Australia, Adelaide).

—— (1984a) 'The Effects of Industrialization on Women: British and Malaysian Experiences', *Kajian Malaysia*, Journal of Malaysian Studies, II(1): 38–58.

—— (1984b) *Class, Gender and Ethnicity in Peninsular Malaysia*, manuscript completed December, 1984.

Purcell, V.W. (1965) *The Chinese in Southeast Asia* (London: Royal Institute of International Affairs and the Institute of Pacific Relations).

Roff, W.R. (1967) *The Origins of Malay Nationalism* (University of Malaya Press: Kuala Lumpur).

Short, A. (1975) *The Communist Insurrection in Malaya, 1948–60* (Frederick Muller: London).

Singh, K.S. (1969) *Indians in Malaya* (Cambridge University Press: London).

Stenson, M.R. (1970) *Industrial Conflict in Malaya* (Oxford University Press: Kuala Lumpur).

—— (1980) *Class, Race and Colonialism in West Malaysia; The Indian Case* (Queensland University Press, St Lucia).

Webster's New Collegiate Dictionary (1956) (G. and C. Merriam Co.; Springfield, Mass.).

Wheelwright, E.L. (1965) *Industrialization in Malaysia* (Melbourne University Press: Melbourne).

Wu, M.A. (1982) *The Industrial Relations Law of Malaysia* (Heinemann Educational Books (Asia) Ltd; Singapore and Hong Kong).

7 The Political Economy of Trade Union – State Relations in Radical and Populist Regimes in Africa

Jon Kraus

Have trade unions in populist and radical regimes in Africa been able to increase the power of workers and trade unions in the national political economy, safeguard and advance the interests of workers, and participate in the political process and in the organisation of production? Have such regimes worked to prevent a weakening of the position of workers in the face of the changing international division of labour?

The first is a relevant question for several reasons. Since the state in most African countries has moved to control narrowly trade unions or to repress them in order to control labour, facilitate capital accumulation, and establish a political hegemony for the ruling group, it is plausible to ask whether trade unions and workers have been able to develop the power and capacity to act in their own interests at least in regimes which appear to be pursuing radical or populist political–economic strategies. (To varying degrees radical and populist regimes are those engaged in altering their international relationships to reduce their political–economic dependency, reducing upper class access to economic resources and political power in favour of broader class segments of the population, possibly developing their political base for policies by mobilising the political participation of and generating organisational resources for the popular classes, introducing redistributive measures which increase socio-economic equality, and pursuing economic development strategies which increase growth in ways in which the popular classes share.) The differences between populist and radical regimes do not appear to have been critical in Africa for shaping trade union–state relations. Second, the question is relevant because, in the increasingly dictatorial and authoritarian regimes in Africa, trade unions are the only mass organisations which have the potential capability of imposing the interests of some segments of the popular classes on state power. Third, in response to the frequent authoritarianism, inegalitarian socio-economic policies, and state controls over trade unions and workers, a radical critique of African trade unions has been offered. It suggests that: the dominant social groups and incipient social classes exercising state power are systematically involved, objectively or subjectively, in exploiting other classes, primarily workers and peasants; associations between trade unions and the state result in the co-optation of trade union leaders, subordination of unions, and policies inimical to workers; union leaders have tended to be readily corrupt, co-optable, and without regard for rank and file interests; union leaders have built trade union bureaucracies which have distanced them from the rank and file in order to entrench and enrich themselves, which reflects their own sharing of interests with the dominant governing class; such union leaders tend to be conservative and to restrain a reflexive populist or working class consciousness among rank and file workers and lower level, workshop union leaders; and, in consequence, trade unions in Africa tend to be obstacles to progressive change and the increased power and well-being of workers (Kraus, 1979, pp. 260–1; Crisp, 1984). There are many problems with this critique, despite the evidence for its propositions that exists: it ignores the fact that trade unions must deal with state power, and this is all the more the case in radical or populist states where major industries have been nationalised or been developed by the state which is highly involved in economic management; it suggests that the wildcat protests and strikes from below do not have implicit union leadership support (though they frequently do) and can have systematic consequences in production, economic, and political relationships. None the less, it is important to know to what extent this radical critique of trade union behaviour is true for unions in radical and populist African regimes.

We will study the political economy of trade union—state relationships in regimes in four African countries: Algeria, Ethiopia under the Derg, Tanzania, and Ghana. (Ghana has had several populist regimes – Nkrumah and the Convention People's Party (1951–66) and the early years of military rule under Col. I.K. Acheampong and the Supreme Military Council (SMC), roughly 1972–5/6–and one radical regime, under Flight Lieutenant Jerry Rawlings and the Provisional National Defence Council (PNDC) government, January 1982–present.) These four countries represent a range of radical and populist regimes, civilian and military, with varying or no colonial inheritance.

Firstly, the impact of both external and internal economic factors upon trade union—state relationships is examined. While economic factors are crucial for structuring social class and political relationships, other variables often have a critical impact upon union–state relationships. This is particularly true for radical and populist regimes in peripheral capitalist countries which are attempting to restructure external economic relations, manage the economy, and construct a new coalition of political support. Thus, the impact of some political factors is also noted. Second, the importance of union and working class strength and autonomy before these regimes appeared is evaluated. Third, we assess in each regime the nature of the trade union–state relationship and its consequences for trade union power and autonomy, worker incomes and employment, and the capacity of workers and unions to participate in the political process and in the organisation and management of the means of production.

THE IMPACT OF ECONOMIC AND POLITICAL FACTORS ON UNION–STATE RELATIONS

The thesis has been offered that the dramatic internationalisation of capital in the post-war period and the spread of multinational corporations into many economic sectors in less developed countries (LDCs) on the capitalist periphery is creating a new international division of labour and has tended to stimulate more rigorous labour control measures to keep down labour costs and thus to foster labour repressive regimes (Southall, 1984, pp. 147–8). While these four countries have not attracted much multinational investment capital for manufacturing for export, there are at least three major senses in which their participation in the international division of labour has imposed external pressures on the economy, real wages, and trade unions: first, through the pressures of existing foreign capital and government desires, at certain points, to attract more foreign capital; second, through their involvement in and dependence upon international markets for export and crucial foreign exchange earnings and thus their exposure to international market fluctuations, recessions, price shocks, and changes in their terms of trade; and, third, given the latter and the rise in balance of payments deficits and debts, the need to accept International Monetary Fund (IMF) policy prescriptions in exchange for new capital invariably has wage-repressive and increased unemployment consequences, at least in the short term.

With respect to the first, in two of these countries, Ghana and Tanzania, foreign capital was heavily involved in labour intensive industries for export which made major contributions to employment and to foreign exchange earnings. Moreover, labour was a crucial cost component in the competitiveness of these industries: gold, produced in Ghana, in the 1950s and 1960s had a fixed value on the world market; and sisal, grown on European-owned plantations in Tanzania which employed about 28 per cent of the wage labour force, faced a highly competitive world market. In Ghana the colonial and Nkrumah governments had been strongly urged by the gold mining companies and the Chamber of Mines to hold down the government minimum wage in the 1950s, since increases in the government minimum led to immediate union pressures to raise theirs as well (Kraus, 1973). An increased minimum wage in 1956–7 precipitated the closure of several marginal mines; the 1960 increase induced several larger but also increasingly marginal mines to prepare to close their operations, until the government purchased the mines to maintain employment and export earnings. In Tanzania worker and union pressures for increased wages generated widespread strikes in the years preceding independence and during the first year of independence, 1962, inducing Nyerere to detain in the rural areas the two leaders of the sisal plantation workers' union until the strikes could be settled. Anti-strike legislation was passed in that same year (Bienefeld, 1979, p. 572). A collective agreement in 1964 provided modest annual wage increments tied to corresponding increases in production (Tanzania, 1967, pp. 22–3; Tanzania, 1967a, 10–11). However, sisal production and employment dropped severely in the 1960s, as did employment and production in gold mining in Ghana. Bienefeld has also argued strongly that the belief of Tanzania's leaders in 1960–3 that they needed to attract foreign private capital was a major motive in the series of steps taken to establish tighter controls over labour. The need to take such measures became more urgent with the developing disaffection of some sectors of the union movement in 1961–4 with TANU government policies with regard to the East African Community, the slow pace and rules with respect to Africanisation of government positions, rising wage demands, insistence upon the right to strike, and differences over international union affiliation (Bienefeld, 1979, 574–8).

Second, the levels of economic activity, employment, and real wages of all of these countries, like other peripheral capitalist countries, are profoundly affected by the broader role of these countries in the international distribution of labour as producers of raw materials selling into semi-oligopolistic world markets, or, as in the case of Algeria in the 1960s, selling oil in a world market whose prices were still determined by the monopolistic agreements of the Seven Sister international oil companies. All except Algeria suffered significantly from the oil price shocks of the 1970s, the subsequent generalised inflation in manufactured goods, food, and other imports, and the recurrent worldwide recessions of the 1970s and early 1980s which reduced the demand for and, frequently, the prices of their exports.

Table 7.1 provides indices of the terms of trade, exports by volume, and imports by volume of Ghana, Algeria, Ethiopia, and Tanzania (1980 = 100 for the three measures). Ghana had severely depressed terms of trade for almost all of the 1960s and also for the 1970s, except for 1977–9. By 1982 its terms of trade had dropped to 39 per cent below its 1960 and 1980 levels. Ghana had expanded its exports significantly during the 1960s, primarily in cocoa, to little avail. While it experienced a high and rising level of imports by volume during 1960–5, and indeed altered their composition to favour capital equipment for investment, since 1965 Ghana has had a declining volume of imports. This import scarcity has severely retarded its growth, generated less employment, and, with other government policies, reduced real wages. The low world prices of cocoa and other exports (in real terms) influenced the

Table 7.1   Terms of trade, export, and import indices

	1960	1962	1965	1970	1975	1980	1982
				1980 = 100			
Ghana							
Terms of trade	100	80	68	109	95	100	61
Volume: Exports	115	142	158	147	136	100	115
Volume: Imports	168	155	196	172	150	100	67
Ethiopa							
Terms of trade	147	134	150	156	120	100	74
Volume: Exports	60	72	89	84	97	100	127
Volume: Imports	60	75	102	109	85	100	108
Algeria							
Terms of trade	19	18	18	18	52	100	106
Volume: Exports	74	109	86	125	104	100	101
Volume: Imports	42	23	21	37	92	100	105
Tanzania							
Terms of trade	107	100	106	107	111	100	86
Volume: Exports	154	154	167	197	126	100	100
Volume: Imports	56	62	71	108	120	100	97

Source: UNCTAD data.

government's real producer price that it paid to cocoa farmers, which contributed to a sharply declining level of cocoa exports in the 1970s. This, in turn, produced lower export revenues and a downward cycle in the economy, with crippling import scarcities, and prompted inflationary government spending with an unremitting downward pressure on real wages (Kraus, 1986).

Ethiopia, whose economy is less integrated with the world market, had relatively even terms of trade during the 1960s and early 1970s. After 1977 the terms dropped sharply and in 1982 were 50 per cent of the 1960 level. A gradual rise in the volume of exports from 1960 to 1973 permitted Ethiopia a gradually rising level of imports. However, drought, land reform, increased peasant consumption, and disruptions caused by civil war and invasions helped to reduce exports during 1974–8 and, hence, imports as well. After 1978 Ethiopia was able to increase its exports significantly, by 59 per cent in volume during 1978–82, but the sharp fall in its terms of trade of 53 per cent affected economic activity and real wages.

Tanzania was also not severely affected by sharply lower terms of trade during 1960–77, despite a brief sharp drop in 1975–6 because of world recession. Its terms of trade varied little during 1960–73 and were slightly higher during 1974–8, but they declined precipitately during 1979–82. Export volume rose significantly during the 1960s and early 1970s, permitting a rising level of imports as well. But since 1974 exports have declined markedly in volume, as have imports, due to recurrent world recession and adjustment shocks from external inflation as well as disruptions in agriculture caused by droughts and the Ujamaa agricultural policies.

Algeria's economic growth – and hence employment and real wages in part – were sharply affected by the economic chaos that accompanied independence and the withdrawal of French capital. Algeria's terms of trade – largely reflecting oil and natural gas prices – were stagnant to 1970, rose somewhat in 1971–3, and then soared in 1974 and again in 1979–80. Rising export volume during 1968–70 financed rising imports, as did increasing terms of trade after 1971. Moreover, Algeria has relied not only upon its rising terms of trade to generate economic activity and marked increases in employment but also on an extraordinary increase in foreign capital borrowing, which saw total external debt outstanding (including undisbursed) climb from $2.2 billion in 1971 to $21.5 billion in 1980.

In summary, therefore, the role of these countries in the international capitalist economy was highly disadvantageous to Ghana and somewhat disadvantageous to Tanzania and Ethiopia during the latter half of the 1970s. Algeria's economy was buoyed by external demand and prices and had less need to pursue labour repressive policies.

One characteristic common to the development strategies of all four countries (Ghana under its populist and radical regimes) has been an attempt to escape this dependence by internally-oriented economic growth policies, to some extent import-substitution in character. These policies have involved nationalisation of foreign industries, new state activities in industry and marketing, state farms or mandatory marketing of produce of farmers and co-operatives through state agencies, and state control over financial and insurance industries. A determination by the political leadership to restrain consumption on behalf of investment in new production and services has also been a major determinant of the state's attitude towards trade union autonomy, power, and representation. In many African states, including Tanzania, Algeria, and Ghana, the governments have sought to establish, more or less explicitly (less in Ghana's case), national pay policies. These were considered legitimate in order to: prevent the diversion of larger and larger proportions of government revenue from development expenditures to recurrent wages; to prevent wages and salaries from becoming so high that they tended to reduce the creation of new jobs; prevent increased inequality between urban wage groups and urban and rural workers; and, as noted, allow export industries (gold and sisal) to remain competitive and profitable. In part these were real and legitimate concerns, especially when the governments first permitted some increases in wage rates, as in Ghana and Tanzania shortly before and after independence. But, the governments' interest in introducing pay policies invariably clashed with and involved the pre-emption of what unions saw as their major function.

However, the initial steps to impose controls over trade unions' rights in several cases preceded the decision to adopt national pay policies or to expand state intervention in the economy: in Ethiopia in 1974, in Algeria in 1963 and recurringly thereafter. In Tanzania the adoption of repressive labour legislation and controls was in part prompted by an explicit pay policy. In Ghana the state's employment of potential controls, in 1960–1, was animated in part by pay policy concerns and a large state investment programme. The consequences of statist efforts to generate economic growth (in terms of employment as well as overall economic activity) by restraining increased wages and consumption among workers on behalf of greater government perogatives in allocating economic surpluses has contributed to a major tendency to develop labour control devices and to restrict union power and autonomy. This propensity has been accentuated as radical/populist governments have expanded state ownership and management of the economy, where worker wage demands involve a direct imposition on state budgets and upon the political leadership's prerogatives in allocating surpluses. In Ghana, Tanzania, Ethiopia, and Algeria the regimes have argued to the workers and unions that trade unions and workers in socialist countries (or in state industries) cannot function as they did under capitalism, as they are obliged to increase production for development.

Clearly such an argument can mask the fact that incumbent political leaders and a rising bureaucratic bourgeoisie have enjoyed salaries and prerequisites out of all proportion to those available to wage earners, the lower salariat, and peasants. However, in most of these states there has been a relatively small economic surplus (Algeria excepted). Competitive claims over its distribution creates the basis for potentially high levels of conflict.

The higher the level of the social differentiation of labour and the crystalisation of diverse social classes or groups which have developed some institutional capacities for promoting their own interests, the greater the possibility for unions and other associational groups to develop and retain autonomous organisational capabilities. Other political factors contribute to or detract from this tendency, including inherited political norms and institutions and the levels of political competition or coercion in society. Higher levels of economic development and social differentiation of labour, articulation of new social classes, inherited (liberal) public norms and institutions, and (at least intermittent) competitiveness in the political environment permitted trade unions in Ghana to develop earlier than in these other states (Algeria apart) and to have a somewhat greater opportunity to struggle for autonomous power, worker rights, and a central role in determining wages and conditions of labour. In Tanzania, the later development of unions, the establishment of a single-party system continuously in power since 1962, and the early emasculation of the independent power of unions have left unions and workers with virtually no power. In Algeria, despite the FLN's and regime's attempts to monopolise political legitimacy and its successful suppression of independent union power, intermittent political factionalism, an older union tradition, and a large proletariat have occasionally permitted a representative union movement to assert itself and articulate strongly worker interests. In

Ethiopia, the late development of non-autonomous unions, low levels of development and social differentiation of labour, an absence of political competition, and the pervasive prevalence of authoritarian public political norms, under the non-participatory Haile Selassie regime and the participatory revolutionary Derg government, have denied workers and unions a capacity for asserting workers' interests.

The thesis that under radical or populist regimes, workers and unions will be a core constituent of the power structure, inducing the regime to pursue pro-worker/union policies, cannot, unfortunately, be sustained by the evidence from the performance of such regimes. Unions and workers have tended to have their organisational capacities to articulate their interests suppressed.

However a more or less serious commitment to populist or radical ideologies or values has distinguished some major political leaders (though by no means all) in the Nkrumah and Rawlings' regimes in Ghana, Nyerere's Tanzania, the Derg in Ethiopia, and Algeria – despite the considerable inequalities that emerged in these regimes as well. These regimes have acted in some distinctive ways in their socio-economic and political strategies to advance popular class interests even when they sought to control union movements. There is inadequate room here for an explicit comparison with non-radical/populist regimes. These regimes have all had a distinctively egalitarian cast in socio-economic terms, in great contrast with a Kenya, Nigeria, Zaire, Ivory Coast, or Tunisia. There was at least some self-conscious attention to limiting the acquisitive propensities of state political and bureaucratic leaders (the top politicos in Nkrumah's regime excepted), e.g., in leadership codes which prevented their involvement in businesses. The radical egalitarianism in Ethiopia under the Derg and in Rawlings' early years are highly distinctive. Corruption does not appear to play the dominant role among political leaders in these regimes that it does in so many other states (Nkrumah's regime excepted). All of these regimes have put enormous resources into education, especially at the primary school level, with great increases in the percentage of primary age children (and of females) in school, expecially in Algeria (98 per cent), Tanzania (104 per cent), Ghana under Nkrumah, and in Ethiopia, which mounted an extensive literacy campaign. Algeria and Ethiopia are the only African states where significant egalitarian land reform has occurred. All these states have made major, successful efforts to increase wage/salary employment as a means of increasing equality, especially Algeria, Ghana (under Nkrumah and Acheampong, 1972–6), and Tanzania.

TRADE UNION STRENGTH AND ORGANISATIONAL AUTONOMY PRIOR TO THE ESTABLISHMENT OF RADICAL AND POPULIST REGIMES

Substantial strength and organisational autonomy of trade unions prior to the establishment of radical and populist regimes should increase the capacity of the trade union movement to retain its independence and to expand its power, unless it confronts overwhelming state coercion, as in Ethiopia. Relevant measures of union strength and autonomy would include: the size and strategic salience of the wage labour force; the age of the movement and thus prior inculcation of trade union or class values and consciousness among members and leaders; development of substantial organisational networks; levels of solidarity among union leaders and rank and file based on prior historical struggles; and the development of internal organisational norms, values, and interests – all of which generate commitments to trade unions as working class organisations.

It is also important to know whether the union movement developed autonomously or emerged in tandem with nationalist or other party organisations and the early character of trade union–political ties.

In Ghana recorded employment was relatively low after the Second World War, with only 131 000 in 1949, with the largest number in the mines and in government services (railways, construction, posts). However, it grew rapidly in the 1950s (1960: 326 664) and under Nkrumah's industrialisation and development programmes in 1960–5. It regressed in size in the 1966–9 period, rose by roughly 20 per cent during 1970–5, and stagnated or declined in the 1970s as the economy experienced severe depression. Ghana's wage labour force as a percentage of total labour was one of the largest in Africa in 1960, at 19.1 per cent (census data), which grew to 24.1 per cent in 1970, with non-agricultural wage labour about three-quarters of the total. The labour force in agriculture declined from 61.8 per cent in 1960 to 51 per cent in 1979. (Doctor and Gallis, 1966, Ghana, 1961, 1983). While mineworkers constituted the single largest wage group in the late 1940s and early 1950s, and were the most militant in strike activity in these years, their distance from main urban centres, the migrant, northern, apolitical character of the underground workers, and their relative lack of solidarity with the rest of the working class meant that their significance was economic rather than political. However, the inability of capital or the state to control them perhaps increased the room for manoeuvre of the rest of the working class. In the towns the railway workers were the most militant in the late 1940s and early 1950s.

The first Ghanaian trade unions to endure appeared in the late 1930s, and the major and most militant expansion of trade unions occurred in the first five to six years after the Second World War. A labour federation, the Trades Union Congress (TUC), with relatively weak powers, was established in 1945. A strongly-supported, country-wide, two week, but unsuccessful general strike in 1950 was followed by massive dismissals, which retarded union organisation and membership growth for some years. Membership was 38 135 (paid members) in 1949, with a much larger number of supporters, and did not recover to that level until 1954; it reached 100 000 only in 1959 (about 27 per cent of non-agricultural wage labour). Though there were a large number of small, weak unions, major unions among railway, public works, mines, municipal, timber, construction, and some commercial workers were reasonably well-established. Several of the unions had established fairly strong traditions of union organisation, strikes, solidarity, and continuous leadership, including the mines, railway, public works, and several municipal unions (Jeffries, 1978; Crisp, 1984; Kraus, 1977, 1979a). Most had voluntary leaders at most if not all levels; many remained in the union movement for many years, providing national level leadership after the unions were reorganised in 1958 and again in the post-Nkrumah era in 1966 and after. Trade union leaders and members overwhelmingly favoured Nkrumah's CPP when it emerged in 1949 and launched, in tandem with an industrial dispute, a general strike with the CPP in behalf of political goals in 1950. But many of the most important unions were anxious to retain their independence and to separate their political and trade union activities. This became a more important issue as they had to bargain with the CPP government (during internal self-rule, 1951–7, and after), and when in the mid-1950s pro-CPP union leaders tried to assert their control over the TUC. Roughly three groupings of unions emerged: the whole-hearted CPP proponents, whose leaders held positions on the CPP's Central Committee and National Executive since 1949, who wished to use an alliance with the governing CPP to strengthen the power of the union movement; some populist and militant leaders in older unions which insisted upon their independence and distrusted the CPP union leaders as a result of conflicts over control of the TUC (railway, mines and hospital workers); and more conservative union leaders, who preferred an a-political posture for their unions, as advocated by the Department of Labour. The CPP leadership of the TUC led the union movement into an alliance with Nkrumah's CPP in 1958 under conditions which promised significant organisational benefits (check-off dues, union shops, requirement that employers bargain collectively) and which did not initially threaten the internal autonomy of the 24 industrial unions which emerged from the 1959 reorganisation. However, the primary commitment of most union leaders remained to their unions (Jeffries, 1978; Sclafani, 1977; Kraus, 1979a).

In Tanzania, a more largely agricultural economy than Ghana's, about 91 per cent of the labour force was in agriculture still in 1967, about 83 per cènt in 1979. Only 10.1 per cent of the labour force were wage workers in 1962, half of those non-agricultural. The largest group of workers were the 110 000 sisal plantation workers in 1960, whose numbers had shrunk to 30 000 by 1970; the second largest employer was government. The labour movement started later than Ghana's, after the abortive attempt of the Dar es Salaam dockworkers' strike in 1950. The first new unions were not registered until 1952. The period of rapid expansion of unions and membership occurred between 1955, when the Tanganyika Federation of Labour (TFL) was formed, and 1960, roughly a decade after Ghana's period of militant expansion. By 1960 there were somewhere between 43 460 and 91 770 union members (Friedland, 1969, pp. 51, 76). In some contrast to Ghana, there were few voluntary leaders (non-paid) and a relatively large number of full-time leaders, union entrepreneurs who supported themselves by collecting membership dues. Unlike Ghana as well, over half the leadership positions were held by appointment rather than election (the latter, 41 per cent). There was an extremely high turnover in leadership, at the local as well as national union levels. For example, of 25 top leaders in 13 unions between 1957 and 1960, 60 per cent were no longer active in union affairs by 1960, most of them being the previously full-time general secretaries (Friedland, 1969, pp. 75–81).

The TANU government's cooptation of two of the TFL's most dynamic leaders, Rashidi Kawawa and Michael Kamaliza, did not strengthen the unions *vis-à-vis* the government. There were no formal linkages between TANU and the TFL until 1961 (introduced in order to reduce conflict). The union movement was founded quite apart from TANU. None the less, a large majority of the full-time union leaders were TANU members, and many of the most important TFL and union leaders held TANU leadership positions (Friedland, 1969, 121–6).

Ethiopia is an almost totally agricultural economy, with an estimated 88 per cent of its labour force in agriculture in 1960, 80 per cent in 1979.

It had an estimated 300 000 non-agricultural wage workers in 1960 (4 per cent of the labour force), of which a small number were in industry, most in construction and government (Doctor and Gallis, 1966).

In Haile Selassie's Ethiopia labour unions were illegal until the early 1960s. They emerged and were recognised in 1962, were confined to the private sector, and were highly cautious and conservative in their behaviour. Strikes were virtually illegal and did not occur. By 1963 there were 42 unions with 10 000 members, by 1966 50 unions with 25 000 members, and by 1974, the year of the revolution, there were 80 000 members. Unions of white-collar, service workers appeared to be predominant. The unions enjoyed a modest independence only by closely confining their activities and demands (Zack, 1966). CELU's first protest statements and demands as the political system opened up suddenly in 1974 in the wake of the army mutinies involved corporate union and wage rather than political demands. Its first successful general strike, of three days, was launched then, but CELU and its member unions were too weak to ensure the implementation of the concessions which the government had made under duress and later withdrew (Ottaway and Ottaway, 1978, 34–9). Either new union leadership in 1974–6 became quickly radicalised by the conflicts in Ethiopia, or else radicals from outside the union movement acquired union positions in order to build strength by which to oppose Derg rule. None the less, there is little to suggest that the unions had acquired substantial strength (numbers apart) or institutional capacities.

In Algeria, dominated by a settler economy and regime up to 1962, roughly 37 per cent of the entire labour force (Algerian and European) was drawn into capitalist wage labour by 1954, 19.7 per cent in non-agricultural jobs. Wage labour employment grew rapidly in the 1950s, especially in construction. There were few large firms, may artisanal, employing ten or less workers. Algerians in the wage labour force rose to 43.3 per cent of the total labour force by 1966 and, following Algeria's intensive industrialisation in the 1970s, to 59.1 per cent by 1977. The number of wage labour jobs grew from 1.06 million to 2.21 million, or 108 per cent, between 1966 and 1977, with the non-agricultural proletariat almost tripling, to 700 000 workers, by 1977 (Doctor and Gallis, 1966; Corten and Tahon, 1982; Palloix, 1980).

Relatively little is known about the strength and activities of the UGTA and its member unions prior to Algeria's independence. Trade unions became active among European workers in Algeria in the 1930s, in branches of the French CGT. While the CGT primarily organised the French or *pieds noirs* working class, some Algerians did become active in the union movement and became leaders in CGT-affiliated unions. Some of the independent-minded UGTA leaders after independence had served leadership roles in CGT unions. A political organisation competitive with the FLN, Messali Hadj's *Mouvement National Algérien* (MNA), launched a trade union movement in February 1956, in Algeria. Some twelve days later, UGTA's formation was announced by ex-CGT union leaders, most of them apparently linked to the FLN, clearly to preempt Messali Hadj's union from claiming the allegiance of Algerian workers.

UGTA leaders were soon forced to go underground, and by 1959 most of the top leaders had fled abroad or died in French prisons. UGTA's attempted eight-day insurrectional strike in January 1957 was quickly crushed by the French army. Thereafter, urban workers as a group and UGTA did not play a significant role in the violent liberation struggle. It would seem improbable that UGTA had much organisation in place when it returned in 1962, though individual unions remained active. On the other hand, whatever its leaders' linkages with the FLN and its commitment to national liberation, UGTA leaders returned to Algeria with the determination to develop an autonomous (but pro-FLN) trade union movement.

On balance, it appears that Ghana's union movement was somewhat stronger and more institutionally developed, with greater commitment by labour leaders, than the unions in Tanzania. It is impossible to evaluate the strength of Algeria's union movement at independence, but the regular re-emergence of leaders as UGTA Secretaries-General in 1965 and 1978 of men who had pre-UGTA union leadership experience with the CGT suggests a strong degree of leadership continuity and commitment in individual unions. The Ethiopian unions had slight institutional abilities prior to 1974 and no significant history of struggle and protest of the kind that creates experienced, committed leaders. These factors influence the character of post-independence union–state relations, as did the level of political competitiveness and factionalism in the political system and political leadership needs and orientations.

THE POLITICAL ECONOMY OF TRADE UNION–STATE RELATIONSHIPS: CONSEQUENCES FOR TRADE UNION AUTONOMY AND POWER, ROLES, POLITICAL PARTICIPATION, AND WORKER INTERESTS

For each country we will assess the character of the trade union–state relationship in terms of the development of state controls over labour and workers, the extent of trade union power and autonomy over time, union ability to protect the interests of workers, and the political participation of unions and workers, especially in terms of participation in management of the means of production.

In Ghana in 1958 John Tettegah, the TUC's Secretary-General, pushed a reluctant government into designing an Industrial Relations Act, which involved a fairly explicit political exchange in which there were benefits as well as costs to the union movement. The benefits were: the reduction of 85–95 relatively small unions to 24 unions in 1959, reduced to 16 in 1960, then to 10 in 1965 (largely because of their continuing financial weakness), then finally back to 17 by 1967, which produced stronger unions and often not much loss of identity though existing strong unions (e.g., mine and railway workers) found the change non-beneficial; establishment of a check-off system for union dues – and in 1960 a union shop provision – which not only greatly increased union membership but for the first time gave the unions a financial base to hire union members not dependent on the employers to organise branches, bargain collectively, and attend to worker grievances; a requirement that employers bargain collectively with the unions, which was of crucial importance since most employers had refused to bargain with the unions. This gave the union movement a permanent and central role in wage/salary negotiations and also, through gains won in collective bargaining, made the private sector the wage leader instead of the government, as in the past. Some unions and the TUC gained political and economic power, status and resources. This also promoted John Tettegah and his chief union lieutenants to a central role in pushing for more radical economic policies by the government, the promotion of state enterprises, and the creation of jobs, which increased rapidly during 1960–5. The costs were not unimportant and were ultimately demoralising; strikes became virtually illegal, and a compulsory conciliation and arbitration system was established, which past experience led workers and unions to consider a benefit; certain powers vested in the TUC gave it power over the member unions, giving the CPP government a strong influence in union actions (but not one which involved changing union leaders except for the position of secretary general); the compulsory membership of civil servants and union shop provisions prevented members from opting out of the unions; and this, the effective ban on new or breakaway unions, irregular elections, compulsory check-off, and anti-strike pressures together significantly reduced membership influence over union leaders (see Crisp, 1984, for the impact of this in the mineworkers' union). The real cost was that when Nkrumah established a dictatorship during 1960–5, it was easier than it might otherwise have been to control the labour movement.

The limits on union autonomy became apparent when the Sekondi– –Takoradi railway and dockworkers launched a strike in September 1961, to protest a compulsory savings law being used to supplement government revenues for investments, despite the fact that workers' real wages were higher than they had ever been (Table 7.3). The major railway and dockworkers unions' deeper grievances involved their forced merger in the TUC and the authoritarianism of the CPP-influenced TUC leadership which failed to support their demands. This seventeen-day strike in Sekondi–Takoradi was a populist protest against the government and TUC autocracy. The workers, joined by opposition politicians, called for the removal of Nkrumah's government. With threats but without violence the government forced the workers back to their jobs; several union leaders were detained (but freed ten months later and never prosecuted), while others fled abroad. Whilst the government had given way to large unruly worker demonstrations from below in mid-1960 in Accra, the capital, and increased wages by 18 per cent, now it strongly discouraged strikes, which fell to almost none during 1962–4. There was also a general antagonism to the union movement among old guard CPP leaders because in 1960–1 Tettegah had sought to build the TUC into an organisation which could rival the CPP. Nkrumah forced new secretary generals on the TUC in 1962 and again in 1964 (Tettegah was dismissed) and imposed close police surveillance on union meetings, demoralising leaders and turning them into government spokesmen although some unions remained active, their leaders fighting to prevent state managers and CPP branches from displacing union influence within firms (see Bartimeus, 1966).

In other instances, however, union leaders themselves used their ties with party and government to suppress harshly the autonomy and militance of their former unions and workplace associations, e.g., Foevie in the Mine Workers Union (Crisp, 1984, pp. 125–49; Jeffries, 1978, pp. 102–9). There was also a significant erosion of the minimum and other wages during 1961–5, especially in 1964–5 (Table 7.3). However, significant fringe benefits were won through collective bargaining. Government pressure also prevented layoffs during the 1964–5 recession.

After 1966 and Nkrumah's overthrow, the union movement was revitalised, union elections held regularly, leadership accountability forced on the leaders by rank and file strikes and protests, and important degrees of autonomy regained. However, the union movement was unable to recover the losses in real wages from the military government (1966–9) or the Busia government which followed in 1969–71 (Table 7.3). Workers and unions went on a sustained series of wildcat strikes, protests and demonstrations during 1968–71 on behalf of wage demands to redress reduced real wages, retrenchments, dismissals, lengthy delays in collective bargaining and in implementing collective bargaining agreements, and often in protest against arbitrary and authoritarian management behaviour – one of the most important causes of strikes (Kraus, 1977). The dynamics of this strike wave (Table 7.2, 1968–71) made the union leadership much more responsive to rank and file claims and wildcat initiatives, decreasing the distance between union leaders and workers but increasing the distance between unions and the state.

The Busia Progress Party (PP) government, an expression of the Ghanaian merchant–managerial–professional bourgeoisie, believed that workers were highly overpaid relative to cocoa farmers (which was inaccurate) and was deeply antagonised by the strikes, especially those against state corporations and the central government. It intervened unsuccessfully in the union movement to get a pro-PP man elected as TUC secretary-general (1970) and with success to support several breakaway unions; it declined to consider an increased minimum wage. Instead, it inaugurated a National Development Levy of 1 per cent on workers' incomes for rural development. When the TUC agitated against the Development Levy, the Busia/PP government rushed through an amendment to the Industrial Relations Act, with the following effects: abolition of the TUC as a legally-mandated institution; unions could be freely formed (to undermine existing unions and TUC unity); check-off of dues ended except on a 'contracting-in' basis; union funds were frozen; strikes remained illegal; strong anti-strike prerogatives were given the Minister of Labour.

Not unnaturally, the unions greeted joyfully the military coup by Colonel Acheampong which overthrew the Busia government in January, 1972. If the Acheampong/SMC government initially mounted drastic pressures on unions to stop strikes, which did drop sharply during 1972–3 (Table 7.2), in many other respects the SMC was decidedly friendly to the trade union movement: it made strikes less necessary by compelling firms to deal promptly with worker/union grievances; it restored the TUC and check-off; it revalued the currency but kept in effect the increase in wages the government had permitted to

Table 3   Real wages in Ghana, Tanzania and Algeria

	Ghana			Tanzania		Algeria Real Gov't minimum wage index (1/1/72=100)	
	Nominal gov't minimum wage ¢	Real gov't minimum index (1963 = 100)	Some unions' minimum index[a] (1963 = 100)	Index of average earnings (1974 = 100)	Real gov't minimum wage index (1963 = 100)	Agric.	Non-agric.
1960	.65	120					
1961	.65	113					
1962	.65	104					
1963	.65	100			100		
1964	.65	90			98.4		
1965	.65	66.4			92.5		
1966	.65	58.3			88.1		
1967	.70	68.6			85.9		
1968	.75	67.9			82.9		
1969	.75	63.5			93.0		
1970	.75	61.2			90.4		
1971	.75	56.0			87.0		
1972	1.00	68.1			111.3	88.2	88.2
1973	1.00	57.1			102.0	84.4	84.4
1974	1.50[b]	73.2	c.150	100	110.8	99.2	95.2
1975	2.00	75.2	c. 96	82	87.0	91.2	87.5
1976	2.00	48.1	c. 67	59	68.1	104.5	93.1
1977	3.00[b]	33.4	c. 51	52	58.3	99.3	87.9
1978	4.00	25.6		31		121.5	106.2

Year						
1979	4.00	16.7	c. 33		130.6	111.0
1980	6.00[b]	16.6	c. 33		140.4	101.3
1981	12.00	15.4		26		
1982	12.00	12.6		25		
1983	21.75[b]	9.9		18		
1984 (10mo)	32.00[b]	11.5				
1985	70.00					

[a] From the early 1970s to late 1970s, some unions were able to win through collective bargaining minimum wages double or more the government minimum wage. See text.

[b] Nominal minimum wages in these years are averages of the minimum at different times during the year.

Sources: for Tanzania, Jackson; for Algeria, computed from World Bank data, agricultural and non-agricultural minimum wages deflated with Algiers cost of living index, with 1 January 1972 = 100; for Ghana, government real wage computed from Ghana, 1974, and various issues of Central Bureau of Statistics, Newsletter.

Table 7.2 Strikes, strikers and man-days lost (MDL): Algeria, Ghana, Tanzania

							[L.F. = Labour Force]									
	1960	1962	1966	1967	1968	1969	1970	1971	1972	1973	1974	1975	1976	1977	1978	1979
Algeria[a]																
Strikes						42 (72)	57 (99)	70 (152)	100 (146)	99	(250)[a]	(175)		(160)	2 mo.	
Strikers						5349	6363	12276	10706	12079						
as % L.F.						0.18	0.21	0.39	0.33	0.36						
MDL ('000)						25.14	25.77	52.16	40.59	5.32						
Ghana																
Strikes			29	24	47	59	58	78	14	14	43	33	45	61	65	50
Strikers			14996	4653	52419	30988	21467	46715	3711	4443	32371	15301	32360	47304	42913	40606
as % L.F.			0.49	0.15	1.64	.95	.64	1.37	0.11	0.13	0.91	0.42	0.87	1.24	1.10	1.01
MDL ('000)			20.43	5.01	156.20	165.57	145.12	133.10	5.28	4.31	64.41	39.41	114.26	205.17	196.17	170.6
Tanzania[b]																
Strikes	203	152	16	25	13	4	3	3[c]	0[c]	0[c]	1[c]	0	0	3		
Strikers	89495	48434	2062	3224	1906	874	357	654	0	0	60	0	0	1773		
as % L.F.	1.95	1.0	0.04	0.06	0.03	0.02	0.01	0.01	—	—	—	—	—	0.03		
MDL ('000)	1494.8	417.5	8.85	7.22	5.76	2.14	0.73	3.03	—	—	0.24	—	—	5.78		

[a] Strikes in parentheses for 1969–77 are from Knauss, see sources, indicating under-reporting by Algeria.

[b] Tanzania counts only those strikes longer than one day, which significantly undercounts the actual number of strikes.

[c] Strike data given for Tanzania, 1971–74, is very inaccurate, failing to count significant number of strikes.

Sources: ILO, *Yearbooks of Labour Statistics*, various years; J. Kraus, 'Strikes and Labor Power in a Post-Colonial African State', paper, Institute of Social Studies, The Hague, 1977; Peter Knauss, 'Algeria under Boumedienne: the Mythical Revolution, 1965–78'; I.J. Mowoe (ed.), *The Performance of Soldiers as Governors* (Washington, D.C.: Univ. Press of America, 1980), 68; Dudley Jackson, 'The Disappearance of Strikes in Tanzania', *Journal of Modern African Studies*, 17, 2 (1979), 220. Labour force data from ILO, Yearbook(s) and IBRD, World Tables (1980), 460–3.

offset the price hikes which devaluation had caused, in effect raising real wages substantially (by over 12 per cent, see Table 7.3); it introduced subsidies on a small range of essential, widely-used food and other imports, it forbade dismissals of over five employees without the permission of the Department of Labour, which was difficult to obtain; and it reintegrated the union splinters of terms favourable to the dissidents.

The distinctly different class thrust of the early Acheampong regime policies made its authoritarian rule, at least initially, appear to be much more just to the working class and trade unions than that of the democratically-elected Busia government. The implicit bargain with the union movement was that it should help to keep industrial peace, whilst the SMC would be attentive to union and worker interests. In the event, however, the SMC measures strengthened union leadership over workers – for example, eliminating protesting splinter unions' dues check-off – in order to enlist union efforts in reducing worker resistance. But after two years when strikes were stifled quickly, from 1974 on the number of strikes, strikers and man-days lost expanded rapidly (Table 7.2). SMC attempts to bully workers, e.g. the railway workers in Sekondi, were ineffectual. Workers in the gold mines violently rejected management attempts to impose labour discipline (Silver, 1978).

Acheampong's SMC government inaugurated a number of policies whose economic nationalism and populist thrust were broadly popular and equitable: the partial repudiation and rescheduling of foreign debts, a self-reliance campaign in agriculture, and the forced takeover of majority equity control of foreign gold mines, banks, insurance, aluminium and timber companies. There were other policies specifically beneficial to labour, which flowed from union bargaining with the state: the extension of the right of unions to bargain collectively on behalf of almost all state workers in parastatals, which brought new (and relatively expensive) benefits: a very large expansion in employment, which was, unfortunately, largely unproductive; and, in the face of rising shortages and worker protests, major TUC and national union roles in allocating scarce commodities to members through co-operatives.

However, the unions sought or were granted these benefits with the implicit but crucial proviso of accepting the SMC's expression of state power, which was extraordinarily destructive of the economy, public institutional life, and any degree of participation and civility in Ghanaian political life. The union movement at no time joined in the increasingly wide-scale public protests against the government in 1977–8 as the economy collapsed all around it (though economic strikes increased). That Busia-era politicians, who had attacked and sought to cripple the labour movement, were prominent in the leadership of the protest movements is not enough to account for union leadership acquiescence to inept, incompetent, increasingly repressive SMC rule. For since 1975–6 SMC rule had become increasingly disastrous to the living conditions and real wages of workers and almost all Ghanaians. In the face of oil price shocks, price inflation in all imported goods, and recurring and extremely severe import scarcities, the economy became more and more unproductive. The government sought to spend massively to sustain economic activity and its own flagging political legitimacy; the result was hyperinflation, blackmarketing and hoarding, smuggling, and the exodus of increasingly large numbers of skilled Ghanaians. Table 7.3 notes that the real government minimum wage index (1963 equals 100) rose by over 12 per cent in Acheampong's first year, then fell in 1973, and rose by 16 per cent in 1974 when the minimum and most other wages and salaries were increased by 100 per cent; then the real government minimum fell like a stone, from 1975 to 1979, when it was worth only 25 per cent of its 1972 value. Real average wages declined as greatly as minimum wages during 1974–9, 74 per cent and 77 per cent respectively. That many unions which had collective bargaining rights obtained a minimum wage up to twice as high as the government's left them in an only marginally better position (Table 7.3). Wildcat strikes, absenteeism, moonlighting, and demoralisation all increased.

Three developments towards the end of SMC rule cast light on the cautious, conservative quality of top union leadership, leadership tendencies to oligarchy, and low responsiveness to rank and file desperation. First, union leaders refused to join the vigorous opposition to military rule, despite economic failure and regime violence against workers. Second, the 1978 TUC quadrennial Congress was delayed, its date withheld, making it purposely difficult to challenge incumbent Secretary General A.M. Issifu. When Richard Baiden of the Maritime and Dockworkers Union (MDU) did so, with calls for a more militant union movement, the other general secretaries rallied around Issifu. Balloting at the Congress gave union leaders control of their delegates' ballots, leading the MDU to leave the Congress in protest. Third, the TUC decided to form a party, the Social Democratic Front (SDF), to contest the 1979 elections. But national union leaders accepted Issifu's choice as presidential nominee of a wealthy Dagomba lawyer and businessman, from a rural area of the country, whose sole qualification was his friendship and alleged silent business partnership with the TUC Secretary General. This bespeaks an incredibly casual attitude among union leaders regarding the possibility of mobilising workers in behalf of their interests. As a result, workers totally ignored the SDF candidates.

During the interregnum of post-Acheampong military rule (August 1978–September 1979), workers and other Ghanaians exploded in protests, strikes and demonstrations against the state, managers and officials. During the short period of democratic rule under the Limann/ People's National Party (PNP) government (September 1979–December 1981), union leadership was somewhat more assertive but no more successful in protecting the interests of workers, partly because the economy continued to regress and the government was incapable of taking coherent remedial measures. Strikes continued at a high level. A government appealing to the unions and workers for wage restraint in order to curtail the rate of inflation permitted its Members of Parliament to vote themselves incredible salaries and perquisites, unleashing worker outrage and demands. An effective strike by sanitation men in Accra, employing excrement strategically, led to a tripling of the minimum and all other wages in 1980. The gains were almost totally eroded by the inflation (120 per cent in 1981). Weak and incoherent attempts by the government to restore market mechanisms (decontrol prices) to provide producer incentives were partly reversed by angry worker protests and a TUC threat to launch a general strike.

The *coup d'état* by Flight Lieutenant Jerry Rawlings and the creation of the Provisional National Defence Council (PNDC) government on 31 December 1981 created a quasi-revolutionary situation in Ghana. Rawlings had led a mutiny in 1979, when the Armed Forces Revolutionary Council ruled for three months and carried out a vigorous assault upon the most culpable leaders of the Acheampong period within the military and state institutions. Rawlings' process of coming to power, in 1979 and again in late 1981, hastened the collapse of the command structure of the Ghanaian military and of already enfeebled state institutions; state and parastatal officials were confronted by lower level workers with accusations of mismanagement, corruption and abuse of office. Rawlings and his unrepresentative PNDC stimulated a burst of popular participation by encouraging people to establish People's Defence Committees (PDCs) and Workers' Defence Committees (EDCs). PDCs enforced the PNDC's renewed price controls, unleashed an assault upon landlords by enforcing rigorously and with physical enthusiasm a new rent control law, and created new power structures composed entirely of people previously without power, status or authority. Open public tribunals were created outside the judicial system to try speedily those accused of crimes.

The PNDC's assault upon the old order had important consequences for the government. Dissident trade unionists were organised by PNDC member and ex-unionist Kwei into an Association of Local Unions (ALU) which mounted a series of demands for the dismissal of all major trade union leaders. While Issifu and a few other union leaders resigned in the face of angry demonstrations from within and outside the movement, the union leaders in self-protection chose Richard Baiden, militant Secretary of the MDU, as its Acting TUC Secretary-General.

Baiden attempted to defend the autonomy of the union movement, but all the old leadership was swept out of the TUC building and into jail or exile by an assault on TUC headquarters by dissident unionists and armed police. Vigorous protests by many union branches and District Councils of Labour may have had the effect of denying the ALU dissidents control of union offices. After some initial confusion, the individual unions were permitted to choose Interim Management Committees (IMCs) with one chosen for the TUC as well. They were under injunction from the PNDC and their unions to carry out reorganisations of the unions, maximise rank and file participation, and contribute to revolutionising Ghanaian society and the workplace. The chairman of the TUC's IMC made this indictment of the condition of the union movement:

> The Executive Board of the Trades Union Congress had developed into a more or less self-perpetuating clique of officials who were only interested in protecting each other and maintaining their offices . . . by 31st December, 1981, the Trades Union Congress as an institution was weighed down heavily by a bureaucratic, opportunist and reformist culture and tradition that was inimical to the genuine interests of the working class. . . . Leaders of the trade unions were separated by a big gulf from the rank and file of workers. . . . The mass of workers in reality did not have much influence over their unions. Many local union leaders elected by their rank and file only played a nominal role (TUC, 1983, pp. 2–3).

While national union leaders were indeed part of a 'bureaucratic, opportunistic and reformist culture', one largely dictated by the circumstances of state and society, a large percentage of the union leaders had been fairly responsive to rank and file demands. Moreover, in most unions the locally elected leaders played a key role in all matters affecting the unions' relationships with the firms and workers. However, the rapidly sinking real wages of workers during 1977–81 had created a desperate frustration among some union militants and branches, increasing their criticisms of and challenges to top leaders, some of whom were too well entrenched.

The union organisations encountered severe competition in their renewal from the Workers' Defence Committees (WDCs), founded in many factories, offices, and business and state institutions. The WDCs carried out aggressive investigations into the existing and prior management. It soon became common for WDCs to eject senior managers, to seek their arrest or investigation, with WDCs attempting to take over the management of the organisation. The PNDC was forced to try to slow the momentum of WDCs as many institutions came grinding to a halt. In several cases where private companies tried to lay off workers, since inputs for production were unavailable, workers took over the factories and sought PNDC sanction for permanent self-management. The most well-known case was the Ghana Textile Printing Company, where some laid-off workers with outside assistance unilaterally dismissed both local union and WDC leaders, who lost their jobs as well. Workers temporarily took over subsidiaries of Cadbury, which had sought to lay off workers on the false pretext of inadequate raw materials, and Air Liquide, which refused demands to dismiss its Ghanaian manager (*West Africa*, 30 April 1984, p. 924). Two WDC and one union representative were appointed to new interim boards of directors in all state corporations. Some among the WDCs and PDCs were also the PNDC's major popular base, and they rallied to the government repeatedly in the face of criticisms, demonstrations of opposition by students and professionals, and the numerous coup attempts against the PNDC government.

While the WDCs were successful in raising the level of participation of some workers in the management of production in 1982–4, many union leaders, old and new, local and national, considered that the WDCs were an immediate threat to the existence of trade unionism. While there was often co-operation and co-ordination between WDCs and local union branches, there were also intense and bitter divisions, with both acting as representatives of workers' interests, with open assaults mounted against union leaders by WDCs on some occasions. WDC leaders agitated regularly against local unions and often sought to coercively dismiss democratically-elected local leaders. Most WDC executives were much less accountable to the rank and file workers than local union leaders. Irritated by the independent initiatives and criticisms of government economic policies by some PDCs and WDCs, in late 1984 the government renamed them Committees for Defence of the Revolution (CDRs), put them directly under government control, and restored full managerial control of parastatals, reducing worker representatives to an advisory role.

In 1983 at seventeen national congresses, five ALU dissident leaders and five leaders ousted in 1982 were elected as general secretaries. The new TUC officers, old guard unionists, elected at the December 1983 Congress, promptly undertook to assert the interests of workers to the government in a somewhat stronger fashion than the IMC of the TUC was able to do, and in a more public fashion. In early 1982 the PNDC had announced that wages would be frozen and the IMCs of the unions should no longer seek to pursue collective bargaining. Subsequently, the trade unions have vigorously defended their right to bargain collectively for wages and conditions of employment, which the PNDC has reluctantly conceded, since it has been trying to slow the rate of inflation and curtail the momentum of wages chasing prices. In April, 1983, the PNDC government reversed its economic policies and undertook, in co-operation with and at the insistence of the IMF, a drastic devaluation and a progressive reduction of the direct and indirect subsidies given by the government. This along with Ghana's worst drought had a severe impact in inflating prices, but it has also drawn vast new inflows of aid, mostly on soft, concessional terms to enable Ghana to rebuild its largely depleted infrastructure and capital equipment. Since 1983 the TUC and national union leadership has been engaged in a running argument with the government over the need to increase dramatically the minimum and other wages and to control prices on essential commodities (*West Africa*, 13 June 1983, p. 1426; 23 January 1984, p. 189; 20 February 1984, p. 409; 5 March 1984, p. 553). There is no doubt that the PNDC has been unable to improve the abysmal level of real wages that all workers now receive. Table 7.3 indicates that the real minimum wage declined still further in 1982 and 1983, to 12.5 per cent and 9.9 per cent, respectively, of its worth in 1963. PNDC wage/salary increases have involved higher percentage increases to lower paid workers to offset high inflation, creating a drastic compression of wages, so that higher level state and other employees have suffered a sharper decline in real wages. The decline in real wages in 1983 was in large measure caused by Ghana's worst drought and subsequent food shortages and 128 per cent inflation. Inflation eased to 28 per cent in 1984, when real wages increased marginally.

By 1985 the union leadership had become increasingly frustrated with PNDC political and economic policies and told Rawlings:

The National Leadership of the TUC cannot justify the present economic, social, and political situation . . . to our mass membership, for we ourselves are at a loss as to what has happened to the [PNDC's] noble objectives. [We condemn] the threats of mass retrenchments of workers; cutbacks in subsidies . . . ; the absence of any proper and consistent channels of participation in decision-making by the mass of the people. (TUC, 1985, p. 2)

Union leaders criticised strongly the PNDC's failure to consult labour and to carry out the measures of mobilisation and relief that it promised, the violation of trade union rights accompanying some retrenchments, and the frequent dismissal of state officials without public explanation. It demanded a reversal of the IMF austerity measures and increased state economic intervention. The PNDC has disparaged angrily some union claims and ignored others. While it has observed most union rights since 1983, it has refused to create a regular channel of communications between unions and government.

In conclusion, after having its leadership decapitated forcefully, new union leadership has resisted the takeover of the union movement by adaptation and the assertion of the legitimacy of elected representatives of the workers, reasserted the central role of the unions in wage determination through collective bargaining, and thrown up new officers through elections who are willing to contest with the PNDC vigorously–though there have been very few strikes. Union leaders threatened a general strike in early 1984 if recent drastic increases in key food prices were not reversed, which they partially were. However, even the relatively weak state in Ghana has a coercive capacity to restrict union independence and assertiveness when confronted with a continu-ing economic crisis. The high level of opposition which students, professionals, the churches, and teachers offered to the PNDC govern-ment in 1983 regarding military violence and a harsh budget may have contributed to the willingness of the PNDC to respect union autonomy and not to interfere in its elections. Thus, the survival of the unions' institutional integrity and central role in wage determination reflects both Ghana's structural conditions of political competitiveness and the investment in and commitment to an autonomous union movement by many leaders and workers. Both the pre-1982 (and re-elected) and new general secretaries share a commitment to an independent, revitalised, and militant union movement.

In Algeria competition between factions within the loosely organised FLN in the early 1960s and, to a lesser degree, in the late 1970s permitted political space for UGTA leaders and unions to struggle for autonomy for worker interests. In addition, the long union experience of some

UGTA militants made it relatively easy for them to distinguish the interests of the workers from those of the Army, the internal guerrillas, FLN *arrivistes*, and the indigenous bourgeoisie and to pursue UGTA's independent and distinct interests (Ottaway and Ottaway, 1970, p. 52). UGTA's most strongly articulated interests involved: its autonomy, though linked with the FLN; workers' right to strike; the development of worker self-management (SM) rather than state ownership of abandoned farms and industries; its right to organise all workers, urban and rural; reopening abandoned enterprises; and nationalisation of expatriate capital. UGTA started organising workers and linking up existing unions in early 1962. It was probably a rival to the FLN in terms of organisation. Though its membership figures were undoubtedly inflated–200 000 in 1963, 250 000 in 1965–its relative size and dynamism made it a force to reckon with in a state with weak and fragmented authority (Ottaway and Ottaway, 1970, p. 57).

UGTA became an early and fierce advocate of SM, led by the Federation of Electricity and Gas Workers, whose leaders and members were strong SM partisans (Boussoumah, 1982, p. 53). The decision of rural workers to continue their jobs though owners had fled became the opportunity to establish workers' SM as the basis of Algerian socialism. An enormous amount of voluntary work and ideological commitment by UGTA and FLN militants occurred during 1962–4 in an effort to establish Management Committees and Workers' Assemblies (Blair, 1970, pp. 54–88; Clegg, 1971, pp. 48–56). Numerous problems in SM arose on the valuable farms, employing 150 000 permanent workers, and contributing 60 per cent of agricultural production, and the 15 000 workers in the 450 SM firms: the same hierarchy of production relations tended to persist, now with ex-foremen as managers and heads of elected Management Committees; the Workers' Assemblies, composed largely of illiterate semi- and unskilled workers, were unprepared for their roles, had little to say in SM, and were largely apolitical; and class struggle between permanent workers of different skills and between permanent and seasonal or casual workers occurred (Blair, 1970, pp. 120–37; Hagel, 1976; Helie, 1973). While there were some major successes in SM enterprises, most because of their original poor condition became heavily dependent on the state for salaries, capital, and marketing, which permitted the state to exert increasing controls over them and to undermine them (Clegg, 1971, pp. 142–61).

The first response of Ben Bella and FLN leader Mohammed Khider to UGTA's growing organisation and assertiveness was to argue that strikes should be improper and illegal in a socialist society and to coercively impose pliant leaders in top UGTA offices in early 1963. However, there was sufficiently strong rank and file support and local union leadership intent on asserting worker interests to make it extremely difficult for a weak FLN to control labour by merely seizing UGTA offices. A high level of rank and file strikes in 1963–4, support for an unofficial leadership that had more legitimacy than the imposed leaders, and Ben Bella's need for labour against Boumedienne persuaded him to encourage the militants to continue to organise new unions and then to permit UGTA to hold another Congress to elect new leaders in 1965 (Ottaway and Ottaway, 1970, pp. 139–42). At the 1965 conference the FLN-imposed leaders were wholly rejected, popular leaders with long union experience elected, and a UGTA-Ben Bella alliance cemented (Ottaway and Ottaway, 1970, pp. 190–1, 211–13).

However, this alliance was shattered by Boumedienne's overthrow of Ben Bella in mid-1965. Confronted with the clearly more conservative orientations of Boumedienne's new government, UGTA leaders muted their protests in order to avoid a showdown and to retain their autonomy, whilst none the less criticising the government's failure to support SM enterprises and to consult with the unions and workers and its non-participatory political and economic strategies. They were partly protected and supported by several allies in Boumedienne's Council of Revolution and government. However, when these were eliminated in the aftermath of the attempted Zbiri coup against Boumedienne in 1967, the government started to impose strong pressures on the existing UGTA and federation leadership. There were intermittent arrests of UGTA leaders, attacks on local unions, divisions within UGTA on how to cope with the government's hostility, and finally the imposition of pliable leaders in UGTA positions in the 1969 Congress, stage-managed by a Boumedienne lieutenant. Disillusion spread in union ranks, and membership fell off sharply.

Although the 1963 Constitution recognised the legality of strikes, an FLN statement of 1965 declared that 'the right to strike has been proscribed purely and simply'. UGTA leaders, sensitive to the anomaly of strikes where workers (theoretically) exercise some power, have tended to consider that strikes in the 'socialist' sector are improper, in the private sector permissible. Several penal codes and the General Statute of Labour, 1978, indicate that to strike is a crime meriting imprisonment (Boussoumah, 1982, pp. 631–4).

During the mid- and late 1970s there was some resurgence of UGTA's power on a modest scale, prompted initially by Boumedienne's need for leftist allies to help implement his agrarian reform programme, which had run up against entrenched interests within FLN local units, and a programme of worker participation in the state corporations, where worker disinterest and bureaucratic authoritarianism and obscurantism yielded extremely poor performance. Some ideological differences within the FLN leadership, extraordinary public discontent with Algeria's bureaucracies (as revealed in the 1975 debate on the National Charter), and some factional competition among Algerian leaders once again opened some political space for a more independent and militant UGTA. When Col. Mohamed Yahyaoui was appointed the *responsable* for the FLN, he and Boumedienne were ready to permit a freer expression of worker representation. Wide-spread wildcat strikes during 1975 and 1977 (Table 7.2) suggest that the incumbent leadership was alienated from the rank and file, some union federations, and some wilaya (regional) organisations. In addition, there was great dissatisfaction with the continued resistance of many of the state corporations to the programme of worker management (*Gestion socialist des entreprises*). The Workers' Assemblies and Management Councils in which worker representatives were supposed to participate had been established in only eleven firms by 1974, 32 firms by 1975, and 51 firms by 1977, with a total of some 700 units among these companies, grouping some 150 000–200 000 workers (Grimaud, 1978). The process of drawing up an agreement with each state corporation, establishing the Assembly, and electing the Management Councils is a profoundly bureaucratised, paternalistic, sanitising exercise. The committee which selects candidates for Management Councils includes FLN leaders and technicians as well as UGTA representatives, leaving workers often dissatisfied with their candidates. UGTA's recurring protests that only UGTA representatives be involved has been ignored (Boussoumah, 1982, pp. 470–5). These institutions were permitting little substantive participation, because of management resistance and because the hyper-centralisation of Algeria's institutions permitted little leeway even to some state corporations (Nellis, 1977, pp. 547–52).

Col. Yahyaoui democratised the 1978 UGTA Congress in a way that had not happened since 1965. In contrast with the 1973 Congress, Yahyaoui insisted on a 'congress of workers and not of cadres' of the UGTA (Grimaud, 1973, 1978) involving self-criticism, resolutions being sent to Wilaya pre-congress for discussion, election of delegates by secret ballot, freedom of all delegates to speak at the Congress, and a Congress long enough (five days) for delegates to deal with the issues in a substantive rather than ritualistic fashion. Of 1000 delegates, representing 650 000 union members, 275 were manual, 144 technicians.

In the election of the 105 member National Executive Committee, the ballot was secret and permitted choices among three candidates. Twelve of the fifteen members elected to the National Secretariat were new, including the Secretary-General, Demene Debbih, an ex-CGT trade unionist and ex-Algerian Communist Party member. Moreover, the opening to the left was also clear in the election of several known members of the illegal Party of the Avant-Garde Socialists (PAGS) to the National Executive and the National Secretariat, (which grouped members of the illegal Communist Party and other leftist dissidents) (Grimaud, 1978).

However, with the death of President Boumedienne and the election of Colonel Chadli Benjadid, factional alignments within the FLN shifted. Colonel Yahyaoui, an UGTA ally, was an unsuccessful contestant for the presidency with Chadli, and Chadli soon removed him from FLN positions. By the sixth UGTA Congress in 1982, President Chadli was ready to curtail sharply the growing autonomy of the UGTA and various of its federations. The FLN press accused the UGTA Secretary-General of allowing militants, especially Marxists, who were not members of the FLN to occupy responsible union positions. At the Congress Debbih was also accused of responsibility for a large increase in strikes in 1980 and 1981 and for incidents of social conflict. These were partly caused by worker apprehensions at the restructuring and economising of state corporations to increase profits. In elections to the National Executive a large number of members lost their positions; Debbih was not re-elected as general secretary. The federations were accused of too much autonomy, headed by people who were elected rather than appointed, and all the federations were abolished, replaced by Secretariat-controlled professional sectors. President Chadli informed the Congress that it was not autonomous but a sector of the FLN (ARB/P, 5 May 1982, p. 6415). Within the FLN leadership under Chadli clearly no legitimacy is attached to the idea of relative union autonomy or elective representation.

It is doubtful that UGTA has played much of a role in advancing or maintaining the workers' standard of living. All state and parastatal salaries for different grades and for agricultural and urban workers are set by the government and not subject to collective bargaining, which occurs only in the small private sector. The Boumedienne government followed a policy of wage restraint and low spending on social services, apart from education, but it did generate enormous increases in employment. Large increases in the guaranteed agricultural and urban minimum and other wages in 1976 (25 per cent and 15.4 per cent, respectively), 1977 (31 per cent both), and 1978 (two increases, totalling 40 per cent and 33 per cent) followed the outbreak of a large number of wildcat strikes and an intensification of highly visible worker protests (Grimaud, 1978; see Table 7.2). The grievances largely involved wage claims. It is clear from the real government minimum wage index that inflation had reduced real wages since 1972 until the 1976 (for rural workers) and 1978 wage increases. The holding of the more open and critical UGTA congress in 1978 prompted the two large wage increases in that year. In 1976 and 1978 rural workers were given larger wage increases than urban workers, so that by 1980 minimum wages in both areas were equivalent – a measure taken to stem rural migration and increase agricultural production. Wage differentials in Algeria have also been kept lower than in many other countries. In brief, the more UGTA and its unions reflect the grievances of rank and file workers, the more coercive and controlling the state becomes. Hence, workers must organise protest activities outside the structure of the union.

In Ethiopia, once the Derg seized power, it outlawed strikes and demonstrations. The Ethiopian labour federation, CELU, had seen in the overthrow of the imperial government the opportunity to acquire the trade union rights that it had been denied – autonomy, the right to strike. It became more political and immediately challenged the Derg's right to rule, demanded a civilian democratic government, and reasserted its economic demands with a new general strike threat. The Derg promptly arrested CELU's top three leaders, and the strike threat vanished.

Virtually all political forces became radicalised in 1974 and after in Ethiopia, and the radicalisation of CELU and some of its unions was reflected in the emergence of a new leadership in 1975, a time of considerable disarray in the union movement. The Derg permitted new elections to be held – to their regret – and more radical leaders emerged, highly hostile to the Derg's monopoly of power. The underground Ethiopian People's Revolutionary Party (EPRP) developed support in some unions, how many is unclear. A September 1975 conference passed resolutions which rejected dictatorial military rule. CELU's resolution took the EPRP line that socialism required democratic rights for all oppressed classes, led by a workers' party (which EPRP was not, originally being composed of students and intellectuals). It threatened a general strike if union activities were obstructed. When workers distributing CELU's resolutions were shot in a mêlée, a partly successful general strike was undertaken. The Derg quickly arrested some 1500 union leaders, students and teachers, effectively eliminating CELU's capacity to act (Ottaway and Ottaway, 1978, pp. 109–11; Markakis and Ayele, 1978, pp. 151–4).

In late 1975 the Derg set up a tightly-controlled All-Ethiopia Trade Union (AETU), which sought to organise primarily among blue collar workers, while CELU had found its largest base of support among white collar and technical workers. By January 1977 AETU announced that it had organised 1341 local branches, with 287 000 members, an organisation greatly helped by the small, pro-Derg and Marxist MEISON party. Pro-CELU and EPRP supporters mounted some rearguard efforts to disrupt AETU organisation, such as assassinating the first two AETU secretary-generals in 1977. In turn, MEISON helped to organise armed defence squads among factory workers who played a crucial role in eliminating EPRP and other leftists from the unions and from the *kebelles* or neighbourhood councils in the period of intense violence during 1977 (Ottaway and Ottaway, 1978, pp. 186–7). CELU's experience illustrates the problems of an unarmed and relatively non-mobilised working class going to war with the state.

In Tanzania where TANU as a single party monopolised political choices and sought to monopolise organisation and legitimacy as well, the development of state controls over labour contrasted sharply with the way in which it occurred in Ghana, where a good deal of explicit and implicit bargaining occurred between union leaders and the state. In response to high strike levels in 1960–2, TANU sought to restrict strikes by introducing several pieces of legislation in 1962 which, in effect, made strikes illegal and substituted a process of conciliation and a labour tribunal (the Industrial Disputes Act, 1962). A Trade Union Act gave the government the power to appoint a federation of trade unions as the sole federation to which unions could belong, an attempt to heal a breach within the TFL. The government's concerns in making strikes illegal appear to have been largely economic at the time. By 1963 the government clearly attributed no value to an independent trade union, when the ex-TFL leader, Michael Kamaliza, now Minister of Labour, broached the possibilty to TFL leaders of integrating the TFL into his Ministry of Labour, an idea the TFL rejected. In early 1964, when the army mutinied and some trade union leaders apparently made known their sympathies, Nyerere had over 200 trade union leaders arrested, most of the existing union leadership. The government then abolished the TFL and all of the unions and established in their stead an almost totally non-elective bureaucratic institution, the National Union of Tanganyika Workers (NUTA), since renamed Jumuiya Ya Wafanyakazi Wa Tanzania (Bienefeld, 1979, pp. 572–3). NUTA is a completely centralised organisation, with no membership unions, only nine industrial sectors which correspond to some of the previous major unions. In addition, virtually all of its positions are appointive rather than elective.

addition, virtually all of its positions are appointive rather than elective.

Within a few years, and in response to NUTA's pursuit of collective bargaining, the government requested an ILO committee to study wages and introduced an income policy which limits pay increases to 5 per cent per annum. This annual increment, originally designed to reward productivity, is now distributed automatically (about 4.5 per cent) to parastatal employees (Valentine, 1983, pp. 56–7). Collective agreements negotiated also had to be submitted to the Permanent Labour Tribunal for approval. This largely took wage determination out of the hands of NUTA. The idea of limiting the size of wage and salary increases was not in itself objectionable, given Tanzania's economic capacities, the large increases won since independence, and the alleged impact on employment (Jackson, 1979, pp. 230–5). (All the fall in employment stemmed from cuts in the sisal workers; other employment grew.) The income policy robbed the workers' presumed representative of a crucial role.

The impact of the government's stringent labour control policy could soon be seen in the decline of strikes (Table 7.2). Strikes, strikers, and man-days lost all declined sharply after 1963–4, until by the early 1970s Tanzania indicated that it was having three strikes or none per year (lasting more than one day), which was clearly not accurate. Despite the flurry of strikes and protests during 1969–73, however, there was undoubtedly a decline in labour protests.

Was all this readily accepted? In 1965–6 worker complaints regarding NUTA's performance were extremely high. President Nyerere duly had an enquiry made into the sources of complaints about NUTA. The presidential commission of enquiry came out with substantial documentation of the widespread sense of NUTA's inadequacy and unresponsiveness (Tanzania, 1967). It was also recommended that the Secretary-General be elected, not appointed by the president. The government rejected all of the Commission's major recommendations but did decide to no longer have one and the same person act as NUTA Secretary-General and Minister of Labour.

Alternating repression with pro-labour policies, the government followed the strike banning legislation with a severance pay act and the dissolution of the union movement with an act to create a provident fund and a security of employment act. This required employers which wished to discipline or sack a worker to submit evidence to a newly created Workers' Committee, to be composed of elected workers.

After strikes in the newly nationalised state companies in 1969, Nyerere issued a directive instituting Workers' Councils, which were to be established in every state corporation in order to give workers some participation in management. However, whilst it is suggested by Jackson (1979, p. 239) that these councils have had a 'useful advisory role' he neglects to mention the workers' total rejection in 1971–2 of the idea that the Workers' Councils were of use or benefit.

The best measure of NUTA'S distance from rank and file workers was the attitude of workers towards NUTA when they took the occasion of the issuance of the party's guidelines on leadership to engage in widespread protests against factory managers. Generally, the workers declined to see NUTA representatives, to which NUTA reacted with increasing hostility. This was the most important outburst of labour unrest and strikes since the early 1960s, with about thirty strikes and protests from early 1971 to mid-1973. When the government complained, the workers ejected the managers and continued to work, in some instances asking the authorities to let the workers run the factory.

The government forced an end to the peaceful strikes and protests and reinstated the managers, jailing some strike leaders (Mapolu, 1972; Maseko, 1976; Mihyo, 1975, 1980). In another study of cases coming before the Labour Tribunal in the late 1960s and early 1970s, in case after case the grievance dragged on for years, with NUTA representatives absent or non-responsive. The grievances were finally brought to the Labour Tribunal only because of highly visible worker demonstrations before NUTA or TANU offices (Nyalali, 1975).

NUTA has not been in a position to safeguard workers' wages and salaries; the Nyerere government did so to some degree from 1963 (following increases) to 1974 but has permitted wages/salaries of all levels of workers to erode drastically since then. Table 7.3 indicates a gradual erosion in the minimum wage from its 1963 high to 1971. Minimum (and other) wage increases in 1972 and 1974 put the real wage above its 1963 base. But from 1974 to 1977 real minimum wages fell by 47 per cent, by 1979 by 57 per cent. Valentine has shown that real disposable income declined sharply during 1969–80 for all income earners (Valentine, 1983, p. 61), as in a desirable effort to create more equal earnings, the government has allowed inflation (plus progressive taxes) to create an enormous compression of wage/salary levels. In the context of real wage losses, this may have had negative consequences for productivity because of demoralisation, lack of incentives, and worker absenteeism to pursue other earnings (Valentine, 1983, pp. 64–6).

Jackson believes that Tanzanian workers have stopped striking because the Tanzanian government has offered them sufficient off-setting wages, benefits, security, and participatory opportunities. Bienefeld also notes the decline in strikes and suggests that it is not a consequence of repression, which he argues is relatively light. He suggests that while workers have lost all faith in NUTA, they continue to have substantial confidence that the TANU government represents fairly their interests (Bienefeld, 1979, pp. 584–5). I would suggest that while TANU can mobilise a great many people for essentially uncompetitive elections (despite the fact that two candidates contest each seat) that much of the mobilisation in Tanzania is ritualistic, without substance, without presentation of criticisms before the public. Even its major deliberative organ, the National Assembly, is almost entirely quiescent, (Kjekshus, 1974). I would suggest that Tanzanian workers do not strike because they have been systematically demobilised by a political system that fears criticism from below and supplements the mysticism of benevolence with adequate coercion.

CONCLUSION

It is relatively clear that trade unions in populist and radical states have had limited success in efforts to increase the power of workers and unions, safeguard or advance significantly the material interests of workers, or extend their political participation or influence over the management of the means of production. UGTA did make some major efforts to have self-management adopted as a significant source of worker power, but a state intent on demobilisation was unwilling to support an experiment that required nurturing. UGTA is pursuing the highly bureaucratised effort at socialist management underway in Algeria, but it permits little worker influence. The worker participation exercises in Tanzania have combined a ritualistic gesture with a co-optive design. The WDCs in Ghana, though inaugurated chaotically, involved a high level of participation by WDC and union representatives in the management of production relations at a time of upheaval, low capacity utilisation, and threats of lay-offs. In most firms union leadership has re-established itself as the pre-eminent representative of workers. Although managerial authority has been legally reinstituted, articulate and conscious union leadership persists, as do some WDCs (renamed CDRs), and has some capacities for mitigating and holding accountable state managers.

We possess too little information on workplace authority relations in Africa. But it appears that, among these cases, it is only the labour movement in Ghana, among some unions, which has had the structure and capacity to attend regularly to grievances at the local level. Algerian unions have intermittently had the capacity to reflect and assert worker interests, but militant representation and independent worker power is illegitimate in Algeria, as it is in Tanzania and Ethiopia where the unions have become solely creatures of their regimes. Algeria's proletariat is large, armed with sufficient experience of union militance, and suffers living conditions poor enough so that it will prove increasingly costly for the state to suppress worker protest without surrendering its disguise of embodying the interests of workers. There is substantial evidence that as a stable proletariat has come into existence there are many workers in Africa with a strong populist and trade union consciousness, more rarely a class consciousness (Sandbrook, 1981; Sandbrook and Arn, 1977; Kongings, 1980; Crisp, 1984). What the radical critique of trade unionism in Africa, discussed in the beginning, fails to take adequately into account is that these trade unions confront states with relatively high levels of coercive and co-optive capabilities and, though in some respects radical or populist, with little regard for the idea and consequences of an independent union and class conscious trade union movement.

Bibliography

African Research Bulletin/Political [ARB/P], monthly.

Bartimeus, B.T. (1963) *Progress Report to First Biennial Convention* (Accra: Industrial, Commercial, and General Workers Union).

Bienefeld, M.A. (1979) 'Trade Unions, the Labour Process, and the Tanzanian State', *Journal of Modern African Studies* 17, 4 (December): 553–93.

Blair, Thomas (1970) *'The Land To Those Who Work It': Algeria's Experiment With Workers' Management* (Garden City: Doubleday and Company).

Boussoumah, Mohammed (1982) *L'Entreprise Socialiste Algérie* (Paris: Economica).

Clegg, Ian (1971) *Workers' Self-Management In Algeria* (New York: Monthly Review Press).

Cohen, John *et al.* (1976) *Revolution and Land Reform In Ethiopia* (Ithaca: Cornell Univ. Rural Development Committee).

Corten, A. and Tahon, M-B. (1982) 'La formation accelerée de la class ouvrière: L'Experience algérienne', *Labour, Capital And Society* 15, 2 (November): 41–57.

Crisp, Jeff (1979) 'Union Atrophy and Worker Revolt: labour protest at Tarkwa Goldfields, Ghana, 1968–1969', *Canadian Journal Of African Studies* 19: 267–93.

Crisp, Jeff (1984) *The Story Of An African Working Class: Ghanaian Miners' Struggles, 1870–1980* (London: Zed Books Ltd).
Doctor, K.C. and Gallis, H. (1966) 'Size and Characteristics of Wage Employment in Africa: Some Statistical Estimates', *International Labour Review* 93, 2 (February): 149–73.
Friedland, William (1969) *Vuta Kamba: The Development Of Trade Unions In Tanganyika* (Stanford University Press).
Ghana (1961) *1961 Statistical Yearbook* (Accra: State Publishing Corporation).
Ghana (1968) *Report Of The Committee Of Enquiry Into The Recent Disturbances At Prestea* (Accra: State Publishing Corporation).
Ghana (1970) *Report Of The Commission Of Enquiry Into Obuasi Disturbances, 1969* (Accra: State Publishing Corporation).
Ghana (1983) *Economic Survey, 1981* (Accra: State Publishing Corporation).
Grimaud, Nicole (1973) 'Evolution du Syndicalisme en Algérie: Le IVe Congrés de L'UGTA', *Maghreb-Machrek*, 56 (April–June): 26–30.
Grimaud, Nicole (1978) 'Les Rélations de Travail en Algérie: Le Cinquième Congrés de L'UGTA', *Maghreb-Machrek*, 80 (April–June): 57–62.
Hagel, John (1976) 'Workers' Self-Management in Algeria: A Review', *Review Of African Political Economy*, 6 (May–August): 96–109.
Helie, Damien (1973) 'Industrial Self-Management In Algeria', *Man, State, And Society In The Contemporary Maghrib*, edited by I.W. Zartman (New York: Praeger), 465–74.
Iliffe, John (1970) 'A History of the Dockworkers of Dar es Salaam', *Tanzania Notes And Records* (71: 119–48).
Jackson, Dudley (1979) 'The Disappearance of Strikes in Tanzania', *The Journal Of Modern African Studies* 17, 2: 219–51.
Jeffries, Richard (1978) *Class, Power, And Ideology In Ghana* (New York: Cambridge University Press).
Jonsson, L. (1978) *La Révolution Agraire En Algérie* (Uppsala: Scandinavian Institute of African Studies).
Kjekshus, Helge (1974) 'Parliament in a One-Party State – the Bunge of Tanzania, 1965–70', *Journal of Modern African Studies* XII, 1 (March): 19–44.
Knauss, Peter (1980) 'Algeria under Boumedienne: the Mythical Revolution, 1965–1978', *The Performance of Soldiers As Governors*, edited by I.J. Mowoe (Washington: Univ. Press of America).
Konings, P. (1980) *The Political Potential of Ghanaian Miners* (Leiden: African Studies Center).
Kraus, Jon (1973) 'The Political Economy of Trade Union – Government Relations in Africa: The Struggle to Raise the Minimum Wage in Ghana', Paper, 'Workers Unions and Development in Africa' conference, Toronto.
Kraus, Jon (1977) 'Strikes and Labour Power in a Post-Colonial African State: the Case of Ghana', Paper, Seminar on Third World Strikes, The Hague.
Kraus, Jon (1979) 'Strikes and Labour Power in Ghana', *Development And Change* 10, 2 (April): 259–86.
Kraus, Jon (1979a) 'The Political Economy of Industrial Relations in Ghana', *Industrial Relations In Africa*, edited by U. Damachi, *et al.*: 106–68.
Kraus, Jon (1986) 'The Political Economy of Agrarian Regression in Ghana', *Africa's Agrarian Crisis*, edited by M. Lofchie and Stephen Commins (Boulder: Lynne Rienner).

Mapolu, Henry (1972) 'Labour Unrest: Irresponsibility or workers' revolution?' *Jenja*, 12: 20–23.

Markakis, John and Ayele, Nega (1978) *Class And Revolution In Ethiopia* (London: Spokesmen Books).

Maseko, I.J. (1976) 'Workers' Participation in TANESCO and Friendship Textile Mill', *Workers And Management*, edited by Henry Mapolu, 228–58. (Dar: Tanzania Publishing House).

Mihyo, Paschal (1974) 'Labour Unrest and the Quest for Workers' Control in Tanzania', *Eastern Africa Law Review* 7, 1: 1–64.

Mihyo, Paschal (1975) 'The Struggle for Workers' Control in Tanzania', *Review of African Political Economy*, 4 (November): 62–84.

Mihyo, Paschal (1980) 'Self-Management in Tanzania's Industrial Relations Experience', Paper, given at McGill University.

Nellis, John (1977) 'Socialist Management in Algeria', *Journal Of Modern African Studies*, XV, 4 (December): 529–54.

Nellis, John (1980) 'Algerian Socialism and Its Critics', *Canadian Journal of African Studies*, XIII, 3.

Nyalali, F.L. (1975) *Aspects of Industrial Conflict: Case Study Of Trade Disputes in Tanzania* (Dar: East African Literature Bureau).

Ottaway, David and Marina (1970) *Algeria: The Politics Of A Socialist Revolution* (Berkeley: University of California Press).

Ottaway, David and Marina (1978) *Ethiopia: Empire in Revolution* (New York: Africana Publishing Company).

Palloix, Christian (1980) 'Un Essai sur la Formation de la Classe Ouvrière Algérienne', *Revue Tiers Mode* XXI, 83 (July–September): 559–74.

Roberts, Thomas (1982) 'The Algerian Bureaucracy', *Review of African Political Economy*, 24 (May–August): 39–54.

Sandbrook, Richard (1975) *Proletarians And African Capitalism: The Kenyan Case* (New York: Cambridge University Press).

Sandbrook, Richard (1981) 'Worker Consciousness and Populist Protest in Tropical Africa', *Research In The Sociology Of Work, I*, edited by R. and H.I. Simpson, 1–36 (Greenwich: Jai Press).

Sandbrook, Richard and Arn, Jack (1977) *The Labouring Poor And Urban Class Formation: The Case Of Greater Accra* (Montreal: Centre for Developing Area Studies).

Scalfani, Joseph (1977) 'Trade Unionism In An African State: The Railway And Ports Workers' Union Of TUC (Ghana)' (Ph.D. thesis, Brown University).

Silver Jim (1978) 'Class Struggles in Ghana's Mining Industry', *Review Of African Political Economy*, 12 (May–August): 67–86.

Southall, Roger (1984) 'Third World Trade Unionism: Prospects for Equity and Democratization in the Changing International Division of Labour', *Canadian Journal of Development Studies*.

Tanzania (1967) *Report Of The Presidential Commission On The National Union Of Tanganyika Workers* (Dar es Salaam: Government Printer).

Tanzania (1967a) *Proposals Of The Tanzania Government On The Recommendations Of The Presidential Commission Of Enquiry Into The National Union Of Tanganyika Workers* (Dar es Salaam: Government Printer).

TUC (Trades Union Congress, Ghana) (1978) 'Report of the Activities of the TUC (Ghana) to the 2nd Quadrennial Congress, Winneba, 18–20, 1978' (Mimeo).

TUC (1983) 'Report of the Interim Management Committee of the TUC (Ghana) Presented by Brother E.E. Aboagye, Chairman, to Extraordinary Delegates Congress, Kumasi, 13–17 December 1983 (Mimeo).

TUC (1985) 'Position Paper on the Present National Situation by The Executive Board of the TUC.' 18 February, addressed to the Chairman, PNDC (Rawlings).

Valentine, Theodore (1983) 'Wage Adjustments, Progressive Tax Rates, and Accelerated Inflation: Issues of Equity in the Wage Sector of Tanzania', *African Studies Review* XXI, 1 (March): 51–71.

West Africa (London), weekly

World Bank (1981) *World Development Report, 1981* (New York: Oxford University Press).

Zack, Arnold (1967) 'Trade Unionism Develops in Ethiopia', *Boston University Papers On Africa*, edited by J. Butler and A.A. Castagno (New York: Praeger) 104–14.

8 Unions, State and Capital in Western India: Structural Determinants of the 1982 Bombay Textile Strike

Debashish Bhattacherjee[1]

'We are the oldest industry. Why should we earn less?' (a worker from Century Mills)

INTRODUCTION

Between January 1982 and February 1983, 250 000 textile workers from sixty-odd mills in Bombay were on strike. According to one estimate, accounting for dependency rates, more than a million people were directly affected (*New York Times*, 4 May 1982). What started as a wage and bonus strike in a few mills in late 1981 spread to the entire industry. Plant-level trade union struggles evolved into a unified political struggle against not only textile capital, but more importantly against the state-recognised union nexus forced on to the industry since 1947. The recognised union saw its membership fall by more than half between October 1981 and March 1982 (*Business India*, 27 September 1982). The strike was costly: a production loss of about 100 million rupees a month, and according to the (then) commerce minister, 58.42 million man-days were lost by August 1983 (*Times of India*, 10 August 1983).

The strike had spillover effects on other occupations in other industries and services. Notably, the city police and public transport workers' sympathy strikes that resulted in violence and arrests. Workers who had returned to their villages created moments of unity with agricultural labourers. Worker–peasant links were forged spontaneously which took the established left by surprise (Bakshi, 1984). Finally, in November 1984, Datta Samant, the man who led the strike and now

211

heads the newly founded *Kamgar Aghadi* (approximately Workers' Party) won a parliamentary seat in New Delhi from a Bombay working class constituency.

The 1982 strike was the longest in Indian urban labour history; it was a political struggle that seemed almost 'inevitable' given the post-independence developmental trajectories both in the political economy of the industry as well as in the labour market and union movement. In this sense, the strike represented a prolonged moment where labour, capital, and state had to confront and overcome 'barriers' created by an objective crisis of accumulation in the industry as well as by a subjective crisis of legitimacy in the labour movement (de Janvry, 1981, p. 1).

The purpose of this chapter is to derive the above trajectories that culminated in the strike by truncating the post-independence developments in the union–state–capital matrix in the Bombay textile mill[2] industry into two periods: the first one from 1947 to about early to mid-sixties, and the second period from the mid-sixties to the present.

Although industrial production in India quadrupled from 1950–75, growth was uneven between those years. Thus from 1951–65, industrial production increased at an average annual rate of 7.7 per cent per year, the rate falling to 3.6 per cent between 1965–75 (Nayyar, 1981), since then rising to 5.1 per cent between 1976–83.[3] Political economists have identified various factors associated with the industrial stagnation in the mid-sixties: the inefficiencies of state regulation (Bhagwati and Srinivasan, 1975), the segmented nature of economic growth (Bagchi, 1978), the structure of demand (Nayyar, 1981), and the terms of trade between agriculture and industry (Mitra, 1977). In the Bombay textile industry all these factors played a role in its crisis. We shall see below how textile capital restructured itself after the mix-sixties aided by the cumulative effects of governmental economic policies and state control over the direction of the union movement and bargaining relationship between capital and labour.

The periodisation fits well tendencies in the overall Indian trade union movement and in the 'industrial relations system' in general. The first period was characterised by state-sponsored unions typically negotiating give-away contracts with relatively homogeneous employer associations or with the state as employer in the public sector. This period saw the growth of legalism, consultationism, 'government' unions, and was a period where 'responsible' unionism was promoted subject to the maintenance of industrial peace. Trade unions were asked to restrain their excessive consumption demands for the sake of economic development (Mehta, 1957) as the state attempted to co-opt a segment of the unionised proletariat under the guise of nationalism. To reduce inter-union rivalries based on differences in political affiliation, the Code of Conduct was passed in 1958. The ruling Congress Party, in close collaboration with its trade union federation, the Indian National Trade Union Congress (INTUC) unilaterally determined the 'representative' union in an industry through verification of membership dues by the regional registrar of trade unions. The latter method invariably led to exaggerated claims, but since INTUC's claims were most often backed up by the legal industrial relations apparatus, it was they who turned out to be the most representative (Chatterjee, 1980). The state adopted a policy of paternalism towards trade unions as democratically run union elections were ruled out.

The second period witnessed the growth of worker and union demands in the form of shopfloor control originating at the *point of production*. Production or factory politics whose object is the 'political apparatus of production' (Buroway, 1982), the latter defined as those institutions, labour laws, and industrial relations machinery that contain and channel the union movement so as to sustain state power over it, emerged as the dominant factor in labour struggles and negotiations, instead of 'governmental' or union-party politics. Inter-union rivalries were more based on plant-level issues than on party affiliations. This trend reflected the changing uneven and combined nature of industrialisation: modern firms in the engineering, transportation, consumer durables, and chemical industries bargained with militant plant-level unions often not affiliated to any parliamentary political party and large wage and non-wage gains were secured. Fractions of capital in the more advanced firms in the capitalist periphery realised both the efficacy and efficiency of bargaining bilaterally with unions that (at least) represented median shopfloor interests rather than the electoral objectives of ruling class parties. Demographic factors have also played an important role in changing worker and union demands in the second period: a growing proportion of the industrial workforce were post-1950 entrants and had not been participants in pre-independence working class struggles (Sane, 1966).

Given the above developments, the Bombay textile strike (as well as on-going labour struggles in Ahmedabad textiles) emphasises at one level worker militancy with regard to a permanent decline affecting a major sector of the Indian textile industry. Demonstration effects from modern, profitable firms in other industries have convinced textile workers of the economic and political advantages of plant-level bargaining, and of leadership rooted at the point of production.

However, to the extent that segmented and disarticulated capitalist development does not expand the industrial proletariat in proportion to the growth in manufacturing output, large segments of the industrial workforce remained locked in old, decaying firms and industries, and in the face of massive urban migration characteristic of peripheral urbanisation, a mode of labour control whereby a ruling class sponsored union is the only one that is recognised, effectively guarantees the intervention of governmental politics into the realm of production politics thereby setting limits on the development of struggles.

Correspondingly, the 1982 strike was a spontaneous and sustained effort on the part of workers to insulate the two levels of politics. The outcome of their attempt is as yet uncertain, but it is likely that it may have differential effects across firms in the industry, depending on their location in the advanced–backward continuum.

This particular strike, the longest and largest strike in modern Indian labour history, took place in an industry which historically had fueled the industrialisation process in India and elsewhere, and in India (specifically Bombay) was the battleground and birthplace of militant trade unionism. The following discussion of the structural determinants of the 1982 strike is a contrast to the extensive work on the Bombay textile proletariat undertaken by Morris (1955) and Ralph James (1958, 1959) in the 1960s which, working within a modernisation and a neoclassical economics discourse, showed the relative ease with which the labour market with its sociological determinants generated a 'committed industrial workforce'. The Bombay mill industry was studied in isolation from broader macroeconomic forces due principally to the writers' central concern about the emergence or making of the Bombay working class.

The present essay describes the effects of macroeconomic shifts on the structure of the industry and the consequences of those effects of the labour process which in turn shape and constrain union goals and activities. Relating the determinants of the strike to broader macro changes enables one to generalise about labour relations and union goals in the Indian economy in the present period where import-substitution policies and paternalistic factory regimes have given way to free market economics and repressive state actions against the labour movement. Segmented industrialisation has led to a fracture within the unionised proletariat: on the one hand, a small but growing proportion of relatively young and educated workers in the modern highly capital-intensive (often multinational) firms bargaining militantly at the plant-level and securing relatively high real wages and exerting considerable influence over working condition outcomes; on the other hand, a large proportion of relatively older workers in dying industries (such as jute and textiles) who, finding themselves steadily more marginalised, have become an increasingly volatile segment of society.

The labour crisis in the Bombay textile mills is like a prism that reflects the possible future of labour–capital relations in India, and provides possible lessons to union activists and rank and file militants about strategic choices and options in firms and industries undergoing similar technological pressures and structural retrogression. The failure of the strike exposed the political opportunism of most of the 'established' trade unions as well as the limitations of sustained union struggle without a coherent political programme and organisational structure as was the case with Samant's Maharashtra Girni Kamgar Union (see Table 8.1). The political and economic benefits that derive from plant-

Table 8.1   Key to unions in Bombay textiles

Girni Kamgar Union	GKU; formed during the struggles in the late twenties, affiliated to the All India Trade Union Congress (AITUC), the union wing of the Communist Party of India.
Rashtriya Mill Mazdoor Sangh	RMMS; formed in 1945, affiliated to the Indian National Trade Union Congress (INTUC), the trade union federation of the Congress Party.
Mill Mazdoor Sabha	MMS: formed in 1948, affiliated to the Socialist Party. Merges with GKU in 1953.
Mumbai Girni Kamgar Union	Organisation of opposition unions formed in 1959. By 1970 all unions leave except the GKU.
Kapad Kamgar Sangathna	KKS; formed in 1968 by the Lal Nishan Party (LNP), a regionally based Communist Party, and affiliated to its trade union wing, the Sarva Shramik Sangh (SSS).
Lal Bavta Mill Mazdoor Union	LBMMU; formed in 1970 when Community Party of India (Marxist) (CPI-(M)) was formed, affiliated to the Centre of Indian Trade Unions (CITU).
Girni Kamgar Sabha	GKS; active briefly in 1979 during the Janata regime; and splits into various factions.
Girni Kamgar Sena	Surfaces as a result of the breakup of GKS, trade union wing of the regionally based communal and reactionary party, the Shiv Sena.
Marharashtra Girni Kamgar Union	MGKU; formed by Datta Samant on the eve of the 1982 strike. MGKU later forms the basis of the Kamgar Aghadi Party (KAP).

level unionism were made amply clear to Bombay's textile workers who reside with workers from other modern firms in working class neighbourhoods. During the post-strike period, factory committees in the more modern textile mills have partially succeeded in negotiating plant-level agreements and the expectation among workers is that an overall pattern will be set for the entire industry based on these agreements.

The discussion below is organised as follows: first, I discuss the economic trajectory of the textile industry, especially the Bombay mills, by identifying factors that affected its evolution in the two periods: the economic effects of government regulation, internal and external determinants of the commodity composition of output, and in the second period, the stratification within the Bombay mills. Second, concurrent developments in the labour market and union movement are discussed in relation to the unchanging nature of state intervention in the labour relations process through the two periods. Third, a sequential description of the events and effects of the strike are discussed. The conclusion offers some reasons as to why the strike failed, why the state mobilised its repressive apparatus in crushing the strike, and comments upon Samant's role in the strike as well as the future possibilities of trade union mobilisation and expansion through the newly formed *Kamgar Aghadi Party* (KAP).

DEVELOPMENTS IN THE INDUSTRY: GROWTH, 'SICKNESS' AND DIFFERENTIATION

In global terms, the continuing importance of the textile industry for peripheral economies can be judged by the fact that in 1976, before international trade restrictions were tightened (Kapoor and Jain, 1982), one third of their exports going to the developed countries were constituted of textiles and clothing (Barrat-Brown, 1982). Even though continuously 'crisis-ridden', the Indian cotton textile industry still maintains its high position in the Indian economic hierarchy in terms of absolute total employment, industrial income, and export earnings that it generates. The majority of the textile firms are owned and operated by Indian capitalists ('business houses') and a growing proportion are state-owned.

Bombay, the industrial and financial hub of India, where blue and white collar workers dominate the city's population, is the centre of textile activity: according to one estimate, 40 per cent of the nation's textile output and almost 60 per cent of India's textile exports are produced here (*India Abroad*, 15 October 1982). According to employment figures collected by the Labour Bureau, close to a quarter of all textile workers in India work in the Bombay mills (*Indian Labour Statistics*, various issues). One third of the weaving capacity is located in Bombay. The single most important factor underlying the setback to industrial production in 1982–3 at the all-India level, contributing to a decline of about 1.3 percentage points in the rate of industrial growth, was the textile strike in Bombay (*Economic Survey 1983–84*, p. 22). Prior to the strike, 47 private mills employed 136 812 workers and 13 state-owned mills employed another 28 314. The *badli* (temporary) workers in the industry amounted to 100 000. Although the proportion of *badli* workers increased rapidly between 1950–80, the number of permanent workers fell by nearly 20 per cent (Anand, 1982).

Before we proceed to a discussion of macroeconomic changes in the textile industry, a comment on the taxonomy of the industry is in order. Textiles are produced in the mill and decentralised sectors. There are three types of mills: spinning, weaving, and composite. The dominant feature of post-independence economic history of the Indian textile industry has been the changing competitive alignment between these sectors, and the uneven development within the mills.

During the early fifties, as the domestic market was effectively protected, the cotton mill industry grew as did per capita cloth consumption[4] and exports. During this period there was little product differentiation, the industry was more competitive, and textile capital relatively homogeneous (Desai, 1983). However, due to the state's priority in building up a strong infrastructural foundation during the first two Five-Year Plans, investment and hence technological change in the consumer goods industry, especially textiles, was forestalled. The state resorted to a planned policy of curbing the growth of the mill sector by discriminating in favour of the handloom and powerloom units since the latter were more labour-intensive. The discrimination took various forms: subsidies, excise duties charged on mill output, a freeze on loomage in 1956, and preventing the emergence of vertically integrated units. Then in 1964, the Controlled Cloth Scheme was introduced whose purpose was to ensure that a part of the total cloth output would be sold at controlled prices.

Pressure from the millowners reduced the obligatory ration from 50 per cent to 25 per cent in 1968, and by 1971 it was made voluntary (Eapen, 1978). A consequence of this scheme was that various private mills were declared 'sick' and taken over by the state-run National Textile Corporation whose specific job was how to rehabilitate these old mills. In addition, this period saw the steady rise of the decentralised sector[5] in terms of cloth production (see col. D, Table 8.2), and the steady decline of the relative profitability of the cotton textile industry.[6] Attempting to resolve this crisis, the government enacted a comprehensive textile policy in 1978 whose new 'multi-fibre' approach shifted the controlled cloth obligation away from the private sector mills to the state run 'sick' sector. In so doing, the state finally yielded to the pressures from the strongest sections of the private sector within the industry which had contested the scheme ever since its initiation (Eapen, 1978).

Analysts commenting on the mill crisis have related the transition from the initial period of technological stagnation to the restructured second period (the mid-sixties onwards) to movements in macroeconomic variables such as the changing terms of trade in favour of

Table 8.2   Trends in selection variables for the cotton textile industry (all-India level data)

Year	A	B	C	D	E
1957	—	—	—	27.13	59.63
1959	—	—	—	31.53	55.44
1961	—	—	119.60	33.53	46.16
1963	111	108	79.41	39.40	41.02
1965	119	114	84.61	39.71	47.25
1967	142	126	79.60	43.70	59.37
1969	171	134	62.35	45.90	63.09
1971	234	162	79.00	46.20	68.13
1973	277	184	60.57	45.90	85.12
1975	277	222	137.27	49.80	130.61
1977	369	229	38.46	53.30	201.18
1979	—	—	—	57.50	141.19
1981	—	—	—	61.20	164.42

A   Index Number of Raw Cotton Prices, 1962 = 100. *Source*: Annual Reports of the Bombay Millowners' Association, 1966, 1972, 1976.

B   Index Number of Cotton Manufacturers' Prices, 1962 = 100. *Source*: As in A above.

C   Ratio of Gross Profit as percentage of total capital employed in cotton textiles to that of all-industry average (in %). *Source*: Reserve Bank of India Bulletin, November 1967 and Indian Textile Bulletin, 1979.

D   Percentage of total cloth production by non-mill (i.e., handloom and powerloom) sectors. *Source*: Indian Textile Industry Annual, 1964 and Handbook of Statistics on Cotton Textile Industry, 1982.

E   Exports of mill-made cotton cloth. Value in crores of rupees (1 crore = 10 million). *Source*: Indian Textile Bulletin, 1970–1979.

agriculture, in this context the prices of raw cotton moving much more rapidly than prices of cotton manufacters (Eapen, 1978; see cols A and B in Table 8.2), and the changing nature of internal demand conditions. The decline in per capita consumption of cotton and the rise in the consumption of synthetic/man-made fibres since the mid-sixties have accelerated divergences within the mills in terms of the changing commodity composition of output. Eapen (1978) links a shift toward finer counts and man-made fibres to the adverse change in the income distribution profile since the mid-sixties, leading to a further spread between the consumption propensities of various income classes, which in turn effected a truncation of the demand structure. Chandrasekhar (1984) criticises this interpretation since it ignores the substitution effect that may have taken place among middle and working class consumers (in the sixties) towards more durable cloth and hence the observed rise of the sum total of fine, superfine, and blended output during 1970−7. Whether it was the adverse income distribution profile or the substitution effect among consumers that led textile capital to shift to finer varieties, there is little doubt that the changing pattern of market demand adversely affected the overall level of profitability of the mills.

As a result of both the cumulative effects of state regulation on the structural direction of the textile industry (Desai, 1983) as well as the effects of cyclical movements of macroeconomic variables, unintended and until the strike, little noticed effects took place on the structure of firms within the industry: differences in productivity, quality, price, advertising, market segments, and the marketing system were observed (Mote and Bijapurkar, 1977; Iyer *et al.*, 1977). As Chandrasekhar (1984, PE30) observes 'the outputs of what are generally termed textile firms cannot be treated as "technical substitutes" (for each other) in the sense that they satisfy broadly similar needs'.

The post-sixties saw the emergence of two sectors almost mutually exclusive in terms of market segments they catered to: an oligopolistic segment, where a few firms produced for the internal upper class and export market, where product differentiation, advertising, and brand name rivalries took precedence over price competition, and high profit margins made technological change possible; and a non-oligopolistic sector where price is determined by market conditions subject to the collusion between producers (Chandrasekhar, 1984). The low level of productivity in the latter pre-empts technological change and hence undermines its competitiveness in relation to the decentralised sector. It is no surprise that while industrial sickness prevails over most of the mills, some of the most successful 'blue chip' firms in India are to be found in this industry[7].

The overall trends are mirrored in Bombay; in fact, the emergence of the modern textile sector in India primarily reflects changes in the Bombay mills beginning in the early sixties. Various researchers have identified two, and even three, groups or strata of firms in Bombay (Union Research Group, 1982). Prior to declaring many of the private sector mills 'sick', large profits were siphoned out, and reinvested either in more profitable non-textile industries[8] or in expanding profitable mills by introducing dyeing and processing facilities (Chandrasekhar, 1984). As a result of these inter-mill dynamics, the mill industry became heavily concentrated: according to Chhachhi and Kurian (1982), nine 'business houses' (the representative unit of Indian capital) control about 70 per cent of the private mills in Bombay.

Prior to the structural inter-mill differentiation, the Bombay Mill-owners' Association was a relatively homogeneous organisation equally representing all the millowners. The private mills that were declared sick and taken over by the state were typically controlled by small capital that could not compete with the powerloom and handloom sectors due to either their inability to mobilise resources for modernisation and expansion or due to the fact that the surplus that they did manage to accumulate was invested in speculative activities. The mills that modernised and diversified their composition of output and survived the crisis are typically controlled by large 'business houses' (e.g., the Tatas, Birlas, and the Mafatlals) with access to investable finances due to their economic control over other areas of productive activity in Indian manufacturing and finance. The private sector mills that did manage to barely survive were compelled to collude with each other due to competitive market pressures. The emergence of the oligopolistic and competitive sectors of the Bombay textile industry has to be understood in terms of their ownership (large versus small capital) and hence their economic power over access to investable resources. One crucial effect of the strike was the creation of permanent division within the Millowners' Association between employers in the modern mills and those in the weaker private mills. The association between these different strata of mills to the events that preceded and followed the strike will be discussed in the section on the strike.

So far the discussion has abstracted from external trade and global parameters in the production of Indian textiles. Data indicate that since the early fifties India's position in the world textile trade has been on the decline: in 1963 India was the fourth largest exporter of textiles but by 1982 it had declined to thirteenth. Similarly, India's share in the EEC market declined from 14.6 per cent in 1963 to a mere 3.8 per cent in 1982, and in the US the share dropped from 25 per cent in 1963 to only 2 per cent in 1982 (*Herald Review*, 2 September 1984). The shrinking external market reflects the dominating presence of Brazil, South Korea, and Taiwan whose industries structurally responded to the worldwide shift in demand for finer varieties of cloth and man-made fibres. Growing protectionism and a complex system of international tariff agreements have made competition fierce.

Textile export earnings as a percentage of total export earnings fell by 15.5 per cent between 1950/1 to 1966/7 rising to record levels in the late 1970s (Nayyar, 1976; see col. E, Table 8.2). Although exports constituted an alternative market source, they were never fully exploited in the first period as profitability in the captive internal luxury market was high and margins were maintained due to oligopolistic practices among mills with exporting potential (Chandrasekhar, 1984). In the 1970s, the blue chip mills have started getting into the export market thanks partly to generous cash subsidies and entitlements for export promotion given by the state.

The uneven development within the mills was one primary structural determinant of the 1982 strike. It was also an important reason for the virtual demise of the 'recognised' union in terms of real worker following, and it challenged union and factory politics of other established unions in the industry.

UNIONS AND THE STATE IN THE LABOUR MARKET

On the eve of independence, the Communist Party of India had widespread influence over the Bombay textile proletariat. The GKU, the communist union (see Table 8.1), became the dominant force claiming a membership in 1945 or approximately 13 per cent of the total work force (Morris, 1955). The new ruling Congress Party, realising the potential political force of the textile proletariat in that it represented at the time of independence something close to ten per cent of the total Indian proletariat and as they were concentrated in a small but crucial geographical area (Morris, 1955), founded the Rashtriya Mill Mazdoor Sangh (RMMS) in 1945 which was to be affiliated to the Indian National Trade Union Congress (INTUC). The unidirectional chain of command between the Congress and its unions affiliated to the INTUC was made clear by Nehru: 'it is imperative that in all political matters all Congressmen working in the INTUC should treat the Congress as its supreme body and abide by its Code of Conduct' (cited in Chatterjee,

1980, p. 152). Since then, affiliated unions when faced with a choice between the party's patronage and a restive working class movement always opted for the former.

It is against this background that the Bombay Industrial Relations Act of 1946 (popularly called the 'Black Act') was passed. This act became the single most important cause of nearly all future conflict in the industry as it denied workers the choice of a democratically elected representative union. The Act simultaneously imposed a bureaucratised form of industry-wide bargaining which actively encouraged the growth of 'sound organisations' which would support state policy of compulsory conciliation and arbitration (Morris, 1955; James, 1958).

The representative union on the shopfloor was decided not on the basis of elections but by verification of membership dues by the registrar of trade unions. Technically, an 'approved' union could become the 'representative' union if it could claim a membership of at least 15 per cent of the industry's work force. The proof lay in the dues' receipts. If the membership fell below this percentage for three consecutive months other 'approved' unions could file for de-recognition. If the registrar de-recognised the RMMS, the Industrial Court would invariably reverse the decision, as it did in 1950 during the bonus struggle led by the Mill Mazdoor Sabha (the socialist union, see Table 8.1). This system of determination coupled with the industry-wide bargaining structure created a zero-sum situation for the opposition unions.[9] The act also put restrictions on strike activity by making a legal strike a virtual impossibility as there was compulsory arbitration over disputes. In addition, any matter referred for conciliation had to traverse a prolonged period of adjudication, during which strikes and other forms of worker protest could not be employed. In brief, the RMMS sacrificed its right to strike in order to secure de facto exclusive bargaining rights.

The state-sponsored system of industry-wide bargaining introduced by the BIR Act aided wage standardisation which was imposed on the labour market in 1947. Then, in 1949, the Decasualisation Scheme eliminated arbitrary hiring practices and jobber power by effectively 'insulating' the industry-wide labour market (James, 1959). At one level, occupational hiring took place to train and control the supply of skilled and semi-skilled workers. In the hiring halls, *badli*[10] or substitute workers served as a reserve army within the industry's labour market picking up the excess demand during high absenteeism and/or business upswings. The structure of the labour market kept wages low and allowed millowners flexibility thereby facilitating technological change. The RMMS achieved marginal wage and working condition gains by bargaining away its right to delay technological change (James, 1959).

The mid-1950s to the mid-1960s saw the growth of legalism with the RMMS entrenched in its pseudo-representative status. Attempts by opposition unions to secure gains were invariably diffused by the RMMS, as in the twelve-day strike in 1966. In 1956, more than half the work force was enrolled in a single day's membership drive by a joint front of opposition unions, but the RMMS continued its monopoly. By the end of the fifties, the opposition unions realised the futility of dislodging the RMMS through legal means (Chhachhi and Kurian, 1982).

The inter-mill differentiation process in the mid-sixties had profound effects on the labour market: (i) the combination of jobs and the abolition of various job categories decreased employment by 16 per cent between 1960 and 1980 (Chhachhi and Kurian, 1982), (ii) women's employment fell from 20 per cent of the total Bombay textile work force in 1950 to 3 per cent in 1971 (Asian Seminar, 1975) as, consequent to technological changes, women workers crowded into unskilled jobs,[11] (iii) the weaker mills competed by increasing third shift operations (see col. E, Table 8.3), and (iv) textile wages relative to other industries fell from 120.2 in 1962 to 99.3 in 1975.[12]

At the all-India level, labour productivity increased by 56 per cent and real wages rose by only 5 per cent between 1951–64 (Chatterjee, 1980). In Bombay, real living standards of the working class fell (see col. B, Table 8.3) and the monthly expenditure of an average textile worker exceeded his disposable income by nearly 50 per cent (Report on an Inquiry into Indebtedness Among the Textile Workers in Greater Bombay, 1975). Even so, the RMMS refused to bargain militantly for changes in the cost-of-living provisions. Thus, although these were revised in 1973, it would seem that the complicated method of calculation involved enabled millowners to give 'with one hand only to take away with the other' (Chhachhi and Kurian, 1982, p. 269).

Certain segmentationist tendencies in the textile labour market began to develop due to the internal reorganisation of the labour process occurring at varying rates between and within the mills. In the early seventies few mills increased their recruitment of apprentices in designated trades under the Apprentices Act (Annual Review of the Labour Situation in the Bombay Cotton Textile Industry, various issues). According to one estimate, a quarter to a third of the total Bombay cotton textile work force in 1981 were employed in these 'blue-chip' mills (*Times of India*, 3 December 1981). The militancy of the more skilled workers in the modern mills enabled them to secure wages above the

Table 8.3   Trends in selected variables in the Bombay mill industry (five-year average)

Years	A	B	C	D	E
1947–51	14.16	—	3766	75 558[†]	11.00
1952–56	10.53	—	1757	7670	17.10
1957–61	8.74	—	2755	4450	22.26
1962–66	14.66	119.0	2286	4655	30.98
1967–71	15.24	173.0	1803	2487	36.10
1972–76	19.04	260.0	708	1418	42.12
1977-81	23.54	364.4	1702*	—	44.34
1982	29.60	490.0	—	—	47.30

A   Absenteeism Rates. *Source:* Annual Reports of the Bombay Millowners' Association, 1972; Maharashtra Labour Gazette, 1976; Indian Labour Journal, 1982.

B   Consumer Price Index for Industrial Workers in Bombay, 1960 = 100. *Source:* Handbook for Labour Statistics, 1973 and 1976; Indian Labour Yearbook, 1980.

C   Average Size of Strikes (= total strikers/total strikes). *Source:* Labour Gazette, Bombay and Annual Review of the Labour Situation in the Bombay Cotton Textile Industry, 1960 to 1977. * refers to 1977 only.

D   Average Duration of Strikes (= total man-days lost/total number of strikes). *Source:* as in C above. † the large average duration between 1947–51 reflects mass participation by the Bombay textile proletariat in the independence movement.

E   Ratio of average daily employment in the third shift to first shift. *Source:* Annual Reports of the Millowners' Association, 1972, 1976, 1983.

industry-wide bargaining agreement. This is partly evidenced by the fact that the ratio of private (a proxy for the modern mills) to public (a proxy for the older mills) sector average annual earnings of cotton textile workers initially fell from 1.88 in 1965 to .92 in 1973, reflecting the power of the RMMS during this period, but then rose to 1.00 in 1979 (Handbook of Labour Statistics, various issues). The latter are all-India level data, and thus may not accurately capture the extent of wage differentials in the Bombay mills. However, more recent data from Bombay suggests the existence of larger wage differentials between the modern and the older mills: for example, a study in 1982 found that inter-firm wages (fixed pay) varied by multiples of 2.5 for similar skilled and semiskilled occupations (Union Research Group, 1982). The linking of bonus payments to productivity and profit in 1975 led to further spreads. Workers in the more progressive mills clearly realised the efficacy of exerting their independent power at the firm level.

The *badli* workers in both sectors of the industry were at the mercy of the RMMS. After working for years as substitute workers, the *badli* could only hope for permanent status if they allied themselves with the RMMS. In a critical sense, the *badli* had the most to gain with the abolishment of the BIR Act and the consequent downfall of the RMMS.

The wage and working condition drifts outside the industry-wide agreement during the mid-seventies reflected a crucial change at the *point of production*: the establishment of a dual centre of power, i.e. informal mill committees (often led by younger workers not affiliated to any of the established unions) militantly bargaining at the plant level. The latter took place in the leading mills, whereas in the backward and state-owned mills, the RMMS collaborated with the employers, exerted forms of economic coercion on the workers,[13] and relied on the state to intervene in all matters of conflict. Workers in the plant-level committees in the leading mills could exert their collective voice at the shopfloor due to the specific skills they had acquired with the machinery that was introduced during the modernisation process. In addition, their residential proximity to workers in other advanced non-textile firms demonstrated to them the political and economic outcomes of militant plant-level bargaining. This demonstration effect is crucial in understanding the initial militancy of the strike.

The crucial coalition of the *badli* workers and those in the modern sector could not turn to the established unions for mobilising workers in the entire industry. The latter were organisationally tied to governmental policies and were structurally dependent on their formal channels of communication with 'outside' leadership. The communist unions had lost considerable credibility due to their misguided opposition to decentralised bargaining (Pendse, 1981), and in their inability to deal with attacks from the right, namely the Girni Kamgar Sena (see Table 8.1). They failed to change their strategies with the changes taking place in the 'hidden abode of underdevelopment' (Buroway, 1982). Consequently, the left unions failed to capture industries that had what Luca Perrone called 'positional power'.

As a result of the BIR Act and the restrictive nature of the industrial relations system, strikes came to involve steadily fewer workers and became progressively shorter, albeit offset by increasing absenteeism (cols A and D, Table 8.3). However, since the mid-1960s such strikes as these were increasingly directed at the RMMS and the coercive industrial relations apparatus in which it took part and thereby promoted. In mid-1979, the RMMS as well as the local Congress leadership were shocked when 70 per cent to 80 per cent of all workers in the industry struck work for a day to protest against the wage agreement that was signed.

Thus, the strike of 1982 represented a culmination of long-run structural tendencies both in the political economy of the industry, reflecting wider economic developments in India, and in turn, the specific changes in worker demands that have occurred since the early to mid-1970s at the point of production.

THE STRIKE OF 1982: EVENTS AND EFFECTS

The 1982 strike was a radical departure from previous (post-independence) strikes insofar as it was totally a strike of the workers, one which they had themselves collectively decided upon independent of the existing unions in the industry. In October 1981, as was usual, workers from a few of the mills in the advanced sector struck for higher bonus payments. Disenchanted with the RMMS during the 1979 negotiations, the workers approached Datta Samant,[14] an ex-physician and by now a powerful union leader in Bombay, to lead the entire industry into what was likely to be a prolonged struggle against the millowners, the RMMS, and the BIR Act. Samant, who initially began to work with the quarry workers, was also part of the INTUC but left the Congress(I) Party when he was refused an election ticket in 1980. Consequently, he decided to organise workers 'independently' and penetrate the Bombay union movement on his own: the colour of his organisation's flag changed from the traditional Congress Party's tri-colour to a fist rising out of a smoke stack.

Prior to the textile strike, the Samant had broken the credibility and strength of various left unions by militantly negotiating significant wage and non-wage increases (often of the magnitude of 50–70 per cent) for workers in the engineering, pharmaceutical, chemical, automobile and consumer goods industries in Bombay (Patankar, 1981). Samant built up a powerful reputation among the Bombay proletariat as his leadership was based on articulating worker demands at the point of production, and rejecting bourgeois legality in the labour courts. His successful strikes (prior to textiles) were mainly, if not exclusively, in the high-profit sector of the economy with low elasticities of demand for labour. All contracts were negotiated at the firm levels.

The textile struggle was to be industry-wide. Samant was initially reluctant; he warned the workers that it was to be a long-drawn-out battle. The workers were militantly prepared and Samant was overwhelmed by their spontaneity[15]. The RMMS leadership predicted that Samant's entry into the textile industry would spell his demise (*Times of India*, 2 December 1981). Realising that the struggle could not be carried out on the bonus issue alone, Samant attracted the two most volatile components of the textile labour force; first, the nearly 100 000 *badli* workers, and second, the younger, more recently recruited workers from the more modernised firms in the industry. His initial demand reflected this coalition in that he required that wage and especially bonus payments should be more closely related to the profitability of the firm and that all *badli* workers should be accorded permanent status[16]. Furthermore, whereas before January 1982, Samant had negotiated bilaterally with a textile processing plant, the possibilities now opened up as he formed his own union, the Maharashtra Girni Kamgar Union (MGKU), which attracted a large number of workers from both the RMMS and the GKS. Indeed during the initial phase of the struggle, all non-INTUC unions (GKU, LBMMU, KKS; see Table 8.1) joined the strike under the aegis of the Trade Union Joint Action Committee (TUJAC), whilst at the national level, INTUC alienated itself from the labour movement by being the only federation not to have supported the All-India General Strike on 18 January 1982 which was called and supported by eight trade union centrals (*Times of India*, 19 January 1982).

It was an unfortunate time to have commenced the strike. During the last quarter of 1981, the economy was in a recession with growing demand stagnation and stockpiles of unsold inventories. The problem was more acute in the Bombay textile industry and the employers estimated that a few weeks of strike would be beneficial as stocks could be sold and profits realised (Parikh-Baruah, 1982). However, as time went on, employers and the state realised that Samant should be kept out of the industry at all costs. Predictably, because the MGKU had not applied for 'legal' recognition, the strike was declared illegal. Meanwhile, an attempt by the MGKU to file for de-recognition received only half-hearted support from the left unions and hence proved futile. The established left unions saw the MGKU as a threat, as they feared competition on what was previously their own terrain. The left unions tied as they were to party directives could not comprehend a mass union struggle without a vanguard. It was clear from the beginning that the trade union bureaucrats in New Delhi wanted to see Samant fall with the crushing of the strike (Bakshi, 1984).

State intervention in the form of armed police and 'central industrial security forces' patrolled the mill areas and the surrounding working-class residential suburbs. But as the connection between the state and the RMMS became increasingly explicit, the strikers' initial economic demands gave way to more far-reaching calls for the removal of the RMMS and the BIR Act, a process of politicisation which was premised on the very high level of solidarity continuously maintained and reproduced throughout the strike. Hence, while mill committees were formed to provide continuous links between the leadership and the rank and file, clerical, supervisory, and technical staff also joined the fray, and such was the level of support that there was not even need for strikers to implement picketing to keep scabs away from work. Rural workers and peasants around Bombay collected funds to support the workers on strike, and the GKU provided money to each worker with school-going children and various other unions in the city together contributed about ten million rupees (*Probe*, August 1982).

By August 1982 about 100 000 workers had left the city[17] and returned to their villages, where many engaged in countering anti-strike propaganda, supporting local peasant and agricultural unions, and organising local textile workers. In response, local RMMS activists who served as a link between the Bombay millowners, the Congress Party, and the local power structure, co-operated with the landed elites and the police to pressurise workers to return to work. At around this time, millowners from the more modern mills began to voice a desire for reaching a quick settlement with Samant on his own terms on a firm-level basis. However, both the Millowners' Association, which was by now fractionalised, and the RMMS remained adamant that both the MGKU and the strike must be broken. It should be pointed out if the employers in the modern mills had settled over the bonus issue earlier on, the strike need not have spilled over to the entire industry. Employers in these mills did not foresee a prolonged struggle; a few months would have cleared their accumulated stocks and business would have been back to normal. For these employers the long strike involved heavy losses. For employers in the backward mills the long strike had generated expectations that the state would bail them out as it had in the past. The duration of the strike heightened the inherent fractionalisation between small and large textile capital represented by the Millowners' Association.

This period was also marked by rising working-class militancy in the city. When the Bombay police strike occurred the army was called in and five people were killed; and when the municipal government employees together with workers in engineering, pharmaceutical, and chemical industries went on strike, the state government called in twenty companies of the Central Reserve Police in addition to the 22 000 strong city police (*The Statesman*, 20 October 1982).

During this period of prolonged struggle, the state widened and tightened political controls over the labour movement. In June 1982, two bills were passed to amend the Indian Trade Union Act of 1926 and the Payment of Wages Act. The latter legitimised the check-off of union dues. This could potentially increase union strength but more likely would lead to a greater collusion between employers and corrupt union leaders (Tulpule, 1982). By the bill amending the Trade Union Act, the state would assume unlimited powers to interfere into the affairs of unions not subservient to it (Tulpule, 1982). By the Settlement of Disputes Bill, employees in hospitals, educational institutions, service and village industries were required to resort to binding arbitration to resolve any conflict. Furthermore, after the police strike, the state declared that policemen would have no trade union rights (*The Statesman*, 11 October 1982). At the tripartite National Labour Conference convened by the central government and held in New Delhi on 18 September 1982, a 'unanimous' recommendation was made that a strike in any firm or industry must have the support of at least 60 per cent of the workers (*The Statesman*, 8 October 1982). Predictably, INTUC was the only union federation attending the conference.

As 1982 passed, the workers became steadily pauperised and by mid-1983, 57 of the mills re-opened and most of the workers resumed work, although the millowners terminated the employment of a large number of workers who had been activists during the strike (*Business Standard*, 23 July 1982). In addition, 15 000 workers were retrenched because of rationalisation of the labour process within the mills (*Business Standard*, 23 July 1982) and another 15 000 migrated to the powerloom sector in Bhiwandi, a few miles outside Bombay (*Economic Times*, 16 September 1983). In sum, the industry shed a quarter to a third of its work force.

Workers who returned to work found that conditions had worsened. Skill distinctions had broken down, work intensity had increased, those who were demoted or retrenched received no compensation, and management began rotating workers on the shopfloor to prevent communication (*Business Standard*, 24 August 1983). Workers in the modernised sector found their wages to be higher than before, but with an increased workload. The Bombay Millowners' Association issued directives to the mills that they refrain from rehiring workers who reported to their unions, thereby forcing the workers to return to work through the RMMS. However, management in the modern and progressive mills started ignoring and censuring the RMMS workers at the shopfloor by forcing them to work rather than merely exercising their coercive power at the factory gates as they had done in the past (*Business Standard*, 21 August 1983). Once more we note the difference between the Associations' position and that of the management in the more modern mills.

The employers cleared their accumulated stocks and rationalised job structures by retrenchment. The losses by way of fixed capital and storage costs were probably offset by savings in wages at a time of stockpiling and recession. The demand for the expansion of looms for export-orientated production was granted (*Business Standard*, 24 August 1983) and the biggest concession in the 1984/5 budget was to the textile industry. During the strike, due to lobbying by cotton growers, price support for raw cotton growers was guaranteed by the state in spite of declining demand (Abraham, 1981).

The state had used a two-pronged strategy to crush the strike: on the one hand it demoralised the workers by denying them the right of public assembly, i.e. Section 144 of the National Security Act was imposed all over the mill area; on the other hand, the police by jailing, harassing, and beating up the leadership, mill committee secretaries, and activists, isolated them from the rank and file.

The strike may have created permanent fissures within the Millowners' Association[18] and negotiations will tell the extent of cohesion left in the organisation. The general secretary of the Association expressed the need for capital to move out of Bombay, a city 'dominated by workers' (*Probe*, August 1982). Although the textile workers may have lost the strike, the Bombay working class gained. In the recent (November 1984) national elections, Samant won as a member of the *Kamgar Aghadi* Party.[19]

CONCLUSION

As discussed earlier, the state during this prolonged struggle mobilised its repressive apparatus in crushing what could have been a political class-based movement articulated through factory-level agitations and massive street 'morchas' (marches). It was the first time that the state witnessed the articulation of worker demands moving upwards from below, and throwing up its own organistion, rather than being instigated by party-affiliated unions trying to capture constituencies for future parliamentary elections. The state-controlled bureaucratised industry-wide bargaining system had in the past enabled the government to buy off worker discontent through RMMS by granting meagre pay raises and/or by taking over 'sick' mills, thereby maintaining employment and hence in a relative sense maintaining industrial peace. The emphasis on the public sector and the concomitant role of the state in maintaining profit levels in the private sector enabled a paternalistic factory regime to rule over the Bombay mills.

The second period, after the structural differentiation within the industry, saw the rise of worker demands of a different nature: grievances originated at the point of production. Workers went on shorter strikes over working conditions, unfair disciplinary action, discrimination against non-RMMS workers, and arbitrary dismissals. It is these phenomena that gave rise to militant informal shopfloor committees. Given the state's reluctance to formulate a new textile policy and its hesitance to take over any more financially abandoned mills, the RMMS began to lose its autocratic control over the workers. The alliance between the *badli* workers and those in the modern mills was a politically explosive situation since it had the potential of spilling into other state-run services and enterprises (for example, the dockyards and the railways) where the state had consistently pursued a policy of segmenting the labour markets of permanent and temporary workers, thereby curtailing unity in their union struggles. In the present period when the Indian state is successfully trying to attract foreign capital in the form of joint collaborations, especially in the high-tech communications industry which requires a fairly disciplined work force, giving in to Samant and the mass of Bombay's textile workers could have had adverse effects on foreign capital inflows. It was a test of power that the Indian state had to win given its ambitions of transposing the Indian social economy into the twentieth century. In a regional political context, the defeat of the RMMS and the formal abolishment of the BIR Act would have meant a humiliating defeat for the Congress Party in Bombay, the centre of Indian capital. The anti-labour legislation that was passed during and after the strike prevented union growth in the service sector and educational institutions, thereby curtailing union solidarity across industrial sectors. They also put severe restrictions on the internal workings of union federations affiliated to opposition parties. A new autocractic factory regime has come into operation that is now being countered with militant firm and plant-based unionism. The rise of 'employees' unions' in the advanced industrial sector of Bombay indicates the new trend in the union movement of dealing with capital at the firm-level and bypassing altogether the state-controlled industrial relations apparatus.

For Bombay's textile capital, the crushing of the strike enabled the industry to undertake a massive rationalisation process. As Mr. Podar, the head of the Podar group of mills admitted: 'The rationalisation and cut-backs in staff which would normally have taken 3–4 years have now been done in one' (*India Today*, 31 July 1983). The rationalisation of job structures and the labour process would enable the advanced mills to compete internationally, especially since the state gave in to their export-orientated production demands.

The crisis in the textile industry in terms of its relative decline in the Indian industrial hierarchy was one important reason by the strike failed. The long duration of the strike had pauperised the workers, and in the absence of sufficient strike funds (in spite of financial support from other labour organisations) the textile workers were forced to return to work due to economic realities that had taken their toll during the prolonged struggle.

In spite of Samant's leadership, the strike was a working-class event. The struggles both at the shopfloor and at the working-class residential suburbs were carried out by workers themselves. At this level one can argue that Samant was only a 'spearhead of an upsurge' (Pendse, 1981) representing the frustration of the textile workers with bourgeois industrial relations norms and ineffective, bureaucratic labour courts. Given that Bombay's working class history is replete with instances of progressive petty-bourgeois activists leading labour struggles (Pendse, 1981), the 'Samant phenomena' has to be understood as a continuation of earlier trends. The *crucial* difference however between earlier labour leaders and Samant is that while the former organisers worked under directives from political parties, the latter represented the coalescence of spontaneous worker struggles rooted at the point of production in the transformed, economically diversified industrial landscape of Bombay. Thus, on founding the KAP, Samant said: 'We have now realised that the workers should have a political party controlled by them rather than be controlled by the parties' (*Illustrated Weekly of India*, 10–16 February 1985).

A criticism of Samant's strategy during the strike needs to be made. The sustained militancy that was required in the city to maintain the political thrust of the strike was clearly undermined by sending the workers back to their villages. Perhaps, Samant should have settled in the sixth month when the employers in the modern mills wanted to reach a quick settlement. These tactical errors were due in part to his misplaced equation of the textile industry with other advanced sector firms where he had attained success. The movement also suffered from a lack of any systematic organisational structure, due partly to Samant's personal reluctance to participate in broader, united struggles over other political issues. However, his reluctance to work with the Trade Union Joint Action Committee was clearly related to the established left's hostility towards him as an 'independent' labour leader.

In spite of the fact that the strike was crushed and many pauperised workers returned to the mills, Samant won a landslide victory from a densely populated working class suburb as a candidate from the KAP in the national elections. Pre-election surveys consistently pointed out that the workers did not blame Samant, and refused to believe that he had destroyed the textile industry (*Bombay*, 7–21 January 1985). The rise of the KAP was a victory not only for the textile workers but for the Bombay working-class movement as a whole. The KAP represents new tendencies in the union movement as it reflects critical changes in the industrial structure, capital–labour bargaining relationship, and changes in union structure in Bombay since the mid-1970s. The proliferation of employees' unions (many of them in Bombay working with Samant and the KAP) and the formation of a few federations of employees' unions poses new possibilities to union activists and worker militants in sectors dominated by subservient and politically-constrained unions. It is important for new Marxist and radical organisations to bore from within the KAP to prevent any ruptures that may occur between party activists and shopfloor militants due to personality cults and political opportunism that may develop among the KAP leadership.

Notes

1. This study is funded by the American Institute of Indian Studies and by the Graduate College of the University of Illinios. The author thanks Annapurna Shaw and Roger Southall for extensive comments on earlier drafts.
2. This essay is about the crisis in the mill industry. Textiles are also produced in the powerloom and handloom sectors, together known as the 'decentralised' sector. Decentralised implies the absence of governmental controls on output and quality, and also implies the absence of any enforcement of existing labour laws. While the handloom sector employs workers in the rural and semi-urban areas and is run by the various state governments, the powerloom sector is largely owned and operated by individual entrepreneurs who often have close economic ties to large capital that control the mills in the private sector. This connection is difficult to prove and is always denied by the millowners. The strike exposed this connection, to the extent that output produced from some of the powerloom mills during the strike

bore the stamp of some of the private mills in Bombay.

3. Computed from *Economic Survey*, 1983–4, p. 1.

4. Per capita availability of cloth (in linear metres) increased from 10.99 in 1951 to 16.85 in 1964 (Chandrasekhar, 1984).

5. Especially in the powerloom sector, due to its 30–40 per cent lower wage rates, low level of trade union organisation, and government protection in the form of lower taxes and 'reserved areas of production'.

6. See col. C. Table 8.2; 1975 was an exceptional year as the emergency declared by Mrs Gandhi disciplined labour demands.

7. Fourteen firms in the industry were among the top industrial giants in India in 1976/7. (See Chandrasekhar, 1984.)

8. Such as consumer durables, upper-class residential construction, etc. (See *Business India*, 2 October 1978.)

9. The INTUC rationalised the BIR Act thus: 'the choice of a union must be a well considered long-term choice, which will be possible only on the basis of an insistence on continuing paid membership of a union. Temporary excitement and propaganda will influence the result of an election by secret ballot' (cited from Karnik, 1966, p. 165).

10. Badli workers served as a 'general, undifferentiated labour power, transferable within work processes and expendable'. (Union Research Group, 1982, p. 67).

11. In 1971, 81 per cent of the women workers were in unskilled occupations (*Asian Seminar on Conditions of Workers*, Bombay, 1975).

12. Ratio of average annual earnings of cotton textile workers to that of the all-industry mean. The data given is all-India level; given Bombay's weightage, these serve as fairly good proxies. (*Indian Labour Statistics*, 1979.)

13. Badli workers often had to pay the RMMS to retain their jobs.

14. The phenomena of Datta Samant in contemporary Bombay labour history is well presented in Pendse (1981). The bonus struggle in the 22 mills was initially led by the Girni Kamgar Sena (see Table 8.1) before the workers approached Samant.

15. One point that Samant never ceased to make in all his interviews at this time was his total amazement at the collective spontaneity of the workers.

16. Samant's initial demands were: (1) a flat wage increase of Rupees 250–400 per month for different categories of workers, (2) permanency to nearly 100 000 badli workers, (3) increase in leave facility, and (4) additional wages to workers deployed by mills having carried out automation and modernisation.

17. According to a survey carried out by the Lal Nishan Party reported in *Probe*, August 1982.

18. Senior officials at the Employers' Federation of India, Bombay (in private communication with the author) suggested that apparently there were only 12–15 members left in the association after the strike. This fact remains unverified.

19. Interestingly, he convincingly defeated Roza Despande, the daughter of the veteran communist S.A. Dange who had led earlier earlier struggles in Bombay textiles, who stood on a Communist Party of India ticket that was supported by the Congress (I) Party.

Bibliography

Abraham, Amrita (1981) 'Textile Industry, Cotton Prices and Datta Samant', *Economic and Political Weekly* 16: 2119–21.

Ahmedabad Institute of Labour Studies (1975) *Report on an Inquiry into Indebtedness Among the Textile Workers in Greater Bombay* (Ahmedabad: AILS).

Anand, Javed (1982) 'The Tenth Month: A Chronology of Events' in *The Tenth Month: Bombay's Historic Textile Strike*, Factsheet 1, 1–14 (Bombay: Centre for Education and Documentation).

Asian Seminar on *Conditions of Workers, especially women workers in textile industries* (1975) (New Delhi: AITUC).

Bagchi, A.K. (1978) 'On the political economy of technological choice and development', *Cambridge Journal of Economics* 2: 215–32.

Bakshi, Rajni (1984) 'Datta Samant, the Left and the Textile Strike', *Imprint* July: 68–75.

Barrat-Brown, Michael (1982) 'Developing Societies as Part of an International Political Economy'. In *Sociology of 'Developing' Societies*, edited by Hamza Alavi and Teodor Shanin, 153–71 (New York: Monthly Review Press).

Bhagwati, Jagdish and T.N. Srinivasan (1975) *Foreign Trade Regimes and Economic Development: India* (New York: Columbia University Press).

Bombay Millowners' Association (various annual issues) *Report of the Mill-owners' Association* (Bombay: BMOA).

Bombay Millowners' Association (various annual issues) *Review of the Labour Situation in the Bombay Cotton Textile Industry* (Bombay: BMOA).

Buroway, Michael (1982) 'The Hidden Abode of Underdevelopment: Labor Process and the State in Zambia', *Politics and Society* 11: 123–68.

Chandrasekhar, C.P. (1984) 'Growth and Technical Change in the Indian Cotton-Mill Industry', *Economic and Political Weekly* 19: PE22–PE39.

Chatterjee, Rakhahari (1980) *Unions, Politics and the State: A Study of Indian Labour Politics* (New Delhi: South Asian Publishers).

Chhachhi, Amrita and Paul Kurian (1982) 'New Phase in Textile Unionism?', *Economic and Political Weekly* 17: 267–72.

Desai, Ashok, V. (1983) 'Technology and Market Structure Under Government Regulation', *Economic and Political Weekly* 18: 150–60.

Eapen, Mridula (1977) 'Emerging Trends in Cotton Textile Consumption', *Social Scientiest* 5: 93–119.

Eapen, Mridula (1978) 'The New Textile Policy', *Social Scientist* 6: 75–8.

Employers' Federation of India (various annual issues) *Handbook of Labour Statistics* (Bombay: Examiner Press).

Government of India, *Economic Survey 1983/84* (New Delhi: Government of India Press).

Government of India, Ministry of Industry, Office of the Textile Commissoner, *Indian Textile Bulletin* (various issues) (Bombay: Government of India Press).

Government of India, Ministry of Industry, Office of the Textile Commissoner, *Indian Textile Bulletin Annual* (various issues) (Bombay: Government of India Press).

Government of India, Ministry of Industry, Office of the Textile Commissoner,

Handbook of Statistics on Cotton Textile Industry (various issues) (Bombay: Government of India Press).

Government of India, Ministry of Labour and Employment, Labour Bureau, *Indian Labour Statistics* (various annual issues) (New Delhi: Government of India Press).

——, *Indian Labour Journal* (various issues) (New Delhi: Government of India Press).

——, *Indian Labour Yearbook* (various annual issues) (New Delhi: Government of India Press).

Government of India, *Reserve Bank of India Bulletin*, November 1967 (New Delhi: Government of India Press).

Government of Maharashtra, Office of the Commissoner of Labour, *Labour Gazette* (various issues) (Bombay: Government of Maharashtra Press).

Iyer, B.V. P.C. Mehta, T. Narasinham and A.R. Garde (1976) 'Product Standardization in Cotton Textile Industry' in *Some Aspects of Textile Policy*, 41–50 (Ahmedabad: Indian Institute of Management).

James, Ralph C. (1958) 'Trade Union Democracy: Indian Textiles', *Western Political Quarterly* 11: 563–73.

James, Ralph C. (1959) 'Labour Market Insulation and Technical Change: Rationalization in Bombay Cotton Textiles', *Economic Weekly Annual* 11: 217–21.

de Janvry, Alain (1981) *The Agrarian Question and Reformism in Latin America* (Baltimore: Johns Hopkins Press).

Kapoor, M.C. and S.K. Jain (1982) 'Changing Patterns of World Production and Trade in Cotton Textiles', *Economic and Political Weekly* 17: M31–M35.

Karnik, V.B. (1966) *Indian Trade Unions: A Survey* (Bombay: Manaktalas).

Mehta, Ashok (1957) 'The Mediating Role of Trade Unions in Underdeveloped Countries', *Economic Development and Cultural Change* 6: 16–23.

Mitra, Ashok (1977) *Terms of Trade and Class Relations* (London: Frank Cass).

Morris, D.M. (1955) 'Labour Discipline, Trade Unions and the State in India', *Journal of Political Economy* 33: 293–308.

Mote, V.L. and Ashoke Bijapurkar (1977) 'Profitability, Cost Structure and Finances of the Cotton Textile Industry' in *Some Aspects of Textile Policy*, 1–28 (Ahmedabad: Indian Institute of Management).

Nayyar, Deepak (1976) *India's Exports and Export Policies in 1960s* (Cambridge: Cambridge University Press).

Nayyar, Deepak (1981) 'Industrial Development in India: Growth or Stagnation?' in *Change and Choice in Indian Industry*, edited by A.K. Bagchi and Nirmala Banerjee (Calcutta: K.P. Bagchi and Co.) 91–118.

Parikh-Baruah, Manju (1982) 'Bombay Textile Strike', *Economic and Political Weekly* 17: 939.

Patankar, Bharat (1981) 'Textile Workers and Datta Samant', *Economic and Political Weekly* 16: 1981–2.

Pendse, Sandeep (1981) 'The Datta Samant Phenomenon', *Economic and Political Weekly* 16: 695–7 and 745–9.

Sane, G.D. (1966) *The Indian Working Class: Size and Shape* (New Delhi: AITUC).

Tulpule, Bagaram (1982) 'Bombay's Textile Workers' Strike: A Different View', *Economic and Political Weekly* 17: 719–21.

Union Research Group (1982) 'The Wages of Wrath', in *The Tenth Month: Bombay's Historic Textile Strike*, Factsheet 1, 60–81. (Bombay: Centre for Education and Documentation).

*In addition to these references, the following newspapers and magazines were used as sources: *Bombay, Business India, Business Standard, Economic Scene, Economic Times, Herald Review, Illustrated Weekly of India, India Abroad, India Today, New York Times, Probe*, the *Statesman*, and the *Times of India*.

9 Women, Work and Collective Labour Action in Africa

Jane L. Parpart

Much has been written about labour and trade unions in Africa, but rarely from the point of view of gender. Yet women in Africa have been drawn into waged labour much less than men. The migrant labour system has depended on unpaid female labour in the rural areas, while peasant producers here benefited from unwaged female labour on family farms. Where women have worked for wages, they have for the most part performed the least skilled, most insecure jobs. Many work without union protection, and when they belong to a union, rarely take a lead in union affairs.

As a result, scholars have generally neglected women when analysing labour and trade unions in Africa. In contrast, this chapter argues that women deserve more attention, both as workers and as protesters. Women workers have frequently supported strikes and other forms of union-directed collective action. Where they have circumvented union officials and sought separate solutions, this has been more a consequence of patriarchal union structures than an absence of worker consciousness or commitment to collective labour action. Also important, workers' wives and women in worker communities have played a crucial, and little studied, role in collective labour protests. These actions throw doubt on assumptions of female passivity and suggest a need to incorporate women into the analysis of African labour. This chapter is an effort in that direction.

WOMEN AND WAGED LABOUR – THE COLONIAL PERIOD

During the colonial period, waged labour was predominantly a male affair. Colonial employers followed western gender stereotypes that typecast women as domestic caretakers rather than waged employees. As a result, most waged jobs were offered to men. The migrant labour system deliberately fostered this sexual division of labour by excluding women at the site of production, leaving them to carry out reproductive work in the rural areas. In peasant economies, women continued to perform both productive and reproductive work, but cash rewards lessened. Male farmers dominated cash crop production, often aided by gender-biased colonial officials. Women worked long hours producing cash crops, but often reaped few benefits (Wright, 1983, pp. 83–4). When machinery was introduced into agriculture, women frequently lost their jobs to machines run by men. The oil mills in Nigeria, for example, undercut traditional female rights to oil kernels, turning oil production into 'man's work' and therefore man's profit (Nwabughuogu, 1981, p. 270).

In protest, some women fled to towns where the male monopoly of waged labour shunted them into the informal sector. Urban women survived on their wits and hard work. They lived by trading goods and services, often including their own bodies. Some became wealthy, but most struggled to survive. Men usually controlled the more lucrative trade, leaving women to live off petty trade in food and beer, and the sale of domestic and sexual services. Beer-making and prostitution were often illegal, and therefore uncertain income sources (White, 1983; Robertson, 1984, pp. 33–52).

Some women earned wages, but usually in unskilled, insecure and badly-paid positions. In Mozambique, for example, women performed the worst jobs in the cashew industry (Penvenne, 1985, p. 4). Women workers predominated in simple agricultural tasks. In 1951, Tanzanian women composed 5 per cent of the total waged labour force, 80 per cent of them employed in the agricultural sector, often for seasonal sorting and minor processing work on harvested crops (Bryceson, 1980, pp. 16–17). In Kenya, women performed much of the drudgery of coffee picking (Presley, 1978, p. 3). More South African women worked in wage labour than any area of sub-Saharan Africa, particularly after the first World War, when secondary manufacturing developed which depended on female labour. Although white women had greater opportunities, and eventually moved more into the service sector, in every category, South African women of all races performed the least skilled, most insecure jobs.

Female wage earners throughout the continent were poorly paid as well. The Kenyan coffee pickers received pitiful and sometimes non-existent wages. Between 1900 and 1933, Mozambique's minimum wage law set women's wages at about 50 per cent of male wages. Women porters, for example earned half the male wage (Presley, 1978, p. 4;

Penvenne, 1985, p. 4). In South Africa, female domestics usually received a third less than their male counterparts. Female factory workers experienced similar wage difficulties (Bradford, 1985, p. 334).

And everywhere on the continent, most women continued to rely on some help from men. Only a few wealthy traders and professionals could support families on their own. Most waged women still depended upon the waged earnings of male relatives and husbands. This dependence had important implications for women's role in labour struggles.

WOMEN AND COLLECTIVE LABOUR ACTION: COLONIAL AFRICA

Because so few women participated in wage labour, and even fewer played a role in trade union activities, African women have been largely ignored in colonial labour studies. Yet a re-examination of the evidence suggests the need for a new approach. Recent studies, and a broader definition of protest, reveal considerably more collective labour protest among women workers than has been assumed. Just as important, workers' wives, female dependants and women in working-class communities strongly supported labour protests, disproving their assumed obliviousness to labour–capital conflicts.

African women working in the informal economy have long understood the importance of collective action to defend economic interests. In the 1920s, West African market women established associations which were explicitly organised to protect their interests. When necessary, these organisations exerted political pressure. Women also organised collectives to improve productivity and profits (Little, 1972, p. 280; Mba, 1982, pp. 188–9). Prostitutes established informal unions which enhanced profits and job security by regulating prices and territory (Little, 1973, pp. 98–9). Sometimes traditional institutions were transformed into economic pressure groups. Margaret Strobel cites an example in the Lelemana Association of Mombasa which became a means for collectively controlling women's affairs in the 1940s (Strobel, 1979, 163–6). In other cases, new institutions lobbied for a better economic deal. The Sudanese Women's Union, established in 1951, promoted equal pay for equal work for urban working women, and fought to extend a seven-day maternity leave to forty days with pay (Fluehr-Lobban, 1977, p. 137).

Sometimes unwaged female producers collectively confronted capitalist innovations which threatened their economic survival. In

1946, women in the Onitsha Province of Nigeria rioted to protest the establishment of Nsula oil mills and managed to get them closed. Four years later, anti-oil mill riots flared up again in Calabar Province, and at Ibiono outraged women beat up the president of the Native Council, boycotted the mills, and by denying them fruit, rendered them economically unviable (Nwabughuogu, 1981, pp. 270–4). These actions reveal women traders' well-developed understanding of collective action's potential benefits.

But did women drawn into waged labour indulge in similar collective action? We have to admit that, except in South Africa, women workers rarely led strikes and were noticeably absent from union leadership. This was no doubt largely due to the precarious nature of their employment, competing reproductive duties, and patriarchal traditions. These impediments are important, and certainly worth studying, but should not blind us to the need to study working women's participation in collective labour action, in whatever form it took.

While plagued by inadequate data, existing evidence indicates that women workers did protest against their working conditions. These early protests were often sporadic and small-scale. Sometimes they included a politicial dimension. In colonial Kenya, women working on coffee plantations rallied to Harry Thuku's cause when he made female labour conditions a major issue of his abortive anti-colonial campaign during the early 1920s. Short work stoppages organised by women workers plagued the Kenyan coffee industry. In 1960, 122 stoppages took place in the agricultural sector, primarily on coffee estates (Presley, 1978, pp. 5, 10). In Mozambique, women working in the cashew-nut industry tried to protest harsh conditions. These efforts largely failed, but indicate a desire to effect change (Penvenne, 1984, 148–53). Given the unorganised and often vulnerable nature of women workers, many of their protests no doubt took more subtle forms, such as slow downs, absenteeism, and uncooperativeness. Much more research is needed.

While the number of women in waged labour increased after the Second World War, we know little about their collective efforts. As unions developed in the 1940s, some women joined, though often with a cynical recognition that male-dominated unions did not always have their interests at heart. In Kenya, although influenced by union leaders after the 1940s, the Kenyan female coffee pickers usually organised strikes and stoppages by themselves (Presley, 1978, pp. 11–13). Some Mombasa nannies joined the Domestic and Hotel Workers' Union in the 1950s, but no female leaders came forward (Stichter, 1975–6, pp. 56–7). Many white-collar workers, especially teachers and nurses, also joined unions. In the Sudan, the Union of Government Elementary School Teachers was established in 1949 and the Nurses' Trade Union was organised in 1950. Women joined both unions in large numbers. While we know little about these women as union members, we do know that the first group of politically active women emerged from this trade union movement (Fluehr-Lobban, 1977, p. 138). Unfortunately, general studies of the Sudan trade union movement, as with other trade unions in Africa, rarely mention the contributions of women members.

But the one area with sufficient data, namely South Africa, amply proves women workers could play an active role in collective labour protest. Initially coloured women predominated, but as manufacturing expanded after the First World War, women of all races entered the work force. Textile and printing manufacturers depended largely on female labour. Women soon joined the unions, and a number of outstanding women leaders (Bettie du Toit, Ray Alexander and Johanna Cornelius, for example) repeatedly raised women's issues in trade union meetings. In 1917 the first predominantly female strike occurred among the unskilled printers' assistants. Two of the strike leaders were women. In 1919 and 1920 female members of the Witwatersrands Tailors' Association joined men in a strike for higher wages. And in 1919 there were enough female workers to prompt an attempt to organise a women's union (albeit mostly white) – the Women's Workers' Industrial Union. It failed, but indicates a growing awareness of the common problems faced by women workers (Walker, 1982, p. 59).

While racial divisions weakened worker solidarity – for example, in 1919 a strike of Cape Town clothing workers brought raises for white female workers while most of the coloured women lost their jobs – (Berger, 1985, 36), a number of white female unionists successfully drew coloured and black women workers into unions. African women could legally join registered unions because, unlike African men, they didn't carry passes. As a result, union activists found it easier to organise black women. Bettie du Toit and Ray Alexander organised African, Indian and coloured workers into several unions. The Garment Workers' Union, under the able leadership of Johanna Cornelius, was particularly determined to overcome racial divisions. Cornelius organised large strikes in the early 1930s during which women workers displayed remarkable discipline and solidarity in the face of deliberate police brutality. The union even sent members to the USSR to learn about non-racial unionism (Walker, 1982, pp. 63–4).

Some black workers responded to South Africa's racial problems by organising their own union, the Industrial and Commercial Workers' Union (ICU). Spurred on by participation in the 1919 general strike, women workers were active in ICU from then on. In the 1920s, the growing political activity of black women, led by Charlotte Maxeke, spilled over into the ICU. In 1920, the ICU tried to initiate a women's branch in Cape Town which Maxeke may have been part of. Unfortunately, the ICU was short-lived, and the women's branch never flourished, but women members were active in many strikes. In 1930, women were among the most militant participants during an ICU-led six-month long strike in East London. However, women rarely took the lead in strikes, and rural women were almost entirely ignored (Berger, 1985, pp. 36–7; Bradford, 1985, p. 314).

After 1940, trade unions expanded rapidly as the South African industrial base grew. More and more women of all races entered the work force. White women moved increasingly into white collar jobs, leaving coloured women in industry and Africans primarily in the service sector, although African women moved into the lowest ranges of factory employment in the 1950s (Walker, 1979, pp. 115–16). Women continued to join unions, but now many became union leaders as well. Coloured and African women emerged as leaders in the garment and food industry unions, especially after the Garment Workers' Union established a separate branch union for coloured workers in 1940. The Food and Canning Workers' Union (FCWU) had a number of articulate women leaders and a large female, mostly African, membership. Black and coloured women were poised to play an important role in worker struggles in the 1950s, when the Nationalist Party victory soon led to an attack on unions, especially multi-racial unions. Women union leaders such as Bettie du Toit, Hilda Watts, Ray Alexander and others, were banned and forced to stop organising. But women workers of all races fought back. They joined the South African Congress of Trade Unions and women's branches of political organisations. Many were politicised in the struggle, and joined the fight for racial justice in South Africa (Walker, 1979, pp. 118–21; Lapchik, 1981, pp. 233–4).

Non-unionised South African women workers protested collectively as well. In 1927, some washerwomen turned to strike action after the ICU failed to protect them from licence increases. Female beer brewers boycotted beer halls all over Natal in 1929. They marched through the streets chanting war songs, raiding beer halls and assaulting male drinkers. A good deal of sexual antagonism was expressed against male workers as well as state officials, suggesting consciousness of patriarchal as well as class antagonisms (Bradford, 1986, pp. 316–18). And throughout this period, women of all races in South Africa worked as domestics, a form of labour particularly resistant to collective and even individual protest. But despite these difficulties, resistance occured. In 1906–08 black female domestics on the Rand joined the Amalaita gangs that roamed the white suburbs attacking employers who mistreated their servants. During the period of widespread worker dissatisfaction and unrest in 1917, the South African newspapers reported growing insubordination among servants. White servants refused hard work, while less-favoured coloured and black nannies used more subtle methods such as slow downs, unresponsiveness, absenteeism and changing employers (Berger, 1985, pp. 40–1). In 1950s, women domestics joined demonstrations against the pass laws in large numbers, and in 1958, 2000 nannies stayed away from work to protest (Cock, 1980, p. 53). Thus, both individually, and less often collectively, non-unionised women organised resistance to employer oppression.

ALTERNATIVE STRATEGIES

Women made other little recognised contributions to collective labour action as well. Wives, daughters and community women often played a crucial role in labour protest. In South Africa, Mary Fitzgerald organised a 'Pickhandle Brigade' of women to assist the Johannesburg tramway workers in their 1911 strike. The Brigade caused a furore by lying on the trolley tracks to dramatise their support. Two years, later, Fitzgerald figured prominently in the white miners' strike on the Rand. During the 1922 miners' strike, wives organised the Women's Active Leagues, and resolutely supported the strikers. They marched in major demonstrations and even attacked scabs. Sixty-two women were among those arrested in the strike's suppression (Berger, 1985, pp. 1, 37–9).

Zambian copper miners' wives supported collective action from the first strike in 1935. In both the 1935 and 1940 strikes, women protested alongside their men. They slept with their husbands on the football fields to maintain worker solidarity and resolve. They promoted unionisation in the late 1940s, and provided crucial support for every strike. They grew extra food, organised neighbourhoods, went to union meetings, and bullied husbands into following union directives. Strikes were called to coincide with food production, and strike leaders made it clear they relied on women to rally behind the union. Household conflicts were shelved while both sexes concentrated on maintaining a united front against capital (Parpart, 1986). Women in other parts of Zambia behaved similarly. Karen Hansen reports a large demonstration of women during one of the railway workers' strikes in the 1950s (Hansen, personal communication).

Similar scenarios emerge elsewhere on the continent. During the 1961 Sekondi–Takoradi strike in Ghana, women carried messages between imprisoned strike leaders and the workers. They also collected money from the community to help imprisoned strikers and their families (Joseph Engwenyu, personal communication). In the 1947 strike, market women gave food to strikers on the assumption that they would benefit from wage increases to their major customers. Since many of these women were married to miners, they had a double reason to support the strike (Crisp, 1984, p. 87). In the 1948 Enugu coal strike, miners' wives turned out in droves to protest the dismissal of 50 hewers. The demonstrators became so angry, they damaged company property. While this didn't settle the dispute, it certainly revealed wives' ready support for collective action. Later, in the Nigerian general strike of 1964, women roundly supported workers for complaining about family living conditions (Ananaba, 1969, pp. 49, 104–5). These are just a few cases from a still very undeveloped literature. No doubt many more occurred.

Workers' wives and female supporters lobbied government officials as well. In 1922, a long procession of women from the Women's Active League of the Krugersdorp area marched on Town Hall to confront the Resident Magistrate. They presented him with a resolution urging the government to end the strike, and called on government to establish new industries to absorb the unemployed (Berger, 1985, pp. 38–9). Zambian miners and their wives appealed to labour officers and government officials to protect them from management. Eventually, men and women in the mining communities turned to nationalist political parties as a way to express working peoples' frustrations and wrest a better deal from management. When miners drew back from politics to avoid dismissal, miners' wives continued their political activity and several became important political leaders (Taylor and Lehmann, 1961, p. 90).

WOMEN AND WORK: INDEPENDENT AFRICA

Women in black Africa have not significantly increased their participation in waged labour since independence, especially in the modern sector. A study of waged labour in Kenya, Ghana and Zambia notes that 'the share of women in modern sector employment is less than 15 per cent . . . in Kenya (about 14 per cent (in 1972)), in Ghana (about 10 per cent (in 1971)), and in Zambia (about 7 per cent (in 1969))' (Akerele, 1979, p. 34). In 1974, women in Tanzania made up 9 per cent of the total waged labour force: only a 4 per cent increase since 1951 (Bryceson, 1980, p. 20). Some Muslim countries report even less; in 1976 only 4.1 per cent of Mali's wage labourers were women. Women are particularly scarce in manufacturing. With the exception of Tunisia, Swaziland and South Africa, women's participation in manufacturing has usually been less than 10 per cent (Bujra, 1983, pp. 6–7). There appears to be no correlation between the size of the modern sector and the proportion of women working in it. This is no doubt partly due to women's reproductive duties and ties to the land, but has been exacerbated by widespread economic stagnation and men's consequent willingness to compete for low-paying jobs. Given sexually equivalent wages, employers generally prefer men (Swantz, 1985, p. 131; Boserup, 1970, p. 113). In Zaire, women face stiff competition from 'school leavers' (Adams, 1980, p. 66) and Zambian women find it increasingly difficult to compete (Hansen, 1984, p. 234). Similar scenarios are reported elsewhere on the continent.

The majority of wage-earning women in Africa work in agriculture, though the percentages vary considerably. In Ghana, only 11.5 per cent of women wage earners worked in agriculture in 1971, as compared to 36.1 per cent in Kenya (Akerele, 1979, p. 39). In 1981, 29 per cent of Malawian female wage labourers worked in agriculture (ILO, 1981), and in South Africa, 43.9 per cent of female waged labourers worked in agriculture in 1970. But in recent years, paid agricultural work for women has declined, and the main growth area for women's employment has been the service sector. Domestic work continues to occupy many women (Stichter, 1986, p. 162; Akerele, 1979, pp. 39, 42). In some countries, women have moved into white collar occupations, especially primary school education, nursing and secretarial jobs. In 1976, over 90 per cent of the secretarial workers and nurses in Kenya were female (Lindsay, 1980, p. 83). Zambia has had a dramatic increase in female clerical workers, although men are increasingly competing for these jobs (Schuster, 1979, pp. 5, 20). Among employed women, only a tiny fraction hold elite positions, usually below 3–4 per cent. In South Africa, for example, 2.7 per cent of the female labour force is in professional and technical jobs (Stichter, 1984, p. 192).

As in the rest of the world, female wage earners in Africa generally hold the most menial, poorly paid, and insecure positions in their occupational category. They process cashew nuts or shrimp, sort and clean coffee, and carry out the least attractive jobs in the processing and manufacture of cotton, textiles, knitted garments, buttons, tobacco and shoes. Women workers are offered low wages and poor promotion prospects on the assumption that they have family support. The large number of female headed households has altered neither employer perceptions, nor the wage structure. Women are also offered poorly paid seasonal work on the assumption that it fits into already busy domestic schedules. Women thus often perform both reproductive and productive labour, but are in no position to challenge this double duty (Mbilinyi, 1984, pp. 177–9).

WOMEN WORKERS AND COLLECTIVE LABOUR ACTION

Independence has not significantly improved women workers' participation in union affairs, especially in leadership roles. Even in Ghana, with its strong progressive labour movement, women have been conspicuously absent from union leadership. In Zambia, very few women participate in union affairs, perhaps explaining the insufficient attention paid to maternity legislation in that country (Akerele, 1979, pp. 58–9). Only one of the 146 executives of the Nigerian Labour Congress is a woman (Pittin, 1984, pp. 77–8). Not surprisingly, women workers have played a relatively unimportant role in Nigerian unionism (Ubeku, 1983, p. 76). South Africa has been the only exception, where in 1974, 9 of the 23 unregistered African trade unions had women as Secretaries–General. But this hardly represents female domination (Van Vuuren, 1979, p. 96).

This limited involvement is due to several factors, the most obvious being patriarchal ideology. Directing large confrontational institutions is seen as 'man's work.' In Nigeria, for example, Abdel Ubeku admits that 'societal norms . . . do not exactly encourage a woman to be a leader of men in the struggle for improvements to the conditions of employment' (Ubeku, 1983, p. 76). Such attitudes pervade the continent, inhibiting women from competing for union leadership (Swantz, 1985, pp. 144–5). But women's double day is also important. Like many other men, Ubeku assumes women workers who are also housewives 'would not really want to be involved in the rigours of trade union activities' (Ubeku, 1983, p. 76). Since most wage earning women also run households, this disqualifies the majority. But more to the point, already overburdened women hardly have the time or energy to take on the demanding life of union leaders. Economically vulnerable women, especially female heads of households, are constrained by fear of dismissal, while women with family support can tolerate lower wages, and so are often reluctant to risk dismissal for only potential gain. Both groups thus approach strike action with some trepidation. In some countries, unions are banned, leaving both men and women with no recourse to institutional protest. In Swaziland, for example, Patricia McFadden discovered a large disaffected female labour force working at Libby's, but could not assess the commitment to unionisation (McFadden, 1982, p. 162).

Despite these limitations, it is important to recognise women workers' contribution to union-directed collective action. Once again, South African women workers have been the most militant female union members on the continent. African women garment and textile workers struck repeatedly during the 1970s and 1980s. Spurred on by low wages during a period of inflation, the largely female garment workers struck in 1973. Despite prohibitions against strikes and registered African unions, women workers have been deeply involved in the mushrooming of factory committees and unregistered trade unions that developed to organise renewed interest in collective labour actions. Even domestic workers joined the trend towards unionisation (Gaitskell *et al.*, 1984, pp. 103–6). Women joined men to battle capital and the state. In the 1980 strike at the Frame-owned factories in Durban, women (who were 70 per cent of the work force) organised into two groups. They confronted strike breakers, enforced discipline, and bore the brunt of considerable violence. The women's hostel became a meeting ground for strike organisers and a platform for building worker solidarity and commitment to the strike (Natal Labour Research Committee 1980, pp. 34–8). In the rest of Africa, inadequate data impedes analysis. Akerele discovered relative inactivity among women in trade unions in Ghana, Tanzania and Zambia (1979, p. 58), but she was looking at union membership and official strike actions. Women's commitment to collective action may have to be measured in more subtle and indirect ways. It also may simply require more research, particularly in the area of white collar unions, where women's employment has been increasing.

At the moment, women workers' commitment to collective action is often best studied outside official union activities. There are some clues explaining why this is true. In union-led struggles, women workers have frequently raised gender-related issues such as equal pay, job security (especially after maternity leaves), and an end to sexual harassment. While union leaders sometimes lobby for these issues, they often disappear at the bargaining table. In Durban, for example, during the 1972 strike, union leaders demanded the removal of wage discrimination against women, but the issue was largely ignored during negotiations. At the relatively progressive firm of Smith and Nephew, workers demanded equal pay for the sexes, but eventually settled for a lower female wage, no doubt 'not unconnected with the intimidating presence of carloads of plain-clothes police at the meeting during which the offer was accepted' (Berger, 1983, p. 61). But while intimidation was a factor, this inaction suggests limited concern for sexual equality in the work place. Nigerian women workers in Zaria voiced similar concerns, claiming unions did little for them. Women workers also report widespread refusal to deal with the issue of sexual harassment. This problem bedevils working women throughout the continent, but receives little attention. Some working women are unfairly labelled as prostitutes (Weeks, 1973, pp. 95–6). Others report experiences such as those of South African women textile workers, where male workers warned them that management would support the men in any sexual harassment cases (Westmore and Townsend, 1975, p. 26; Pittin, 1984, p. 75).

It is not surprising then that wage-earning women have often circumvented or ignored union officials when lodging complaints. At the Electricity Meter Company (Nigeria) Ltd. in Zaria, for example, women workers were so frustrated by union leaders, they approached management directly, both individually and in small groups. These complaints fell on deaf ears; the Personnel Manager sided with the union. While male workers were disillusioned with the pro-management union as well, women workers felt doubly betrayed. They were ignored both as women and as workers. In other parts of the continent, women workers often prefer individual action to union activism. Some women see education as the best escape from low-paying positions (Swantz, 1985, pp. 1944–5), while female white collar workers often prefer attaching themselves to powerful boyfriends or cultivating personal networks (Dinan, 1977, p. 168; Schuster, 1979, p. 74).

Non-unionised women workers have launched strikes by themselves as well. In Senegal, the management at a large agri-business owned by BUD (a Brussels-based holding company) imposed a piece-rate system on the female packing-shed workers who had been on an hourly wage. This annoyed them, and the women refused to work, eventually winning their cases (Mackintosh, 1977). Women workers at a BUD agri-business in Zaria organised a successful strike for higher wages as well (Jackson, 1980, pp. 25ff). Domestic workers have rarely organised strikes, but employ a variety of strategems to improve their working conditions. Go-slows, absenteeism and insubordination protect them from oppressive employers (Cock, 1980, pp. 7–8, 53). Much more research is needed, but women workers' willingness to organise collective labour protests should not be in doubt.

Wage earning women have also resorted to political organisation in order to improve their economic lot, but their traditional reticence often gets in the way. Swantz reported that although two-thirds of the women workers belonged to the Tanzanian African National Union (TANU), they rarely spoke at meetings. 'The cleaners . . . said they preferred just to listen. They were still inhibited by centuries of customary deference to men.' And TANU's women's organisation was dominated by elite women, who were wary of single working women (1985, pp. 145, 160).

ALTERNATIVE STRATEGIES

As in the colonial period, women continue to protest their position in waged labour by pulling out. In the rural areas, they have withdrawn from cash crop production, concentrating on food production instead (Mbilinyi, 1984, p. 182). In town, women enter petty commodity production and trade, rather than remain in the most disadvantaged sectors of the waged labour force. This popular strategy reduces female commitment to unionisation as waged labour becomes only a temporary means to acquire capital (Peil, 1972, p. 109; Jackson, 1980, p. 21; Hansen, 1984, p. 231). While this pattern also occurs among men, particularly in West Africa (Peace, 1979, p. 78; Weeks, 1973, p. 78), it is more prevalent among women, who after all, have more reason to leave wage labour.

But women continue to support male workers' struggles with management, and often the state, as a strategy for survival as well. Higher wages bring the possibility of better lives to women who depend (at least partially) on male earnings. While strike action has often been blocked by the state, where strikes have occurred, support from wives and community women has often played an important, and under-recognised, role. In Zambia, for example, the copper miners' wives participated in the first large strike against the new government in 1966. Women helped with food distribution and organised neighbourhood committees. At one of the mine compounds, about forty women demonstrated outside the compound offices demanding money for their children and pay for hospitalised husbands (*Times of Zambia*, 6 April 1966). Later on, miners' wives joined other protests. In 1979, they beat empty pots, pans and plates in front of government offices, demanding that they be filled with food (Luchembe, 1982, p. 517). Two years later, over 3000 miners' wives demonstrated outside the Konkola mine (in Chililabombwe) complaining vociferously about mealie meal shortages and the company's threat to stop credit for mealie meal. When company officials tried to stop them, the women booed, refused to listen, sang songs of defiance and threw stones at the speakers. The strike started when the morning shift workers obeyed their wives and stayed away from work. The wives, dressed in overalls and hard hats, forced those trying to get to work to return. Picketing wives and their older children barricaded the main roads with steel pipes. The strike spread to other mines, with both men and women involved. At one mine, men, women and children stoned the police. The strike ended without solving the mealie meal question, but it disproves any notion of female passivity. At one of the mines, 28 of the 32 people arrested were women (*Times of Zambia*, 6–10 July 1981).

Other workers found their wives' support crucial as well. In 1982, laid-off workers from the Bancroft Transport Company in Zambia brought their wives to the district labour office to complain. The workers threatened to stay with their wives until they received their severance pay (*Times of Zambia*, 22 July 1982).

Workers have often gained support from community women as well. Many of these women make their living selling goods and services to male wage earners, so have a vested interest in higher wages. In Ghana, for example, market women supported railway workers during the 1961 and 1971 strikes. The market women were ardent supporters of the 1961 strike. They saw the 1961 strike as a means to both protest their own marginalisation, and to improve their major customers' buying power. Throughout the 17-day strike, they encouraged the workers to hold out and raised morale by supplying free food. The market women identified with the railway workers' struggle against the centralising tendencies of the TUC, which they likened to the government's hated oligopoly of the market-trade. Their strike assistance thus embodied both general protest against government corruption and a desire to improve immediate conditions, particularly wages. The market women supported the railway workers again in 1971 (Jeffries, 1978, pp. 73–4, 95–6, 138). In that same year, Adrian Peace reported widespread community support for strikers who lived in Agege, but worked in the neighbouring Ikeja Industrial Estate. Self-employed townspeople gave the strikers food, money and moral support throughout the strike. Again, this was both a general protest and a way to increase potential spending-power

(Peace, 1979, pp. 175–6). Further research will undoubtedly reveal more such examples.

CONCLUSION

Women have been ignored by scholars of African labour for two reasons: their limited involvement in waged labour and their even more limited participation in trade union affairs. This combination conveniently reinforces gender-stereotypes which emphasise women's peripheral role in labour matters. Whether workers or wives, women have been dismissed as unimportant by-standers in labour–capital relations.

While the facts are correct–many African women neither work for wages nor belong to unions–ignoring women's role in labour struggles mystifies reality. From the beginning of the colonial period women have sought to protect their economic interests through collective action. Market women, prostitutes, domestics and other women have organised collective protests–often in the face of great odds and frightening vulnerability. There can be no doubt that women understand the need for collective struggle. And the South African case certainly proves that women workers willingly join unions and engage in union-led collective action. At the same time, patriarchal-bias among union leaders and members has held back whole-hearted female support, thus impeding worker solidarity and effective collective action. By refusing to face this problem, women workers' potential contribution to unions and collective labour action has been both undermined and underestimated.

Workers' wives and unwaged women living in worker communities have also played a little recognised role in collective labour action. The Copperbelt case clearly disproves the notion that only productive workers understand worker consciousness and the need for collective action. Indeed, the copper miners' wives have sometimes seemed more committed to collective labour struggles than their men. The genders might fight later over the division of the spoils, but during a strike collective solidarity took precedence and women proved worthy allies against capital.

We need to know much more about these struggles before we can truly assess women's contribution to collective labour action in Africa. At this point we can only reiterate the need for a more inclusive approach to African labour studies, one that examines both gender and class struggles, and consequently both reproductive and productive labour.

Jane L. Parpart 253

Bibliography

t
Adams, Lois (1980) 'Women in Zaire: Disparate Status and Roles' in *Comparative Perspectives of Third World Women: the impact of race, sex and class*, edited by Beverly Lindsay (New York: Praeger).

Akerele, O. (1979) *Women Workers in Ghana, Kenya, Zambia: A Comparative Analysis of Women's Employment in the Modern Wage Sector* (Addis Ababa: ECA/ATRCW/SDD/RESO2/79).

Ananaba, Wogu (1969) *The Trade Union Movement in Nigeria* (Benin City: Ethiopia Publishing Corporation).

Berger, Iris (1983) 'Sources of Class Consciousness: South African Women in Recent Labor Struggles', *International Journal of African Historical Studies* 16, 1: 49–66.

Berger, Iris (1985) 'A Regrettable Aversion: Women and Wage Labor in South Africa, 1900–1925' (Mimeo).

Boserup, Ester (1970) *Women's Role in Economic Development* (New York: St. Martin's Press).

Bradford, Helen (1985) 'Beer Protests in Natal, 1929–1930: Sexually-Differentiated Patterns of Resistance' (Mimeo).

Bryceson, Deborah F. (1980) 'The Proletarianization of Women in Tanzania', *Review of African Political Economy (ROAPE)* 17: 4–27.

Bujra, Janet (1983) 'Urging Women to Redouble their Efforts . . . : Class, Gender and Capitalist Transformation in Africa' (Mimeo).

Cock, Jacklyn (1980) *Of Maids and Madams* (Johannesburg: Raven Press).

Crisp, Jeff (1984) *The Story of an African Working Class: Ghanaian Miners' Struggles, 1870–1980* (London: Zed Press).

Date-Bah, Eugenia (1983) 'Female and Male Factory Workers in Accra' in *Female and Male in West Africa*, edited by C. Oppong (London: Allan).

Dennis, Carolyne (1984) 'Capitalist Development and Women's Work: a Nigerian Case Study', *ROAPE* 27/28: 109–19.

Di Domenico, C.M. (1983) 'Male and Female Factory Workers in Ibadan' in *Female and Male in West Africa*, edited by C. Oppong (London: Allan).

Dinan, Carmel (1977) 'Pragmatists or Feminists? The Professional "Single" Women of Accra, Ghana', *Cahiers d'Etudes africaines* 65, XVII: 155–176.

Fleuhr-Lobban, Carolyn (1977) 'Agitation for Change in the Sudan' in *Sexual Stratification: A Cross-Cultural View*, edited by Alice Schlegel (New York: Columbia University Press).

Gaitskell, Deborah, Judy Kimble, Moira Maconachie and Elaine Untehalter (1984) 'Class, Race and Gender: Domestic Workers in South Africa', *ROAPE* 27/28; 86–108.

Hansen, Karen T. (1984) 'Negotiating Sex and Gender in Urban Zambia', *Journal of Southern African Studies (JSAS)* 10,2.

International Labour Organisation (1981) *Yearbook of Labour Statistics*.

Jackson, Sam (1980) 'Hausa Women in Strike', *ROAPE* 13: 21–36.

Jeffries, Richard (1978) *Class, Power and Ideology in Ghana: the Railwaymen of Sekondi* (Cambridge: Cambridge University Press).

Lapchik, Richard E. (1981) 'The Role of Women in the Struggle against

Apartheid in South Africa' in *The Black Woman Cross-Culturally*, edited by Filomina Steady (Cambridge: Schenkman Publishing).

Lindsay, Beverly (1980) 'Issues confronting Professional African Women: Illustrations from Kenya' in *Comparative Perspectives of Third World Women: the Impact of Race, Sex and Class*, edited by Lindsay (New York: Praeger).

Little, Kenneth (1972) 'Voluntary Associations and Social Mobility among West African Women', *Canadian Journal of African Studies* 6, 2: 275–88.

Little, Kenneth (1973) *African Women in Towns* (Cambridge: Cambridge University Press).

Luchembe, C. (1982) 'Finance Capital and Mine Labor: a Comparative Study of Copperminers in Zambia and Peru, 1870–1980', Ph.D., University of California, Los Angeles.

MacKintosh, M. (1977) 'The men form a union, the women go on strike: sexual contradictions and labour conflict on a West African estate farm' (Mimeo).

Mba, Nina (1982) *Nigerian Women Mobilized* (Berkeley: Institute of International Studies, University of California).

Mbilinyi, Marjorie (1981) 'The Future of Women in Africa' (Mimeo).

Mbilinyi, Marjorie (1984) 'The Changing Position of Women in the African Labour Force' in *African Projected*, edited by T.M. Shaw and O. Aluko (London: Macmillan) 170–86.

McFadden, Patricia (1982) 'Agriculture', *South African Labour Bulletin (SALB)* 7, 6: 140–66.

Natal Labour Research Committee (1980) 'Control over a Workforce–the Frame case', *SALB* 6, 5: 17–47.

Nwabughuogu, Anthony (1981) 'Political Change, Social Response and Economic Development: the Dynamics of Change in Eastern Nigeria, 1930–1950', Ph.D., Dalhousie University.

Parpart, Jane L. (1986) 'The Household and the Mine Shaft: Gender and Class Struggles on the Zambian Copperbelt, 1924–66', *JSAS*.

Peace, Adrian (1979) *Choice, Class and Conflict: A Study of Southern Nigerian Factory Workers* (Brighton: Harvester Press).

Peil, Margaret (1972) *The Ghanaian Factory Worker: Industrial Man in Africa* (Cambridge: Cambridge University Press).

Penvenne, Jeanne (1985) 'Making our Own Way: Women Working in Lourenco Marques, 1900–1933'. mimeo.

Pittin, Renee (1984) 'Gender and Class in a Nigerian Industrial Setting', *ROAPE* 31: 72–81.

Presley, Cora (1978) 'Labor unrest among Kikuyu women in colonial Kenya'. mimeo.

Remy, Dorothy (1975) 'Underdevelopment and the Experience of Women: A Nigerian Case Study', in *Towards an Anthropology of Women*, edited by Rayna R. Reiter, 358–71 (New York: Monthly Review Press).

Robertson, Claire (1984) 'Women in the Urban economy', in *African Women South of the Sahara*, edited by Jean Hay and Sharon Stichter (London: Longman).

Schuster, Ilsa M.G. (1979) *New Women of Lusaka* (Palo Alto: Mayfield Publishing Co.).

Steady, Filomina (1982) 'African Women, Industrialization and another Development', *Development Dialogue*, 1–2: 51–64.

Stichter, Sharon (1975–6) 'Women and the Labor Force in Kenya 1895–1964', *Rural Africana* 29: 45–67.

Stichter, Sharon (1984) 'Some selected statistics on African women', in *African Women South of the Sahara*, edited by Margaret Jean Hay and Sharon Stichter (London: Longman).

Stichter, Sharon (1985) *Migrant Laborers* (Cambridge: Cambridge University Press).

Strobel, Margaret (1979) *Muslim Women in Mombasa, 1890–1975* (New Haven: Yale University Press).

Swantz, Marja-Liisa (1985) *Women in Development: A Creative Role Denied?* (London: C. Hurst & Company).

Taylor, John V. and Lehmann, Dorothea (1961) *Christians of the Copperbelt* (London: SCM Press Ltd).

Ubeku, Abel K. (1979) *Industrial Relations in Developing Countries: the Case of Nigeria* (New York: St. Martin's Press).

Van Vuuren, Nancy (1979) *Women against Apartheid: the Fight for Freedom in South Africa* (Palo Alto: R and E Associates).

Walker, Cherryl (1982) *Women and Resistance in South Africa* (London: Onyx Press).

Weeks, Dorothy C.R. (1973) 'Adaptive Strategies of Men and Women in Zaria, Nigeria: Industrial Workers and their Wives', Ph.D., University of Michigan.

Westmore, Jean and Pat Townsend (1975) 'The African Women Workers in the Textile Industry in Durban', *SALB*, 2, 4.

White, Louise (1983) 'Vice and Vagrants: Prostitution, Housing, and Casual Labor in Nairobi in the mid-1930s' (Mimeo).

Wright, Marcia (1983) 'Technology, Marriage and Women's Work in the History of Maize-Growers in Mazabuka, Zambia: a Reconnaissance', *JSAS* 10, 1: 73–5.

Index